A PRACTICAL GUIDE TO

Organizational Ombuds

How They Help People and Organizations

CHARLES L. HOWARD

AMERICAN BAR ASSOCIATION
Dispute Resolution Section

Cover design by Amanda Fry/ABA Design

Printed in the United States of America.

25 24 23   5 4 3 2

Library of Congress Cataloging-in-Publication Data

Names: Howard, Charles L., 1950– author.

Title: A practical guide to organizational ombuds / Charles L. Howard.

Description: Chicago : American Bar Association, 2022. | Includes bibliographical references and index. | Summary: "Many people and organizations do not understand what organizational ombuds are and how they work. They want to know what value these programs really add, and they frequently express skepticism about ombuds' claim of confidentiality and how these programs can operate independently within an organization when an ombuds may be an employee of the organization. This book is a practical guide for those who have questions such as these about organizational ombuds programs and how they operate"—Provided by publisher.

Identifiers: LCCN 2021041022 (print) | LCCN 2021041023 (ebook) | ISBN 9781639050536 (hardcover) | ISBN 9781639050543 (ebook)

Subjects: LCSH: Ombudspersons—United States. | Personnel management—United States. | Abuse of administrative power—UnitedStates.

Classification: LCC KF5423.H69 2022 (print) | LCC KF5423 (ebook) | DDC 342.73/0667—dc23

LC record available at https://lccn.loc.gov/2021041022

LC ebook record available at https://lccn.loc.gov/2021041023

Discounts are available for books ordered in bulk. Special consideration is given to state bars, CLE programs, and other bar-related organizations. Inquire at Book Publishing, ABA Publishing, American Bar Association, 321 N. Clark Street, Chicago, Illinois 60654-7598.

www.shopABA.org

This book is dedicated to Joan, Brian, and Katharine, whose abiding love, support, and encouragement are more than anyone could ever hope for, and to my late mother, who taught me the importance of principles,

and

to the Ombuds who shared their stories with me so I can help you understand why I admire them so much for the work that they do.

Contents

Acknowledgments

I want to express appreciation to the many people who provided me with the opportunity to learn about organizational ombuds and the work that they do. Most of the insights and conclusions I offer in this book are from my experience representing organizational ombuds programs throughout the United States and around the world. I am deeply indebted to my former clients for the opportunity to work with them. That is how I first learned about the positive impact ombuds can have on people and organizations. I am also indebted to my former law firm, Shipman & Goodwin, for allowing me to continue representing ombuds programs despite other areas of my practice that were more lucrative.

I want to give special thanks to those brave ombuds who trusted me to tell the stories of the work they do. Virtually all of the ombuds who assisted me have far more work to do than they can reasonably manage. My request for assistance for this book only added to that burden, and I am extremely grateful for their willingness to share so I could collect and tell their stories. This book would not exist but for them.

Several other people were extremely helpful in bringing this book to life. The opinions and any errors are mine alone, but the final product was made much better by the assistance, thoughtful comments, and editorial suggestions of Dori Antonetti, Chuck Doran, Carolyn Esposito, Julie Fay, Vaughan Finn, Jim Hostettler, Melanie Jagneaux, Jon McBride, Rachel Osmundsen, Arthur Pearlstein, and Julie Weber. Special thanks go to Katharine Howard and Brian Howard for their helpful suggestions. I also greatly appreciate the assistance of Kim Johnson, who helped me compile the actual ombuds examples in the categories that you see in this book, and Harry Burgess, who has assisted me for many years in monitoring the continued development of ombuds case law and who provided invaluable assistance with the citations in this book. And finally, I appreciate the guidance and encouragement of Sarah Craig, Executive Editor at ABA Publishing.

I am deeply grateful to you all for your help.

About the Author

Chuck Howard served as the Executive Director of the International Ombuds Association from 2019 through 2021. Previously, he was a Partner and General Counsel of the law firm of Shipman & Goodwin LLP. For almost thirty years Chuck represented ombuds offices at major corporations, universities, research facilities, and other organizations throughout the United States as independent counsel. He is the author of *The Organizational Ombudsman: Origins, Roles, and Operations—A Legal Guide*, published by the American Bar Association in January 2010, and has long been a frequent presenter and writer on ombuds issues.

From 1985 to 2000, Chuck was Chair of Shipman & Goodwin's Litigation Department. His litigation practice included business and intellectual property litigation, as well as the representation of public, quasi-public, and state governmental entities in a wide range of matters, including in more than seventy-five appeals. He was included in Best Lawyers in America® in the practice areas of Commercial Litigation, Arbitration, and Mediation and was recognized as a Connecticut Super Lawyer® in the Intellectual Property Litigation practice area.

Throughout his career, Chuck has been active in numerous civic and professional activities. Among these was his service from 2002 to 2004 on the Ad Hoc Advisory Group to the United States Sentencing Commission, which recommended revisions to the federal organizational sentencing guidelines. From 2014 to 2018, he served as the Chair and then Co-Chair of the Ombuds Committee of the Dispute Resolution Section of the American Bar Association and was on the Dispute Resolution Section Council.

In 2012 he received an Award of Special Recognition from the International Ombuds Association for "his significant contributions to, and effort in support of, the organizational ombudsman profession."

In 2019, he was awarded the Lifetime Achievement Award by the *Connecticut Law Tribune* for his legal accomplishments and civic activities. Also in 2019, he received the New England Trailblazer Award by Law.com and the *Connecticut Law Tribune* for his advocacy on behalf of organizational ombuds programs.

He is a graduate of the School for Public and International Affairs at Princeton University and the University of Virginia School of Law.

Stories are the most powerful form of human communication

—Peg C. Neuhauser, Corporate Legends and Lore

Reports convey information. Stories create experience. Reports transfer knowledge. Stories transport the reader, crossing boundaries of time, space and imagination. The report points us there. The story puts us there.

—Roy Peter Clark, Writing Tools

Humans are not ideally set up to understand logic; they are ideally set up to understand stories.

—Roger C. Schank, cognitive scientist

A picture may be worth a thousand words, but a good story can bring a picture to life.

—Anonymous

Introduction

Many people and organizations do not understand what organizational ombuds are and how they work. When confronted with requests to create these programs, those in charge often raise questions about the need for yet another overhead expense that does not produce revenue. They want to know what value these programs really add, and they frequently express skepticism about ombuds' claim of confidentiality and how these programs can operate independently within an organization when an ombuds may be an employee of the organization.

I want this book to be a practical guide for those who have questions such as these about organizational ombuds programs and how they operate. To accomplish this purpose, the book has two very different but complementary parts. In part I, I respond directly to the many difficult questions that ombuds and I have been asked over the years—questions about what organizational ombuds offices are, why they fill a need that other functions cannot address, why confidentiality is important, and why the office's structure is important to achieving that confidentiality. My goal for part I is to present a discussion on these issues that is both accessible and readable so that it can be read in one or two sessions.

Because part I is structured around answers to important questions, it does not have to be read like a novel, from start to finish (though I think that reading from the beginning is best). If you know what organizational ombuds programs are, you may wish to begin by reviewing the chapter titles and section headings listed in the table of contents. If there is a question that you would like answered first, feel free to start with the corresponding chapter or section. For example, if you are wondering why some people think ombuds programs are necessary or why they gave you a copy of this book, you might want to start with the questions in chapter 2 on why ombuds programs are needed. Hopefully, you will find that discussion compelling and go on to review the sections on other important questions.

Part II of the book approaches the topic in a completely different way. It consists solely of stories that provide actual examples of what ombuds do. These examples are all absolutely real—not composite or hypothetical—and they are organized into thirty-three categories. Part II, in effect, illustrates my answers to the hard questions by bringing the work of ombuds to life through a large collection of real stories. Any explanation by me about ombuds work pales in comparison with the illuminating power of these stories to reveal the types of issues that ombuds address and how they do so. I have long thought that telling real stories about what ombuds do makes concrete what a discussion only reveals in abstract. While only a limited number of these stories could be included in the print edition of this book, a full compilation of them—more than 600 pages in all—is available for download in PDFs using the URL provided at the end of the Introduction to part II. Again, you should feel free to start by reviewing some of the examples printed in part II of the book, and you can then go from there.

I believe that this practical guide to organizational ombuds will be a useful resource for both decision-makers about ombuds programs and ombuds. A little more than ten years ago, I wrote a book on ombuds programs, *The Organizational Ombudsman: Origins, Roles, and Operations—A Legal Guide,* that was published by the American Bar Association (ABA) Dispute Resolution Section (DRS). Although it remains the leading treatise on this subject, that book dealt primarily with *legal* issues and included an extensive history on the evolution of the organizational ombuds role and information about many areas of law that ombuds may encounter. It is not easily accessible or understood by nonlawyers, regardless of whether they are ombuds or senior managers with whom ombuds interact. I remain confident of the analysis presented there, but it did not have either the informative or the persuasive impact I had hoped for. Many organizations still fail to recognize the benefits of these programs, understand how they should be structured, or trust ombuds to do the work that must be done confidentially to be effective. As a result, this book has a more modest focus; it is designed to answer questions directly and illustrate ombuds work with real examples. It also does not have (many) footnotes. If you are looking for a detailed legal analysis or lots of citations to authority, you are invited to refer to *The Organizational Ombudsman*.

I admit that I believe the need for these programs has never been greater. People throughout the world have endured a pandemic in 2020–2021 that resulted in record unemployment, killed millions of people and—for those who still have jobs—strained their ability to work remotely and take care of and educate their children while living in quarantine conditions. As if that crisis were not enough, this has occurred against the backdrop of a national and international crisis over race, institutional and scientific distrust, and political dysfunction. The impact of these issues has disproportionally affected some people more than others, but most would agree that these challenges—whatever one's particular experience has been—are a reason to pause and think about how much people and organizations need help navigating their way through such a new and unfamiliar world.

I hope you find this book both readable and compelling. Organizational ombuds offices can improve the lives of people in our educational, work, social, and civic organizations and can help improve those organizations by surfacing and resolving many issues that are not being—and that would likely never be—brought to the organization's attention. Time is passing and the need is great.

Part I

1

What Is an Organizational Ombuds?

Organizational ombuds help both people and organizations. They help people resolve conflict and surface issues by providing information, offering coaching and guidance, and assisting people in developing options for taking action. They also help organizations by providing feedback to an organization's senior leadership about systemic issues and trends in the organization without disclosing the identities of or any confidential communications with those who consult with the ombuds (commonly called "visitors").

The ombuds (or ombudsman or ombudsperson) concept is relatively new in the United States, having first been introduced in the early 1960s and subsequently evolving in divergent ways in government, colleges and universities, and business organizations.[1] As a result, there are other types of ombuds who function differently from organizational ombuds, but these differences are not well understood, with the result that many people believe or assume erroneously that all ombuds are the same, when they are not. This has led to confusion about what an organizational ombuds is and does. Because this book is focused solely on *organizational* ombuds, however, it is important to begin by

---

[1] For more background on the history and evolution of ombuds programs, *see* Charles L. Howard, The Organizational Ombudsman: Origins, Roles, and Operations—A Legal Guide 1–75 (2010).

summarizing what organizational ombuds programs are and what they do and do not do.

The work and structure of organizational ombuds programs are based on compliance with four key practice principles: **independence, impartiality, informality,** and **confidentiality.** These principles are embodied in the International Ombuds Association's (IOA's) Code of Ethics and Standards of Practice.[2]

Ombuds programs that comply with the IOA Code of Ethics and Standards of Practice operate independent of management, reporting to the highest level possible in the organization. Though most frequently embedded in an organization, they can be created as external resources under a contract with an organization. They are designed to be neutral and impartial, neither part of management nor advocating for employees or other groups served by them. They advocate only for fair process. They are a valuable ADR (alternate dispute resolution) mechanism, using tools such as mediation, facilitated conversations, supplying information, and coaching to help people resolve conflict. As such, they operate informally.[3] They do not maintain business records for their organizations, and they are not a "formal channel" of the organization to be used to notify the organization if someone wants to assert a claim against it. Because organizational ombuds are independent, impartial, and informal, they also can have the superpower of being confidential—which both makes them distinct and unique compared to formal channels and makes them a safe place and ideally suited to help people resolve conflict or surface issues that they are unwilling or afraid to bring to formal channels.

The practices of organizational ombuds programs grounded on these principles have transcended the organizational settings in which they operate. Organizational ombuds—whether in corporations, universities, or government—now function in remarkably similar ways.

Even though the practices of organizational ombuds have coalesced around the IOA Standards of Practice, a final point about these ombuds is important: ombuds services today can be delivered in a wide variety of ways that can be adapted to the needs of an organization and the

[2] The IOA Code of Ethics and Standards of Practice are publicly available on the IOA website: https://www.ombudsassociation.org/.

[3] Chapter 2 discusses "formal" and "informal" channels in greater detail.

context in which they operate. There is more information about this in chapter 3, but ombuds can be employees or external services providers, they can be full time or part time, they can be created in multinational corporations and small organizations, and they can be created in virtually any organizational setting. While the daily work of an ombuds might vary somewhat depending on the organization and the constituents served, organizations should understand that they can design a program that complies with the IOA Standards of Practice to meet virtually any organization's needs and objectives.

For simplicity and clarity, let me summarize what organizational ombuds do and do not do. **Organizational ombuds DO the following as a confidential resource**:

- Assist people at all levels in the organization as an easily accessible ("no-barrier") resource
- Listen to people to help them sort or frame issues to navigate situations
- Serve as a source of information or a sounding board for visitors with sensitive or confidential concerns
- Explain process, policies, and procedures and advocate for fair process
- Provide assistance on a full spectrum of issues
- Provide a safe place where people can develop options **BEFORE** taking action to address their concerns
- Help people consider and evaluate formal and informal strategies to resolve conflict or report misconduct
- Provide coaching on virtually any organization-related matter, including on how visitors can best articulate concerns
- Provide mediation and facilitated conversations with the permission of the participants
- Provide trend and reporting of systemic issues to senior leadership of the organization both on an "as needed" basis and through annual reports
- Serve as an early warning "listening post" for the organization to identify emerging issues
- Maintain confidentiality, except in very limited situations such as where the ombuds determines there to be an imminent threat

of serious harm or the visitor gives permission and the ombuds agrees to make a disclosure

- Provide conflict resolution training and education for the organization
- Complement formal channels—such as managers, human resources and compliance personnel—by helping people who will not or who are afraid to go directly to those channels

As important as it is to understand what organizational ombuds do, it is just as important to know what they do not do. **Organizational ombuds DO NOT:**

- Have authority to receive notice of claims against the organization
- Have management responsibility except for their own office
- Have authority to conduct investigations or engage in fact finding
- Have authority to make management decisions or policy
- Advocate or take sides between management and employees or leadership and other constituencies
- Maintain business records of confidential communications for their organization
- Serve as a substitute for formal channels
- Testify or produce documents with respect to confidential communications in formal, legal, or administrative proceedings.

With this overview of what organizational ombuds are and do, let's move on to answering important questions about organizational ombuds.

2

Why Should an Organization Establish an Ombuds Office?

Ombuds are skilled professionals who help people resolve interpersonal conflict and develop options for taking action on organizational issues that concern them, including what may be misconduct. As the name implies, *organizational* ombuds are created by organizations for a specific constituency.

Focusing on the constituencies served is a good starting point to explain why ombuds programs should be created because even in normal times conflict between or among people is part of human nature and inevitable in any organization where people come together. Most people have neither training nor experience in how to resolve conflict and are not comfortable dealing with it on their own even though it can be incredibly damaging to themselves or others or both. Interpersonal conflict can also disrupt and impair an organization. Likewise, most people are not trained or experienced in how to report misconduct, and they often fear what might happen to them if they were to do so or if they are wrong. Ombuds are a confidential safe space to help people with both of these types of issues and more besides. With expertise in how to deal with these issues, ombuds serve as an information source, coach, or guide to help people navigate their way in organizations and address these types of issues.

Fundamental changes on several fronts in our organizations and society over the past few decades have resulted in a "new normal" that has made the need for an ombuds resource more important than ever. These include changes in demographics, the role of immigration, and the increasing and central role of people of color and women; the size and scope of many of our organizations (including universities and corporations), as well as what the law and society expect of them; the role of technology and the rise of the gig economy; the impact of the recession of 2007–2008 and the pandemic of 2020–2021 on how we work and interact; and the simultaneous social and political tribalism and divisions.

One result of all of this change is that we have a more diverse population, larger institutions with often a global reach (or, at least, a workforce, student body, or constituents from around the globe). Another result is that workers and people in those organizations have less tenure, loyalty, and connection with their organizations. Consequently, we have the potential for more conflict and a greater need for assistance in resolving conflict and reporting possible misconduct than ever before. At the same time, the usual channels for dealing with these issues have not been sufficient to provide the confidential guidance, information, and assistance that many people need or want.

The case for creating an ombuds office, however, is about more than just helping people, though that is a worthy goal in itself. An organization itself also can greatly benefit from an effective ombuds office.

A. The Big Picture: What Are the Societal Changes in Our Society and Organizations That Call for Ombuds Offices?

While many people have a general understanding that demographic changes are occurring, they may not realize how profound these changes are. My focus is on the United States; but the points that I make also apply to other parts of the world, as the demographic effects of vastly increased immigration worldwide also have transformed the cultures and societies of many countries, some of them even more so than in the United States.

In 1950 the US population was 90 percent white.[1] By 2020, it had become far more diverse, both racially and ethnically, with only about 60 percent of the population being classified as "white alone, not Hispanic or Latino."[2] Nearly 45 million immigrants were living in the United States in 2018, or somewhat less than 14 percent of a total population of about 330 million. The trajectory of this increased diversity is particularly apparent in younger generations: as of 2020, only 52 percent of the post-millennial generation were non-Hispanic whites.[3] That trend will continue. In other words, increased diversity is not only our present; it is our future.

The advantages arising from this increased diversity have been widely recognized by most major organizations. Cognizant of the inexorable demographic changes, efforts have been made almost everywhere to recruit and promote diverse people. Most major corporations, universities, and civic organizations now want fully to embrace diversity as an important goal. Not only does the mix of different cultures, perspectives, and background make for a stronger and more creative environment or workforce but embracing and promoting diversity attracts talent and helps organizations to compete and perform more successfully.[4]

Yet, organizations and the people in them have been struggling with how to address the unsettling effects of assimilating a growing influx of different peoples and cultures. Among these effects is the frustration of newly recruited diverse employees because of a lack of

---

[1] Charles L. Howard, The Organizational Ombudsman: Origins, Roles, and Operations—A Legal Guide (2010).

[2] U.S. Census Bureau Quick Facts, https://www.census.gov/quickfacts/fact/table/US/PST045219 (last accessed July 23, 2021).

[3] Richard Fry & Kim Parker, *Early Benchmarks Show 'Post-Millennials' on Track to Be Most Diverse, Best-Educated Generation Yet*, Pew Research Center (November 15, 2018), https://www.pewresearch.org/social-trends/2018/11/15/early-benchmarks-show-post-millennials-on-track-to-be-most-diverse-best-educated-generation-yet/ (last accessed July 23, 2021).

[4] Katherine W. Phillips, *How Diversity Makes Us Smarter*, Scientific American (October 1, 2014), https://www.scientificamerican.com/article/how-diversity-makes-us-smarter/ (last accessed March 15, 2021).

promotion opportunities, mentor relations, and support in general.[5] Consequently, organizations are finding that even though they try very hard to recruit new diverse employees, those employees frequently do not stay. In contrast to the broad recognition that there is a need to recruit diverse employees, there is not broad recognition of the need for more measures inside organizations to make diversity efforts sustainable and successful. Recruitment is not enough. To achieve the full potential of diversity initiatives, organizations need to provide people with additional resources to help them be successful once they are in the organization.

This observation is also true about the role of women in our organizations. Whether as a goal itself or as part of the goal of promoting greater diversity, most major organizations now also recognize that they need to recruit, promote, and incorporate the perspectives of women in decision making. And, as with efforts to promote other diversity goals, the results have been uneven because of existing cultural attitudes and patterns of conduct.

Even before the global pandemic began in 2020, sexual harassment and discrimination of women in organizations were major issues for women who also frequently bear the brunt of balancing work-life commitments with home-life obligations. The rise of the #MeToo movement and the highly publicized scandals of prominent men with a history of harassing women or discriminating against them shined a bright spotlight on this issue. The pandemic has exacerbated these matters as women also frequently have shouldered the burden of supervising and assisting children in virtual education programs.

Several publications, as recently as 2018–2020, discussed this widespread problem facing women and concluded that ombuds programs

---

[5] Race in the Workplace: The Black Experience in the US Private Sector, McKinsey & Company, February 2021, https://www.mckinsey.com/featured-insights/diversity-and-inclusion/Race-in-the-workplace-The-Black-experience-in-the-US-private-sector?cid=app (last accessed March 15, 2021). *See also,* Vanessa Fuhrmans & Te-Ping Chen, *What's Keeping Black Workers from Moving Up the Corporate Ladder?* Wall Street Journal, February 21, 2021 (reporting on the McKinsey Report), https://www.wsj.com/articles/whats-keeping-black-workers-from-moving-up-the-corporate-ladder-11613926801 (last accessed March 15, 2021).

could help.[6] For example, in a research report by the Urban Institute that focused on STEM workplaces,[7] the authors (one of whom was a former vice chair of the US Equal Employment Opportunity Commission) cited previous research reports to support their conclusion that "the fact that so few [women] come forward to report harassment suggests that they feel unsafe or uncomfortable in doing so." A study cited in the Urban Institute report found that "the majority of respondents who had previously reported harassment said that they would never come forward again" and that "research shows workers who come forward with concerns actually fare worse: they leave the organization sooner, face barriers to advancement, and often feel like they have ended their careers." If that were not damning enough, the Urban Institute report also cited studies that "have found that the majority of employee workplace harassment complaints were met with retaliation." The report noted that ombuds help victims avoid reliving the trauma of sexual harassment brought on by investigations: "given the confidential, informal, and impartial nature of the [ombuds'] role, targets [women experiencing harassment or discrimination] can share what they feel

---

[6] *See*, Sexual Harassment of Women: Climate, Culture, and Consequences in Academic Sciences, Engineering, and Medicine—A Consensus Study Report of the National Academies of Science, Engineering, and Medicine (Paula A. Johnson, Sheila E. Widnall, & Frazier F. Benya, Eds.) The National Academies Press (2018), https://www.academia.edu/36849378/Sexual_Harassment_of_Women_Climate_Culture_and_Consequences_in_Academic_Sciences_Engineering_and_Medicine (last visited March 15, 2021); *see also*, Frank Dobbin & Alexandra Kalev, *Why Sexual Harassment Programs Backfire*, Harv. Bus. Rev., May-June 2020, at 3; Frank Dobbin & Alexandra Kalev, *Chapter 3. Making Discrimination and Complaint Systems Better*, in What Works? Evidence-Based Ideas to Increase Diversity, Equity, and Inclusion in the Workplace, Center for Employment Equity, University of Massachusetts Amherst (2020), https://www.umass.edu/employmentequity/what-works-evidence-based-ideas-increase-diversity-equity-and-inclusion-workplace (last accessed March 15, 2021); Charles L. Howard, *What Happens When an Employee Calls the Ombudsman?* Harv. Bus. Rev., May-June 2020, at 17; and U.S. Commission on Civil Rights, Federal #MeToo: Examining Sexual Harassment in Government Workplaces, April 2020, https://www.usccr.gov/pubs/2020/04-01-Federal-Me-Too.pdf (last accessed March 15, 2020).

[7] STEM refers to the disciplines of science, technology, engineering, and mathematics.

comfortable sharing, knowing that it does not commit them to anything, and they retain control over what happens next."[8]

As with efforts to promote diversity, increasing efforts to fully integrate women in our organizations at every level are likely to fall short of the mark without additional resources that help them navigate their way through issues like sexual harassment and discrimination that are a barrier to progress. Though it may seem counterintuitive, if one of these additional resources were an ombuds office, it would be able to assist both women facing these issues and those who may feel threatened or disadvantaged by the promotion of women or who may be part of a culture that perpetuates unacceptable behavior. Ombuds are available to help *all* people. Their utility and ability to help some people is not diminished by their assistance to other people.

Another significant source of change and disruption in our society and organizations is the retirement of the baby boom generation from the workforce and concomitant replacement by Gen X, millennials, and Gen Z. These younger cohorts have different expectations about work-life balance, different approaches to style and modes of communication, and different perceptions of hierarchy, among many other differences. These differences can surface in ways that may catch some of us by surprise. For example, an employment lawyer shared a situation in which a millennial manager wanted to fire a baby boomer employee he supervised because the employee would try to speak with him in person about work issues. The manager thought the employee was wasting his time since the employee could have easily texted or emailed his concerns.

Many Americans in these younger generations have come of age amid greater diversity and with more acceptance—both legally and socially—of same-sex marriages and differences in gender identity and expression. This has enabled many LGBTQ persons to participate more fully in many facets of educational, social, political, and economic life. Some individuals may be indifferent to these societal changes and others

---

[8] Jenny R. Yang & Batia Katz, Promising Practices for Addressing Harassment in the STEM Workplace: How to Lead in Today's Environment, Urban Institute Research Report, March 2020, https://www.urban.org/sites/default/files/publication/102045/promising-practices-for-addressing-harassment-in-the-stem-workplace_0.pdf (last accessed March 15, 2021).

may be supportive of colleagues and others within the LGBTQ community. And yet, like many societal changes described above, not everyone is accepting of or comfortable with these changes and new roles, so our educational and workplace organizations are a battle ground where leaders frequently struggle to find ways to promote common community and protect the rights of all.

Changes wrought by demographic transformations have not occurred in isolation. There also have been fundamental changes in the way we work. Gone are the days when it was common for someone to have the same employer for thirty-eight years, as I did. Gone also is a strong sense of loyalty to one employer, as large numbers of people have experienced layoffs or difficulty in getting jobs. A whole generation was caught in the maw of the 2008 Recession and then again in the 2020–2021 pandemic. With union membership in the private sector in 2020 barely above 6 percent of the workforce, it is not surprising that many employees feel estranged from their employers and that there is no one to advocate for or help them.[9]

In some ways, even the concept of "employment" on a full-time basis with benefits is beyond the reach of many. The pandemic accelerated a trend that had been building for many years: the "gig economy." The tenuous and often temporary relationship of these gig workers with the organization for which they work presents greater difficulty in dealing with organizational issues than those faced by employees. The problem is not only that they may not know where to go to seek assistance; it is also that they are afraid or unwilling to jeopardize their fragile economic lifeline. Speaking with an ombuds is a no-risk way to seek guidance for people in this situation.

Compounding the upheavals caused by these demographic and work-life changes has been a transformative change in how we communicate. Even before the pandemic in 2020, the rise of social media, the ubiquity of the Internet, and the increase in remote learning and working were significant social forces that changed almost everything about the way people interact. Just to name the most obvious examples, email, texting, remote access, cloud computing, and video conferencing have

---

[9] US Department of Labor, Bureau of Labor Statistics, News Release, January 22, 2021 at 2, https://www.bls.gov/news.release/pdf/union2.pdf (last accessed July 23, 2021).

changed much about our lives. While all of these developments have served to facilitate increased connectivity and communication, they also—paradoxically—have reduced a sense of "connection" to an organization or among people. They have reduced opportunities for personal interaction but not necessarily the need for personal contact.

Finally, a clear picture of who we are now as an American society would not be complete without also addressing the polarizing social and political shifts that have been occurring for many years, but which accelerated after the 2016 presidential election. The effects of the demographic transformations, workforce and work-life challenges, and technological developments have not been experienced in the same ways by all regions, races and ethnicities, and economic levels of society. Whether described as "red" states v. "blue" states, urban v. rural, rich v. poor, college educated v. blue collar, Black and Brown v. White, East and West Coasts v. Middle America, immigrant v. nonimmigrant, or on some other dichotomy axis, it is clear that American society has become polarized and intolerant in many different ways. Beyond any disagreement over what are "facts" or "fake news," these political, economic, and social lines of division have resulted in a tribalism that has increased conflict and made the task of coming together for common purpose or with mutual toleration and appreciation for each other much more challenging. For many of us, these divisions have leached into our thinking and our ways of interacting with others. The events in the aftermath of the 2020 presidential election destroyed any belief that the polarizing forces of division would soon abate.

The key point for purposes of this analysis is that these demographic, social, political, economic, and technological upheavals are not just occurring in our broad, vaguely defined "society"; they are having an impact *inside* our most basic institutions, our schools and universities, our workplaces, and in our civic organizations. How could it be otherwise? It is really a perfect storm resulting from all of the other changes going on around us. If we want to begin the process of trying to restore a sense of unity, learning again to treat people as neighbors rather than adversaries, and listening to each other, our organizations must be part of the solution. They need to be champions for more peaceful and constructive conflict resolution and modes of interaction, and they need to model these values by incorporating resources into their operations, such as organizational ombuds, to provide support and assistance to *all people.*

"All people" means everyone in the organization who has issues or concerns. People on any side of any of the divides described above can feel threatened and afraid. Because ombuds are a safe place to discuss concerns and issues, they can be especially valuable to women and people of color in dealing with conflict, discrimination, and harassment. At the same time, they are also equally available to people who may feel that they have been disadvantaged by an organizational emphasis on women and people of color. Ombuds are ideally adapted to deal with people and organizations in turmoil, and their commitment to impartiality allows them to be a resource for everyone. For that reason, they are an important complement to diversity and inclusion programs. Increasing diversity on any dimension where there might be perceived "winners" and "losers" without also providing a resource to help anyone with uncertainties and conflict is to invite frustration, departures, and outcomes that fall short of desired goals.

"All people" also includes senior leaders. Ombuds can be of great assistance to senior leaders in dealing with the issues that they and their organizations are facing as a result of all the upheaval described above. Today's organizational leaders, in virtually every sector, have to juggle strategic, financial, environmental, societal, and governmental priorities, all of which take on equal importance in the eyes of an ever-broadening constituency of stakeholders: customers, employees, communities, regulators, the press, and a very involved and watchful public. If that were not enough, senior leaders and their organizations also face ever more threats from external disruptions such as public health crises, environmental crises, cyber-attacks, and political uprisings.

As a result, leadership must be agile and able to pivot and respond as necessary to address these issues and threats. This requires that they understand what is happening in their organization to maximize the engagement of human capital and manage risk across all areas of the organization. Those with a seat at the table driving their organizations through all of this chaos—whether on the board, in the C-suite, or as senior leaders below them—need every advantage they can get to deal with the challenges they face and should see ombuds as an added and thoughtful resource to bring a deeper level of listening and support to a changing and highly stressed workforce or constituency while also providing objective information and insights to leadership.

All of this is to say that life for many Americans—and for virtually the entire world—has not been and will not be business as usual. The changes described above are monumental and have been hard adjustments for most people and organizations. It is not surprising then, that the conflict, uncertainty, distrust for institutions, sense of lack of support, and unfamiliarity with different people, cultures, and roles have increased the general level of angst in our society. It has affected all institutions, but particularly those where we spend the most time: our educational institutions and our workplaces. We all should be asking ourselves how organizations should best address these disruptive forces of change. What has been done to date and is it enough?

B. Do We Really Need an Organizational Ombuds Office if We Already Have Formal Functions Like Human Resources, Compliance, Internal Audit, and a Hotline; and Whistleblower Protection and Antiretaliation Laws and Policies Are Widespread?

1. Formal and Informal Channels

Let's start by looking at the difference between "formal" and "informal" channels. Functions such as Human Resources (HR), compliance, internal audit, and a hotline or helpline are formal channels. That is, these functions are part of the management of an organization because they have a specialized duty to perform on behalf of the organization. They are the organization's "agents" for accomplishing their respective management tasks. If someone were to report a sexual harassment claim to HR, for example, the organization would legally be "on notice" of that claim and, under the law, have a duty to investigate it and take appropriate corrective action. Likewise, if a fraud claim were reported to compliance or internal audit, notice of this claim would be "imputed" to the organization such that if the organization did not investigate and respond to it, the organization itself could be legally liable. An organization in today's world could not function properly without the training and specialized knowledge that is required for each of these formal functions.

Likewise, an organization could not function without managers. An organization requires people to direct its work, and those who have significant management responsibility (managers, senior executives, officers, deans and other senior administrators, and boards of directors or trustees) also have a duty to function as a formal channel. Reporting something to a company manager, senior executive, officer, or board member; to a law firm partner; or to a university department chair, officer, or dean is tantamount to putting the respective organization on notice of the claim, which under the law, creates a duty for them to take appropriate action to address the issue that is reported.

In contrast, the power and singular utility of an organizational ombuds office derives from its being structured as an "informal" channel. Unlike raising an issue with a formal channel, telling a coworker about something that one thinks may be a problem does not place the organization on notice because the coworker has neither management responsibilities nor specialized management obligations and hence no duty to act on that information. In this sense, an ombuds office is no different. The useful work of an ombuds depends on their **not** being a "formal" channel so that communications to or with an ombuds will not be imputed to the organization and thus not create a legal duty to act on behalf of the organization. Given all of the other formal channels, organizations do not need their ombuds to function as yet another one.[10]

Merely saying that something is an informal channel and not subject to imputed notice to the organization, however, does not make it so. Two important considerations—one structural and one legal—support an ombuds' claim to being an informal channel. These concepts help clarify why properly structured ombuds programs legitimately are able to assert that they are not a formal channel.

2. The Importance of Structure for an Informal, Independent Channel

The first of these is structural. Ombuds offices are created by an organization, which gives the organization the ability to dictate the basis (the terms, conditions, and principles) on which an ombuds office is created. Because management serves as an agent for the organization for imputing notice of claims to the organization, it is important for certain structural elements to be in place to prevent ombuds

[10] I also address various issues relating to ombuds' confidentiality and how it can legally be asserted and protected in chapter 4.

from being considered to be managers or part of management and to distinguish the role of the ombuds from that of a formal channel. For example, ombuds should not have any management responsibility (except for the internal operation of the ombuds office). Ombuds also should expressly be established as "independent" offices, so this lack of management responsibility is clear. This is accomplished by the provisions of an ombuds office charter. The charter is essentially a "terms and conditions" contractual understanding between the organization and the ombuds office and sets forth the principles and bases on which the office is authorized to operate. The constituencies served by the office are, in effect, third-party beneficiaries of this agreement and have the right to expect both the organization and the ombuds to abide by the provisions of the charter. A well-written charter makes it clear what the ombuds office is expected to do and how it should operate within the organization. The charter is therefore the foundation for the claim that regardless of whether an ombuds is employed by and exists within the organization, they function independently of it. For external ombuds, both a charter and an ombuds services agreement with the organization accomplish the same purpose.

In keeping with the requirement of independence, ombuds should also operate informally. This means that the ombuds' charter should specifically state what the ombuds is ***not*** authorized to do—such as serve as a place to notify the organization of claims against it. The ombuds should have no authority to make business or policy decisions or to conduct investigations on behalf of the organization and does not testify or produce documents relating to confidential communications. Not only does this help make the contrast between the formal channels and the ombuds office clear, but it also serves to make that distinction plain to any people who might consider consulting with an ombuds.

Ombuds offices that are compliant with the IOA's Code of Ethics and Standards of Practice are required to be impartial or neutral, meaning that they do not advocate either for constituents entitled to use the office (such as employees or students) or for the organization. As explained more fully in chapter 4, compliance with the principles of independence, informality, and impartiality are critical to the fourth principle on which ombuds programs are established: confidentiality. If an ombuds has management responsibilities or is responsible for making business decisions or implementing organizational policy, any claim of confidentiality would likely not be credible or recognized in a court challenge. The ombuds' claim of confidentiality rests on a foundation, embodied in a charter, that enables an ombuds to function in compliance with the principles that are key to an ombuds being an informal channel.

The ability to set up an ombuds office as an informal channel is almost entirely within the control of the organization. Yet some issues are of such significant public importance that laws have been enacted in various jurisdictions that create a mandatory reporting obligation in some circumstances. Child and elder abuse are two examples. In these situations, even the proper establishment of an ombuds office cannot alter the fact that ombuds may be required to comply with some of these statutes. Fortunately, the obligations imposed by these laws are relatively few and generally do not interfere with the normal functioning of an ombuds office. Some organizations have, however, sought to expand the scope of mandatory reporting for ombuds beyond that which is *required* by law. Awareness of possible sexual harassment or reporting under the Clery Act (for campus violence) are two such examples. All of these issues are addressed in chapter 4 but expanding the scope of ombuds as mandatory reporters beyond that absolutely required by law is counterproductive. Especially when this is done in connection with harassment and discrimination issues, expanding an ombuds' reporting obligations severely impinges on an organization's ability to help those affected because it deprives those people an opportunity to seek information, guidance, and options from a skilled professional.

3. Actual and Apparent Authority

The second concept relevant to an ombuds' entitlement to be considered an informal resource is based on "agency" principles, which are often used in law to analyze whether notice to one person or entity (the "agent") should be imputed to an organization in which the agent functions. Here, there are two parts to the analysis. The first is the notion of "actual authority." Formal channels such as HR, management, compliance, internal audit, and the board of directors (or trustees) are specifically granted authority to act on behalf of the organization in their sphere of responsibility, or that authority is inherent in the function served. To eliminate any confusion over the ombuds' informal status, a charter should be clear that the ombuds has "no authority" to investigate or make business or policy decisions for the organization. Likewise, a charter should specifically prohibit the ombuds from having any authority to act as an agent of the organization for receiving notice of claims asserted against the organization. Not only is this good for the ombuds, but it is also good for the other formal channels and the organization itself. It is far better for the organization to require any such claims that a person or entity may want to assert to be channeled to those functions and offices that have the specialized training, expertise, and responsibility to deal with them. The ombuds' role, therefore, is limited to providing a visitor with information, guidance, or options on such issues. The ombuds is not a place to notify the organization of a claim.

The second element of agency principles is that of "apparent authority." Regardless of whether an agent of an organization has "actual" authority to act (or receive notice of claims) on behalf of an organization, the law generally permits an organization still to be liable if an agent has "apparent" authority. This means that if a reasonable person could believe that the agent in question had such actual authority to act or receive notice—even when they did not, in fact, have such authority—the organization can be held liable. This certainly would be a problem for the organization if the ombuds were seen as having "apparent" authority to act on behalf of the organization but was also bound by confidentiality not to disclose to the organization information that the ombuds acquires in confidential communications. Because of this concern, it is especially important that a charter specify both what the ombuds is authorized to do as well as what the ombuds is not authorized to do (e.g., accept notice of claims on behalf of the organization) **AND** (this is the key point for an apparent authority analysis) the charter and related documents, such as brochures, website descriptions of the office, and FAQs, should be widely publicized or available inside the organization. Publicizing the lack of authority of the ombuds to act as an agent of the organization for notice purposes is what makes it unreasonable for anyone to believe that the ombuds office would have authority to do something that it specifically and expressly does not have authority to do.

I hope that the discussion above makes it clear why legal concepts of actual and apparent authority, as well as critical elements in the structure of an organizational ombuds program, are so crucial to the ability to assert that an organization's ombuds program is an informal channel. Additional information related to this issue is provided in chapter 4.

4. The Limitations of Formal Channels

With this understanding of the differences between formal and informal channels, let's now focus on a key assumption about formal channels that does not withstand close scrutiny. Specialty functions like HR, compliance, internal audit, management, and hotlines are almost always designated as places where people can report misconduct, failures, and other claims or concerns, and these functions are designed to then investigate and recommend corrective action for the matters brought to their attention.

Many, if not most, organizations also have whistleblower and non-retaliation policies that supplement similar statutory protections that ostensibly protect people from retaliation for raising issues.

Given all of this, why is there a need for an informal channel that offers an opportunity for confidential communication about such issues, but which has no corresponding duty to report relevant information to a formal channel? The answer is that all of the formal channels rely on an assumption that people will use them when they have issues that come within the purview of those formal channels. A closer look at this assumption reveals that it has significant limitations.

One such limitation to this assumption is that sometimes formal channels fail either to act or take appropriate action when matters are brought to their attention. Numerous examples in multiple categories in part II reveal instances where people went to the ombuds with an issue only after nothing was done when they first brought the matter to a formal channel. When this occurs, what is the failsafe means to raise an issue or "check" the indifference or failure of the formal channel to act?

Other people are reluctant to go to a formal channel with an issue or, even worse, they refuse to do so. It is especially hard for many leaders in organizations with robust business conduct policies that create a duty on the part of all employees to report misconduct, to realize that, as good as all the formal channels and polices are or can be, there still is a failure—or even a refusal—of some people to use them, and especially so for matters that are significant. The problem is not due to any design flaw in the structure or functioning of these formal channels. Rather, the problem is inherent in human nature and a result of social and cultural conditioning that we all experience. To better explain this limitation, we should consider the common cultural aversion to reporting on others, as well as the influence of uncertainty and fear that inhibit people from coming forward.

5. The Blue Uniform Problem

One way to understand the failure or refusal of people to report to formal channels is to view this aspect of human nature in an analogous context: reporting to the police, which is why I call it the blue uniform problem. Formal channels have a duty to act on what is reported to them, much like police have a duty to enforce the law. Formal channels investigate complaints of reported suspicions of misconduct, and the results of their work are used to take corrective action in the form of reprimands, dismissals, or referrals to the authorities. While such actions may be necessary to comply with the law, enforce organizational policy, or ensure effective operation of the organization, these actions are, or are perceived to be, punishments. The nub of the problem is that, in this sense, formal channels function very much like the police.

Do we really think that citizens are likely in all, or even most, cases to report matters that they know or suspect to the police? From an early age we are taught not to "tattle" or "rat" on others; and once we come of age, fear and uncertainty of what might happen to us personally if we do only reinforce this tendency not to get involved or "stick our neck out" if we don't have to. It is often not possible to have a confidential discussion with either the police or a formal channel about a concern or what to do, because they cannot legitimately promise confidentiality. It does not take long for most people to realize that while HR, for example, is designed to address employment issues, HR is there to act for the employer on those issues, not for the employee. To raise the issue with a formal channel is to bring it to their attention, and they must act on that information. When that occurs, the investigative machinery is engaged and will roll on and over people until the investigation is complete. Left with the choice of either reporting or not reporting something, a significant percentage of people will simply not report, regardless of policies making it mandatory or organizational cultures that purportedly encourage it.

Why is it that people will not report concerns, even if reporting is mandatory? First, when people are uncertain, they are reluctant to come forward. Uncertainty can arise in a variety of ways. It can be because of youth, inexperience, cultural background, or a lack of knowing or understanding all the facts or even the process. Certainly, with the demographic changes described above there are many segments of our workforce or society who do not trust the police or others who exercise formal authority.

They also may not have experience in dealing with a problematic issue or have a long enough tenure with an organization to have seen that reporting misconduct is not punished (or maybe they previously have seen that it is punished). It is part of our human nature not to act when we are uncertain. The easiest and simplest thing to do is to remain silent, particularly if doing so helps you avoid becoming involved in an investigation.

A second manifestation of uncertainty—and perhaps the most significant one—is the "Am I right?" syndrome. "Am I right?" is only the lead question. Related questions compound a person's insecurity and therefore reluctance to raise an issue: "Are there things that I do not know?" "What if I am wrong?" "What will happen to me (or my job or connections with other people) if I do report something?" If someone only suspects that something may be amiss but is not sure, or if there is a significant power differential between the one who suspects misconduct and the person suspected of inappropriate conduct, a more junior, younger, or inexperienced person is not likely to come forward.

And finally, in today's organizations we have people who come from diverse cultures and backgrounds, and some of those cultures and backgrounds have a history that has made people strongly resistant to reporting on others. Nothing in the media coverage of stories of police misconduct has in any way ameliorated this concern. Accordingly, formal channels in organizations should assume that, at least for a significant segment of people, there is a blue uniform problem: an unwillingness or refusal of some people to report to formal channels.

The failure to report driven by uncertainty has at least two consequences that should be of concern to any organization. The first is that the more significant the issue that someone is concerned about, the greater the influence of uncertainty on discouraging the person from coming forward. From the organization's perspective, this relationship should be just the opposite: the more significant the issue, the more important it is that it be raised for the good of the order. The second is that when the dissonance created by uncertainly reaches a certain point, instead of reporting an issue notwithstanding the fear of uncertainty, a common response is just to leave the organization. This will vary with the individual but may be sooner rather than later with younger people, people with less tenure in the organization, and for some people of color. Examples in part II illustrate this point.

6. Hotlines and Helplines

But aren't hotlines designed to be a reporting channel for people who are not sure and just want to raise an issue anonymously? The answer is yes, but reality here also often falls short of design expectations.

These services, often subcontracted to outside venders, are indeed places where people can raise issues anonymously, giving them the ability to help someone who desires to remain anonymous because of uncertainty. Yet, despite the involvement of outsiders and a promise of anonymity, these are still formal channels because the information collected is invariably reported back to a general counsel, a compliance officer, or a similar formal channel, and if appropriate, an investigation commences. It does not take a person long to realize that that if their uncertainty is due to a lack of knowledge of what will happen or happen to them if an investigation ensues, this may not be quite the user-friendly resource as advertised.

I presented a significant amount of data on the actual usage of hotlines and helplines in *The Organizational Ombudsman,* and I am not aware of any significant changes in the reality of organizations' experience with them. Despite the fact that the impetus for creating these resources as a means of confidential or anonymous reporting was for issues relating to accounting, financial, and similar fraud issues, experience confirms that they are rarely used for these purposes. Of the issues raised in reports to hotlines or helplines, a large percentage of them typically involve employment, compensation, and similar issues, rather than the type of fraud reporting that was the initial justification for creating these programs. These nonfraud issues are best addressed by counseling and discussion, not an impersonal communication through a hotline. And even when hotlines are used for their intended purpose, a desire to preserve anonymity can result in too little information being disclosed to be useful in prompting or guiding an investigation of an issue. In addition, hotlines are rarely used at all by significant demographic groups, including people from international backgrounds or cultures that have had adverse experiences with such anonymous reporting.

In sum, hotlines and helplines function to supplement the outreach of other formal channels by permitting anonymous reporting. They are better to have than not. Still, a hotline is a formal channel in the sense that the information received is forwarded to other formal channels for investigation and action. While these resources may address the fear of uncertainty in some people, it is hard to provide enough information to initiate an investigation without providing too much (which could identify the person wishing to remain anonymous). In the final analysis, hotlines have been found to be culturally nonresponsive for some demographic groups. The actual usage is skewed toward employment issues that can be better dealt with through discussion and interaction, which require a confidential setting to be effective.

7. Fear of Retaliation and the Limitations of Whistleblower and Nonretaliation Laws and Policies

The fear of retaliation is even more powerful than fear caused by uncertainty in inhibiting people from coming forward to report issues or suspicions of misconduct. To respond to this concern, jurisdictions around the world have responded with laws designed to encourage reporting and protect those who do. Whistleblower laws (and similar policies adopted by organizations) encourage and/or reward people for bringing issues of suspected misconduct to a formal channel. In the United States and the individual states, there are hundreds of such laws. There are also other laws (and policies adopted by organizations) that prohibit retaliation against those who do come forward in good faith to report their concerns. In theory and as a foundation to express important public policy (that people who come forward should not be punished), these whistleblower and antiretaliation laws and policies absolutely make sense. A closer look at what they can do—but more importantly at what they cannot do—reveals that there is still a gap in providing assistance for people who are reluctant or unwilling to report an issue because of fear of retaliation.

The explanation of this phenomenon begins with a simple observation: just as any organization cannot function without people to do the work, people in virtually every organization function in a hierarchy in which others are in positions of authority over them (be it a dean, department head, or a "boss"). People being people, some supervisors or bosses are receptive to criticism and some are not; some are vindictive and some are not. People with authority over others have many ways to punish or express displeasure with a subordinate within the wide range of discretion that they must have to do their jobs. This fact alone makes it hard for any law or policy to interfere with or micromanage a particular situation. Who knows if not getting the next good assignment is the result of a supervisor's displeasure over some report or just because someone else is better suited or more available? It could be either, neither, or both. Yet, to a person who has raised an issue that could be seen as a criticism or attack on the status quo, such a sequence is often *perceived* in cause-and-effect terms: I did not get this assignment *because* I brought forward the issue that criticized my supervisor, the organization, etc. I call this "below the radar" retaliation but acknowledge that it may, in fact, involve no retaliation at all. If conduct might be perceived by a person as retaliation, it has the same effect; the fear of reporting is not assuaged despite whistleblower laws and policies that ostensibly protect that person.

Two other common types of perceived retaliation are also not responsive to or ameliorated by whistleblower and antiretaliation laws and policies: peer retaliation and what I call "ripple" retaliation. Regardless of what either the law or polices provide, they cannot provide reliable protection to someone who reports something to a formal channel. Not only does taking such a bold step break ranks with peers, it can have consequences that extend beyond the organizational context and have an adverse effect on life outside the organization or on family members who also may be excluded from friendships or other activities. For that reason, the power of intermingled work and personal peer networks to punish someone (and their family) who breaks ranks to report possible misconduct or other issues must be recognized as a factor that can inhibit people from coming forward regardless of any official policy.

Similarly, awareness from press reports, gossip, or some other source about adverse consequences to whistleblowers generally can have a profound inhibiting effect. The circumstances in which someone else suffered adverse consequences for coming forward might be very different from a potential reporter's own circumstances inside his or her own organization. Even though there is nothing that any organization can do about what has happened or may happen elsewhere, the effect of what happens in larger society does influence and affect people by increasing their reluctance to come forward. That is why I call this ripple retaliation. A perfect example of this is the publicity that surrounded the presidential impeachment whistleblower (and many of the witnesses who also came forward) in 2019 and 2020. The observation that these people suffered adverse consequences as a result of coming forward despite a right to legal protection was not lost on many people. Such an observation will likely be generalized and applied to potentially quite different situations and circumstances. It is extremely hard for any organization to combat the common assumption that all whistleblowers always get screwed. I was so concerned about the potential ripple effect of the impeachment experience on potential whistleblowers that I wrote an op-ed explaining that while whistleblower laws and policies are necessary, instead of focusing on how we can protect a whistleblower (we really can't), the better question is how we can help people raise issues without having to become a whistleblower.[11] (HINT: ombuds can help.)

There are two additional considerations that also cannot be adequately addressed by whistleblower and antiretaliation laws and policies. First, longevity with an organization or senior status does not insulate one from the various types of retaliation or perceived retaliation described above: below-the-radar, peer, or ripple. In fact, because more senior people have more to lose, the inhibiting power of the fear of retaliation for a person with senior status or a longtime presence in an organization is arguably even greater.

---

[11] Charles L. Howard, *INSIGHT: Avoid Being a Whistleblower with Safe Place Ombudsman Programs,* Bloomberglaw.com, US Law Week, https://news.bloomberglaw.com/us-law-week/insight-avoid-being-a-whistleblower-with-safe-place-ombudsman-programs, Dec. 2, 2019 (last accessed September 4, 2021).

Second, the remedy for a claim of retaliation for being a whistleblower is a legal process. Whether it involves purely internal administrative procedures or a lawsuit, the machinery and concern for due process involve legal issues and technicalities, and the mere process of resolving a claim of whistleblower retaliation will take an extended period of time. That puts a whistleblower in a position directly adverse to their organization and many of the people in it and often for years. The cost, including attorneys' fees, personal toll, delay, publicity, and extended uncertainty are real considerations for those who might consider coming forward with an issue. These potentially severe and perverse adverse consequences of a process designed to protect people who come forward often outweigh any financial reward or desire to comply with the law or an organization's policies.

The Organizational Ombudsman has much supporting data for these observations, but one of the most powerful studies documenting the failings of whistleblower laws and antiretaliation protections was published afterward and in a somewhat surprising publication: *The New England Journal of Medicine.* In an article entitled "Whistle-Blowers' Experiences in Fraud Litigation against Pharmaceutical Companies" published in 2010, the authors interviewed twenty-six federal False Claim Act plaintiffs (called "relators") and reported on the adverse consequences they experienced. All of these relators were successful in their whistleblower claims, resulting in significant personal recoveries net of attorneys' fees and taxes ranging from $100,000 to $42 million (with five receiving less than $1 million, thirteen receiving from $1 million to $5 million; and seven receiving more than $5 million). Twenty-two of these relators were insiders at their organizations who first tried to report their issues through reporting channels inside their organizations but were unsuccessful in getting the organization to act. When they finally did file a False Claims Act complaint, the median time from filing to closure was 4.9 years. At a personal level, that is a long time to be in a position adverse to one's employer.

This study illustrates many of the points addressed above, including the time to vindicate one's rights and the personal toll on whistleblowers. The authors reported that of the twenty-two insiders, only two were still employed by the organization when their matters (successfully) concluded and the "prevailing sentiment was that the payoff had not been worth the personal cost."

> Eighteen insiders (82%) reported being subject to various pressures by the company in response to their complaints. . . . For at least eight insiders, the financial consequences were reportedly devastating. One said, "I just wasn't able to get a job. It went on longer and longer. Then I lost—I had a rental house that my kids were (using to go) to school. I had to sell the house. Then I had to sell the personal home that I was in. I had my cars repossessed. I just went—financially I went under. Then once you are financially under? Then no help. Then it really gets difficult. I lost my 401(k). I lost everything. Absolutely everything." (Relator 17)
>
> Financial difficulties were associated with personal problems. Six relators (all insiders) reported divorces, severe marital strain, or other family conflicts during this time. Thirteen relators reported having stress-related health problems, including shingles, psoriasis, autoimmune disorders, panic attacks, asthma, insomnia, temporomandibular joint disorder, migraine headaches, and generalized anxiety.[12]

In sum, neither the law nor a policy can really protect a whistleblower because they do not address common types of retaliation or perceived retaliation that people fear and experience. Existing formal channels, including specialized functions like HR, compliance, internal audit, and a hotline, as well as whistleblower protection and antiretaliation laws and policies, are necessary but insufficient to address the needs of people who fear retaliation or who are uncertain about what to do or what will happen to them if they were to raise issues.

C. An Ombuds Program Fills the Gap

If one were to design a function to address the gap not served well by formal channels, what should it look like? First, it must not be a formal channel. If uncertainty and fear of reporting or retaliation are strong inhibiting forces, any potential remedy must not also trigger a "blue uniform" reason for not raising an issue. Second, it must be confidential.

---

[12] Aaron S. Kesselheim, David Studdert, & Michelle M. Mello, *Whistle-Blowers' Experiences in Fraud Litigation against Pharmaceutical Companies,* New Engl. J. Med., no.19, 1832, 1836 (May 13, 2010).

Confidentiality is really the only thing that has been proven to be responsive to uncertainty and fear because it creates a safe space to discuss issues, ask questions, and seek guidance without prompting an investigation, a record, or compelling action. Exhortation and creating obligations to come forward, as expressed in many business conduct policies, do not address this gap. While hotlines can be anonymous, and in this sense are confidential, they are cumbersome mechanisms for anything other than tips that misconduct is occurring and should be investigated. They do not provide either coaching or creative responses on how issues could be raised without disclosing the identity of the person raising them.

And finally, any effective remedy should address what often seem to be the empty promises in whistleblower laws and policies of protection from retaliation. A whistleblower law may provide a bounty for reporting misconduct, but incentives to do something often are no match against the fear of doing it, as introductory psychology courses teach. This is particularly true when the sources of retaliation—or more accurately, *perceived* retaliation—are beyond the ability of the organization to address, as is the case with peer, below the radar, and ripple retaliation.

Compounding all of these considerations is the fact that many people have to sue their organizations and the people who have retaliated against them to obtain the protection of the nonretaliation laws and policies. This is not a good remedy, though it is frequently the only one available. A remedy should not require a victim to endure the cost and perils of litigation, with virtually the entire organization in opposition, just to vindicate a right to protection that laws and policies purport to provide. More is needed to overcome these gaps.

A properly structured organizational ombuds office does address this gap. If it is structured to be independent, neutral, impartial, and confidential, an ombuds office can serve as a "no-barrier" resource for people. People can come to the ombuds to seek information. Even when they could obtain the same information from another source, such as HR, they may not want a formal channel to know that they are asking. For example, is drug testing really mandatory?

The power of confidentiality—the ombuds superpower—cannot be overstated. Ombuds protect the confidentiality and the identity of the people who consult with them. If no one knows that you are meeting with an ombuds, the fear of reporting is not an issue, and neither is the fear of retaliation. Confidentiality creates this safe space, and within this safe space, a person can discuss options for dealing with an issue while maintaining control over whether and how they chose to act.

This type of coaching or strategizing on how to report a problem or deal with a conflict on any issue is very important. Leaders and formal channels in organizations sometimes view issues in silos. For instance, they may ask: Is it a compliance or an HR issue? Yet, for many people, serious workplace or organizational issues are rare, and it is not uncommon for people to know that they have a problem but not be sure what "type" it is and where to go or what to do about it. Likewise, most people have not had any training on how to best deal with interpersonal conflicts. They may know that they have a conflict but have no idea how best to address such an issue. In this sense, ombuds serve as "one-stop shopping" resources. They can listen and provide a range of services from information to coaching to options for action on virtually any issue that touches life in the organization. There is no need to consider in advance if it is an HR or compliance problem or something entirely different.

An often-overlooked advantage of ombuds programs stems from their impartial role. Since they are neither part of management nor advocates for employees, they are seen as honest brokers of information and guidance. They advocate only for fair process, which should be a goal of any legitimate organization. Do not mistake this impartiality for passivity. It is true that ombuds have no formal managerial power, but they can be both proactive and impartial. I am aware of many circumstances in which ombuds persisted in their efforts to work with visitors to find creative options for their visitors to act on even when at first no solution appeared in sight.

A good ombuds is a knowledgeable resource who has considerable peripheral vision. They are skilled and experienced in helping people with interpersonal conflicts and problem resolution. In this sense, they are ideally adapted to deal with people and organizations in turmoil. Because they offer a safe place to raise issues, they can be especially valuable to women and people of color in dealing with conflict, discrimination, and harassment. At the same time, their commitment to impartiality allows them to be a resource for everyone. They are an important complement to diversity and inclusion programs because increasing diversity on any dimension without also providing a resource to those potentially advantaged and disadvantaged thereby to help with uncertainties and conflict is to invite frustration and employee departures. That results in outcomes that fall short of desired goals.

1. But How Does All of This Really Help the Organization?

Even when I think I have been successful in explaining why formal channels are not sufficient regardless of how good or well supported they are, there is a final topic on the minds of organizational leaders when considering the need for an ombuds office. Though rarely expressed in the cynical terms I use here, this inquiry is based on a perfectly legitimate core consideration: "Yes, I can understand how ombuds might be helpful for employees or the other people in our organization, but they are an overhead expense (and produce no revenue) so how do ombuds really benefit the organization itself?"

I want to respond to this question by beginning at the most fundamental level before moving to the practical level. The fundamental issue provides context necessary for a response about the benefits in practice.

At the most basic level, I believe we collectively want and expect our organizations and institutions to comply with the law and operate in ethical ways. Yes, this is required, but it is also desired. In effect, we want our organizations to do the "right thing." But sometimes it can be hard to determine what the right thing is, as there are conflicting laws, policies, or pressures on an organization; and even well-intentioned people can disagree over what the right or legal thing is. Organizations can only act through people, and people sometimes are not well-intentioned, fall short of expectations, and make mistakes. In so doing, they cause the organization not to comply with the law or to engage in unethical conduct, or perhaps even worse, to actively engage in wrongdoing. One category of examples in part II contains examples where formal channels are part of the problem. When that occurs, as it will from time to time, what is a failsafe way to catch those issues? For large organizations, it is not a question of whether people acting on behalf of an organization will make errors or engage in misconduct; it is only a question of where, when, and how.

This fundamental principle motivated the United States Sentencing Commission to develop a scheme of guidelines for dealing with the sentencing for organizations convicted of criminal misconduct. The guidelines for organizations had to be different from those for individuals because, unlike individuals, organizations themselves cannot be punished with prison terms. The objective was a system of disincentives to discourage organizations from tolerating criminal conduct and incentives to encourage them to try to prevent it or, if criminal conduct did occur, to take remedial action by reporting it and accepting responsibility for it. Without going into all of the details, one of the incentives in the Federal Sentencing Guidelines for Organizations (FSGO) is to have an "effective compliance and ethics program." The goal has been to encourage organizations to promote a culture in the organization that encourages ethical conduct and compliance with the law. One of the elements necessary for receiving credit for doing so is "to have and publicize a system, *which may include mechanisms that allow for anonymity or confidentiality*, whereby the organization's employees and agents may report *or seek guidance* regarding potential or actual criminal conduct *without fear of retaliation*."[13]

The promulgation of the FSGO was one of the major factors that resulted in compliance offices becoming a standard feature of the modern governance of major organizations. The assumptions that underlay it have global acceptance. But if the fear of retaliation is too great for many people to report misconduct, or if misconduct sometimes involves formal channels as shown above and amply demonstrated in the examples in part II, it is time to give full meaning to the need for a resource that allows people to "seek guidance."

An ombuds office does that. It also serves the fundamental purpose of a "check" on the organization's conduct in that it can collect and present information about troubling behavior, systemic issues, or trends in a way that bypasses the organizational hierarchy and flows directly to those in charge. Even though an ombuds may, in doing so, be received with the enthusiasm of a skunk at a garden party, an ombuds—functioning in the quotidian role of helping people—will inevitably become aware of issues that senior management should know about but doesn't.

---

[13] UNITED STATES SENTENCING MANUAL, § 8B2.1(b)(5)(C) (Nov. 1, 2018) (emphasis added), https://www.ussc.gov/sites/default/files/pdf/guidelines-manual/2018/GLMFull.pdf (last accessed March 15, 2021).

When many leaders are asked what keeps them up at night, a frequent response is that they worry about what they don't know. And the key point—at the most basic level—is that the ombuds' role as a listening post and change agent can be of great service to an organization and its senior leadership by informing senior leadership of issues and situations that they may not know about. In this sense, an ombuds function should be seen as a critical element of good organizational governance even though, as an informal channel, it definitely is *not part of* management.

Moving to more practical issues, a good ombuds office assists the organization with the resolution of interpersonal conflict and surfacing issues. It is a superb alternative dispute resolution mechanism, using tools such as counseling, coaching, and facilitation and mediation. An ombuds office demonstrates that the organization cares about people and wants to assist them so that they can be fully heard. If appropriate baseline measures are noted at the commencement of an ombuds program, over time they should reflect a positive impact of the ombuds office on grievances and employment litigation. An ombuds office should also improve employee engagement, morale, retention, and loyalty. When ombuds survey their visitors and ask, "what would you have done if you had not gone to the ombuds?" there is almost always a significant number who respond that they would have filed a lawsuit or left the organization. A review of the examples in part II supports the conclusion that ombuds are often helpful in resolving issues that otherwise might have ended up in litigation against the organization. These represent real and tangible cost savings in terms of both direct outlays (not having to retain lawyers as much to defend grievances or litigation) and cost avoidance, such as freeing up the time of administrators and leaders from having to address these issues. For example, some very busy HR departments regularly refer people to the ombuds when the issues presented do not rise to the level of policy or legal violations. These referrals result in more assistance for people and allow HR to concentrate on matters that they must handle.

Another and possibly surprising benefit of an ombuds office is assistance that ombuds provide to middle and senior managers. Senior leaders commonly assume that an ombuds exists primarily for the benefit of lower-level employees or other lower ranks in the organization hierarchy. That is not the case. Part II contains example of senior leaders who have sought guidance from an ombuds. Beyond the assistance ombuds can provide to an organization's most senior leaders, I learned through many years of experience representing multiple ombuds programs that where there are significant numbers of engineers, scientists, academics, or other professional people, approximately 35 percent to 40 percent of the inquiries to ombuds come from those ranks. Many of the people in these groups are themselves middle managers of people, and the guidance and coaching that they receive from the ombuds helps them do their jobs better. It is just these categories of "yeomen" that are the operational backbone and the most important human capital of many organizations, and money spent to retain them and better equip them to do their jobs is money well spent.

Three additional benefits to the organization itself deserve mention. First, the ombuds function should not be seen as competing with formal channels but as extending their reach and enhancing their ability to do their jobs. The issue is not whether to have formal channels or an ombuds function. Formal channels are absolutely necessary. Ombuds offices provide a "check" function when formal channels are part of the problem but also are able to enhance and work cooperatively with formal channels for the benefit of the organization. There are examples in part II in each of these categories. Although formal channels are part of the problem infrequently, it does happen, and an ombuds can be a resource that can help address those circumstances. By far, however, the more compelling collection of examples is where the ombuds work cooperatively with formal channels. If one of the major failings of formal channels is the uncertainty and fear of reporting or retaliation that prevents people from going to them, then with the guidance and creativity of the ombuds, issues will be raised—sometimes directly and sometimes indirectly—to those formal channels that otherwise would not have been raised. The formal channels can then do what they were created to do: investigate and take appropriate action.

Second, organizations often are either not aware or underestimate how significant a contribution the ombuds can make to so many facets of an organization. For the cost of an ombuds, the organization gets a consummate generalist who can serve in the roles of listener, conflict coach, mediator, trainer, organizational design specialist, triage counselor, facilitator, and thought partner. Because ombuds deal with issues from across the entire organization, they have a unique bird's-eye view of the organization. This helps ombuds connect the dots about systems, teams, conflict, and issues; and once the dots are connected, they can then bring this information to senior leadership while still preserving confidentiality. These observations can help them in their role as a change agent to develop recommendations for positive change in practices and policy that can be of substantial benefit to the organization. Ombuds can, and often do, have a prominent role in organizational training, while building conflict resolution capacity in the organization and assisting visitors with actual conflicts. This type of training covers many critical areas, including conflict management, how to have difficult conversations, how to give and receive feedback, active bystander training, mentor-mentee relationships, assumption making, and building emotional intelligence.

While ombuds routinely provide upward feedback to senior leaders, ombuds also can be on the receiving end of the two-way line of communication with senior leadership. This is a role that is underutilized by both senior leadership and ombuds. Senior leadership, however, can ask the ombuds to assist them by sharing issues that are on the minds of the leaders and such things as programs and opportunities available to people in the organization which the ombuds can then share with visitors. Senior leaders can also use the ombuds as sounding boards or engage with them as "thought resources" on issues that may have systemic or significant impact on the organization.

Finally, few things are as important to an organization as its reputation and brand. Admittedly, this intangible is hard to quantify but there are examples in part II about issues brought to the ombuds and subsequently raised with formal channels that could have resulted in embarrassing litigation or had a devastating impact on an organization's reputation. These examples are collected in the categories of "Working Cooperatively with Formal Channels" and "High Impact Cases/Potential Litigation/Threats to Organizational Reputation." When added to all of the other benefits described above and in light of the known limitations of the formal channels, having an ombuds should provide relief to an organization leader who is worried at night about what he or she does not know. Ombuds are not necessarily in a position to catch every issue that could imperil an organization's reputation, but they can promise that they will be able to identify some issues that likely would never have been raised to the organization's formal channels.

3

What Should Organizations Consider in Creating and Operating an Ombuds Program?

We covered the "why" of creating an ombuds office in the previous chapter—but what about the "how"? This compilation of questions and answers is not exhaustive, but because my objective is to provide a practical guide, these are some of the most frequently asked and important programmatic questions.

A. Who Should Be Hired as an Ombuds?

This is only the lead question, and behind it are several subordinate questions, all of which touch upon the subject. These related questions include whether an ombuds should be hired as an employee or as an external service provider; what an organization should do if it is too small to dedicate a full-time person to the position; if a person can be the ombuds while also having other job responsibilities at the organization; and what professional and personal qualities an organization should consider in hiring an ombuds.

The answers to these questions, as one would suspect, vary depending on the facts and circumstances of each organization and how it wants the ombuds program to function. As I mentioned at the end of chapter 1, ombuds programs that comply with the IOA Standards of Practice can be tailored to fit virtually any organization of any size in any context. With this disclaimer that one answer does not fit all circumstances, I am offering my thoughts. I hope at the very least that they will be a useful guide and a starting point for further examination.

1. Internal v. External

Perhaps the most important structural question in determining who to hire turns on whether the program will be staffed by an employee of the organization or by an external service provider under contract with the organization. All things considered, I favor having an internal program, provided that the organization is sufficiently large to support a full-time person (or multiple persons) in this role. There are many advantages of this approach, including the fact that an insider generally is easier to access, with fewer barriers, because (except for COVID) they have a constant presence in the organization, whereas contacting an external service provider requires a visitor to contact someone outside the organization, an unknown, and therefore a barrier that may discourage some. In addition, an internal ombuds may more readily develop ongoing relationships with people, formal channels, and senior leadership that can enhance the reputation and credibility of the ombuds function; an insider may know or may more easily learn the norms and other intricacies of the organization's culture that will enable the ombuds to provide more value and insight into the options that the ombuds can present to and discuss with a visitor; and it may be easier for the knowledge of issues and concerns raised by visitors to be concentrated in one person (or among a small group of ombuds in an office) rather than being dispersed among the multiple people who might be on the staff of an external service provider. This last point may also enable an inside ombuds to provide more meaningful feedback to senior leadership. While all of these observations obviously depend on the abilities of the ombuds involved, it almost certainly would be the case that an internal ombuds would have more hours available to devote to ombuds work than would a contract external service provider.

There are, of course, downsides to having an internal employee ombuds. The most obvious is that some other employees or members of the constituency served may see the ombuds as just another staff person, in effect no different from those serving as formal channels. It may be harder in this situation for the ombuds to be—and to be seen as—independent, especially if the ombuds does not have a charter. I call this the "you get the same paycheck as everyone else" concern, and this perception can be a barrier to trusting an internal ombuds. In addition, with just an internally employed ombuds, much of the success of the program depends on the personal qualities and abilities of that person, so while much can be gained with an internal resource, the program's effectiveness can be adversely affected if the person hired does not perform well.

Even if an organization were to conclude that it would like to have an internal ombuds, a question frequently asked is whether the ombuds should be hired from within the organization or from the outside. Again, there is no perfect answer to this question, but if there is a person currently employed who has knowledge of and experience in the organization, who has earned the respect of people at all levels of the organization, and whose personality is suited to the work of an ombuds, that may be a good choice. Ombuds training can come as part of the transition to the new position. In other organizations, the nature of the issues that exist and the perception of the existing organizational culture may be such that it would almost certainly mean that anyone hired from the inside would automatically not be seen as credible or trusted by the constituency served. For those organizations, an external service provider or hiring from outside the organization would likely be better options. Any organization planning to create an ombuds program must honestly address these questions for itself. Insights and perspectives from middle managers and people outside of the leadership group can be an important part of that self-inquiry.

Turning to the question of a potential external ombuds service provider, there are also advantages and disadvantages. Some of the downsides of an external ombuds are described above: External ombuds also probably will have more difficulty in acquiring a good understanding of the culture and idiosyncrasies of an organization, and the limitations on their ability to interact with senior leaders and formal channels (because they do not have a continuing presence in the organization) may make it harder for them to be fully effective. In my experience there is another—and perhaps the most significant—downside of an external ombuds: much more limited access to internal "marketing" opportunities. For an ombuds program to be really effective, people must know about it and understand how it works. There are many opportunities for an internal resource to accomplish this, including, for example, participating in meetings with all new employees, adding notices or articles to organizational newsletters, participating in other trainings and non-management meetings, and having an actual office or presence that is a visible reminder of the existence of the office.

All of that is much harder for an external ombuds to achieve, though not impossible. Yet, I have seen senior leaders resist such "soft" marketing by an external ombuds on the grounds that they are paying the ombuds on an hourly basis and see such activities as both an hourly expense that is not necessary and an activity that they cynically see as designed to drum up business for the ombuds that would lead to further cost. If an organization determines that an external ombuds program is the appropriate choice for the organization, it should make a concomitant commitment to provide a budget for the ombuds to engage in activities to learn about the organization and to increase awareness of the office. It serves no purpose to have an ombuds office if people are not made aware of it and do not know what it does.

On the plus side, because there is a contractual relationship between an external ombuds and the organization, it is easier as a legal matter to require and preserve confidentiality and to document that understanding and arrangement. Having an external resource also generally is an effective answer to the "you get the same paycheck as everyone else" concern. An external program also offers scalability and flexibility. If the need is for someone only part-time or a few days a week the contract can provide for that. An external service provider may be able to offer people access to a team of ombuds who represent age, racial, and gender diversity to allow people to consult with someone they might feel more comfortable with or can better relate to, all without the organization incurring the cost of full-time salaries to present this array of diversity.

Sometimes external service providers have multiple ombuds services contracts, which gives them peripheral vision on issues and how to deal with them that someone whose experience is limited to a single constituency base may not have. And finally, an external service provider may be the best option for an organization that is too small to justify employing a full-time ombuds or where distrust of insiders is an issue. The smallness of an organization may be such that hiring a third party is the best way to assure that the ombuds is independent and seen as a safe and confidential resource. The only other option for a small organization may be to have an ombuds who has other job responsibilities for the organization, so let's turn to that.

2. Collateral Duty Ombuds

"Collateral duty ombuds" is the term applied to an employee who, in addition to other work responsibilities, takes on the role of serving as the organization's ombuds. This approach has been used by some universities and other organizations where there is a belief that having an ombuds with technical or other expertise and an understanding of or respect by the constituent base will aid them in this work. A prime example is having faculty members (often emeritus) serve as ombuds for university faculty members. My advice on this issue is less even-handed than it is on the internal v. external ombuds question. I think there are certain actions that are not best practices and that in this context must be avoided.

The appointment of someone to the role of a collateral duty ombuds who also has either management responsibilities or a role as a formal channel absolutely should be avoided. I have had to advise organizations that they should not, as they had done, have someone in the role of a half-time Equal Employment Opportunity Officer and half-time ombuds or in the role of a dean of students while also being an ombuds for students. The same would be true for someone whose job responsibilities included being a Title IX Coordinator and an ombuds. These types of dual responsibilities are mutually incompatible in that the person is a part-time formal channel and purportedly a part-time informal channel. This does not work in practice and is indefensible from a legal perspective. This combination also is directly contrary to the IOA Standards of Practice that require any other collateral duties of an ombuds not to interfere with the ombuds' compliance with the four practice principles that underlie organizational ombuds practice: independence, informality, impartiality, and confidentiality. One cannot have a duty to act for an organization on matters that one becomes aware of and also comply with these principles.

With that said, it may be possible for people with specialized expertise to serve in a dual role. Emeritus faculty members often can perform in this role quite effectively since they may have no other significant responsibilities and yet have knowledge and experience that can be very helpful. For any collateral duty ombuds, the key question is whether the ombuds' other role or involvement with an issue presents a conflict of interest. The IOA Code of Ethics and Standards of Practice direct that ombuds should not become involved in matters in which they have, or appear to others to have, a conflict of interest. Where that is not likely to occur, a collateral duty ombuds may work; otherwise, it is best to look to another source for an ombuds.

3. Qualifications and Personal Qualities

No one specific professional background is necessary to be a good ombuds. Many highly effective ombuds have law degrees, a master's degree in a related field such as social work or dispute resolution, or doctoral degrees in an academic subject. Others have no postgraduate education at all. Some of these advanced study avenues, though, may be very advantageous to ombuds work. For example, a law degree may provide an ombuds with a greater understanding of the legal context for what they do, boost their perceived standing or credibility, and provide them with a better understanding of the demands made on the formal channels with whom they work. That training alone, however, is not sufficient and should not necessarily be a prerequisite, as many good ombuds do not have legal training, and there are many lawyers who, despite their legal training, do not have the personal qualities to be a good ombuds. Likewise, a master's degree in social work or in dispute resolution, for example, may be of real benefit in that it is evidence of training and experience in how to deal with people or resolve disputes. But those are only two of the many types of skills that an ombuds needs to master to be effective.

Apart from any particular academic credential, there are trainings and experience that should be required, such as basic training in mediation (offered in 40-hour courses by many organizations) and actually having mediation experience. Taking the IOA Foundations course and other basic practice courses should also be a must. The IOA also offers certification as a Certified Organizational Ombuds Practitioner® (CO-OP®), which demonstrates a high level of accomplishment, training, and knowledge in IOA-compliant programs. For career ombuds, this is certainly a worthy objective.

The personal qualities appropriate for ombuds work are harder to articulate but no less important. People with more experience and gravitas traditionally have been seen as a preferred pool of potential candidates. This is not about having grey hair or additional degrees. Rather, it is because of the experience they have obtained over the years in organizations that may help give them more credibility with senior leaders as well as others they assist. For many ombuds, the move to an ombuds position is a second or third career, and they are able to draw upon their prior experiences and bring a richness to the assistance they can provide. On the other hand, it may be appropriate to balance the need for experience in the role with a consideration of the demographic trends described in chapter 2. These trends increasingly make it appropriate for organizations to consider carefully the population profile of the group intended to be served. It may be appropriate to recruit younger and more diverse ombuds who are more likely to been seen as generational peers of the people they serve and who are more likely to have a first-hand understanding of the issues that may be brought forward. The good news is that there is already a good pool of such candidates, and that pool will only increase in size over time. And certainly, where a program contemplates more than one ombuds, having age/generational diversity, as well as gender and racial diversity facilitates more people being able to relate to the people in the ombuds role.

Aside from the age, experience, gender, demographic, or academic profile of a potential ombuds, there are some criteria that I think are essential for a good ombuds. Ombuds must, first and foremost, be empathetic and able to engage in active listening. They should have cultural humility and competence so that they are able to speak with people from diverse backgrounds at any time. They must be honest, truthful, and either widely respected or capable of engendering wide respect. They must be able to communicate effectively with people in both the highest levels in the organization and the lowest levels and, to paraphrase Rudyard Kipling, able to treat all of them with respect and dignity. High emotional intelligence, strong relationship-building skills, and a deep caring for fundamental fairness are extremely important. A mindset that values helping others is absolutely essential. There is no substitute for an ombuds having a spark of creativity to be able to find new ways to help people and the organization. A heavy dose of both courage and finesse is necessary for an ombuds to be willing and able to be "the skunk at the garden party" by bringing issues and bad news to people who may not want to hear it while still retaining their respect. And finally, an ombuds must be able to deal with the ombuds' paradox: working largely alone with visitors most of the time but also being able to collaborate with formal channels in constructive ways while preserving the independence and confidentiality required by their profession.

B. What Is the Best Reporting Structure for an Ombuds Office?

1. Reporting

The IOA Code of Ethics and Standards of Practice state that an ombuds should report to the highest level possible in an organization. Just as importantly, these documents also provide that an ombuds should not report to a function or entity that could affect or be perceived as affecting the ombuds' independence.

The ideal is to have the ombuds report to the CEO of the organization, with the ability to report as needed to a board of directors or trustees. The IOA Code of Ethics and Standards of Practice recognize that this may not always be possible, particularly for very large organizations, though I am familiar with a large multinational corporation where the ombuds meets directly with the organization's board of directors twice a year. Where reporting to the very top of an organization is not possible, reporting should be to the next level down or to the highest level achievable in that organizational culture such as, for example, to a COO or a university provost, again with the ability to take an issue higher if need be. This last caveat is rarely invoked but having that option available is very important. One of the examples in part II presents the challenging question of where a vice president goes when they have concerns about the president of an organization.

As an organization considers the most appropriate reporting channel, it should also be aware of the impact that the selection will have on the broader perception of the status of the ombuds office and the value that the organization places on it. The higher the reporting line, the more likely it is that the ombuds program will be seen by those in the organization as something that the organization values. It will make it easier for the ombuds to obtain cooperation from formal channels and others who might need to provide information to the ombuds. It also will facilitate the ombuds' ability to provide, and be seen as providing, valuable assistance both to the constituency served and to the leadership of the organization.

Having an ombuds report to a formal channel such as a compliance office or a general counsel can be very problematic, but that has been done, though rarely. When this is done, it makes the case for the ombuds' independence (and thus confidentiality) much harder to articulate and defend. Notwithstanding this concern, I am aware of good ombuds offices that have reported to these formal functions. In each case, the reporting was for administrative purposes only, not to direct or control the work of the ombuds, and other safeguards for the ombuds' independence were implemented. If the culture and existing operations of an organization strongly suggest that the ombuds report to a formal channel, an organization should understand that this is not a best practice and should take extra precautions to document and publicize that reporting is for administrative purposes only and that the ombuds is expected to remain independent and confidential.

If the culture of an organization leads it to conclude that one of these types of formal channels is the best reporting authority for an ombuds, the organization should also seriously consider whether, in that context, such a reporting line *will be perceived* as compromising the ombuds' ability to comply with their four practice principles. Where these formal channels are seen as very strong and effective, such a perception may be inescapable. If so, an organization should find another way. Regardless, it is important for the organization to have an appropriate charter addressing the reporting relationship and practice expectations that the ombuds' confidentiality will not be compromised. It is also all the more important in this context to publicize this information to the entire organization.

A final word about reporting relationships is necessary. It is never a good idea to force someone who does not believe in the role of an ombuds or who does not want to do so to be the person to whom an ombuds reports. I understand that people in these roles change, but there is a strong likelihood that such a cramdown of reporting responsibility will undermine the role of the ombuds and ultimately render it ineffective. I have seen this occur. Even if the consequence of this consideration is a reporting structure that results in reporting to a somewhat lower level, having access to and support from the person to whom the ombuds reports may be more effective. As new people are brought into an organization at senior levels, revisiting the issue of the ombuds' reporting relationship to make sure that the ombuds still has access to and support from senior leadership is also important.

2. Supervision and Evaluation

The duty to maintain confidentiality no doubt complicates the task of supervising and evaluating an ombuds because so much of what they do is behind a curtain of confidentiality. Issues can be resolved by a visitor on their own with the assistance of an ombuds, but no one besides the visitor and the ombuds will know what role the ombuds played in that result. The same is true where an ombuds helps a visitor raise an issue anonymously through a formal channel or in some other indirect way. Nevertheless, there are ways that a leader can obtain input on an ombuds' effectiveness without compromising confidentiality.

A good place to start is with basic statistics: the volume and issue types of the matters handled by the ombuds and any insights that this data offers about what is going on or changing in the organization. The same goes for the levels in the organization of people who are going to the ombuds for assistance. A spike in use by middle managers, for example, may present an opportunity to make recommendations to assist that cohort more systematically. Also, the overall usage of the ombuds office is an important statistic. Well-established offices typically serve 3 percent to 6 percent of the constituent base annually.

Many ombuds track cases in broad categories by significance (either in terms of potential cost, litigation, or brand/reputation risk). This is a practice that all ombuds should consider. Where the number of cases in these broad categories (especially potentially high-impact cases) is reported, it becomes a data point that a leader (and an ombuds) can use to compare with other data points, such as employee attrition or the number of grievances, employment litigation matters, or risk management claims, for example. An effective ombuds program may have an impact on some or all of these and similar statistics.

A final category of information that an ombuds can collect and present to management about the effectiveness of the office is from anonymous survey data of people who have used the office. A wise ombuds should collect and present some of these anonymous testimonials on the value of the office. Responses to such questions as "What would you have done in the absence of the ombuds office?" and "Are you aware of the ombuds office and would you use it if you had a workplace concern?" can be helpful in demonstrating that a significant percentage of people know about the office and would use it if they had a concern and otherwise would have either left the organization or brought suit against it (these conclusions are typically the case). While the ombuds office may not be a revenue-producing function, it can certainly have an impact by substantially reducing costs that might otherwise have been incurred by other functions in the organization.

Aside from the information available from an ombuds and the ombuds office, a senior leader can consider information available from other places in the organization and the input of others with whom an ombuds has interacted. What kind of newsletter articles, new employee presentations, and other trainings has the ombuds prepared or undertaken and how well done were they? Has the ombuds interacted with formal channels on any matters and what observations, if any, do they have?

Another way that the effectiveness of an ombuds can be evaluated is an assessment of the quality of observations and recommendations made by the ombuds to senior leaders on systemic issues and in trend reports. Are the insights helpful? Does the ombuds come with recommendations that the organization or a senior manager can actually use and that are responsive to these concerns? In these, often oral, reporting sessions, does the ombuds convey a sense of purpose, gravitas, and responsibility, and does the senior manager get the sense that the ombuds communicates well and has a good grasp on what is going on in the organization?

In most cases, these sources of information are sufficient for an organizational leader to know whether the ombuds can be trusted to do what the ombuds says they do and to abide by the IOA Code of Ethics and Standards of Practice. If there is any doubt in that trust relationship, there is yet another way that a supervisor can get a better handle on what is going on behind the confidentiality: an external consultant can be retained to evaluate the program. There are several experienced and highly regarded people who could be retained under a contractual assurance of confidentiality to review both the programmatic documentation and the operational practices of an ombuds office. In effect, this is the same type of auditing role that an organization employs for its financial reporting. A resulting evaluation letter to management or the ombuds, while not revealing ombuds-visitor confidential communications to management, can provide an independent third-party assessment of the office and might include recommendations for improvement in program documentation as well as in ombuds practices. It might even address action that the organization itself should consider taking to improve or enhance the ombuds function. Even if there is no seed of doubt about the ombuds office, having such an outside review periodically can be a healthy exercise for both the ombuds program and the organization. It can help the ombuds and senior leadership identify or confirm best practices and validate the work of the ombuds.

C. What Are Recordkeeping and Data Best Practices for Ombuds?

Recordkeeping and data protection practices for ombuds are intended to complement an ombuds' obligation to comply with practice principles in the IOA Code of Ethics and Standards of Practice. The Standards of Practice provide that an ombuds should keep no permanent records containing identifying information for the organization. Information such as notes, phone messages, and appointment calendars are to be kept in a secure manner, and ombuds should have a consistent and standard practice of destroying this information. And finally, confidentiality should be protected with respect to data and reports maintained by the ombuds office as well as the inevitable digital and electronic information that exists outside of the ombuds office that might inadvertently reveal confidential ombuds matters. In this regard, both the ombuds and the organization have a shared responsibility to protect ombuds confidentiality.

1. Ombuds Are Not Appropriate Keepers of Business Records

This IOA guidance on recordkeeping is based on two important premises. First, ombuds should not be a "business record keeper" for an organization. While HR, compliance, and the other formal channels are the agents of the organization for their specialized functions and must be business recordkeepers within the areas of their authority, ombuds are an informal channel. If properly structured, ombuds should have no official business-recordkeeping obligation. This is why ombuds do not require visitors to sign agreements to abide by the confidentiality terms under which the office is created. Maintaining those records would be tantamount to maintaining agreements to mediate an issue and would both reveal who used the office and would create a need for the ombuds to be the recordkeeper for those signed agreements on behalf of the organization. This they should not do. It is far better to state in the charter that visitors will be deemed to have agreed to abide by the terms under which ombuds services are provided. When that is done, no specific agreements need to be kept by the office for business purposes of the organization and yet the contractual claim of confidentiality is not endangered.

The second premise of this recordkeeping Standard of Practice is that routine practices support confidentiality. If ombuds are not required either to create or maintain records for the organization, then doing so only puts the promise of confidentiality at risk of being compromised by others in the organization or in a potential subsequent dispute or lawsuit. If such records of confidential communications are not required or needed, why keep them? The minimal and temporary information necessarily created in the normal course in order for ombuds to do their jobs includes information such as temporary notes, phone messages, and appointment calendars. For this type of information, once a matter has concluded, there is no need for it to be retained, and best practices provide that this type of information should be purged or destroyed regularly.[1]

2. Statistical Information, Policies, and Procedures

The best way to articulate the kind of information that should be maintained by an ombuds program is that it includes information that does not compromise ombuds' confidentiality. Thus, for example, ombuds can and should maintain statistical compilations of the types of issues

---

[1] Ombuds in public sector programs may be subject to recordkeeping requirements of freedom of information laws that limit their ability to destroy documents, thus placing more pressure on them not to create these types of documents in the first place. *See*, Charles L. Howard, The Organizational Ombudsman: Origins, Roles, and Operations—A Legal Guide 389–405 (2010).

presented to the program that are stripped of any reference to the identity of visitors or other revealing information. Any such data does not prove that there is a factual basis for those issues, however, as ombuds base their issue reporting on what people tell them rather than on the basis of any investigation or factual determination by the ombuds. This statistical information is the core embodiment of ombuds' work and serves as the source of information for systemic reports to the organization. While this data typically is not disclosed in any detail outside of the ombuds office, trends or other conclusions can be drawn from it that can provide useful insights into the organization. Other documents, such as the charter and any policies or procedures adopted to document how the office works, also should be maintained. A prime example of an important policy is the document destruction policy itself. Likewise, confidentiality agreements with non-ombuds service providers (ombuds' administrative staff, information technology (IT) consultants, interpreter and translation services, etc.) should be retained. None of these documents reveal confidential information, and all of them help establish how the office works. While an ombuds should resist any effort to compel discovery of confidential information about visitors, disclosure of this type of information related to how an ombuds program was established and how it operates would typically not be opposed.

I also advise ombuds programs to maintain a final category of information: historical documents and information such as copies of annual reports, presentations, brochures, and any other documentation or presentations that ombuds have generated or used in connection with their offices. While the ombuds may not need to refer to these historical documents on any regular basis, this information can be incredibly useful to an ombuds' lawyer in the event there is a legal challenge to the program. A lawyer may need to come up to speed quickly and may need to support court filings with affidavits and factual presentations to demonstrate how a program was created, operated, and publicized. I have used this type of data on many occasions. In fact, I once had an occasion where data was available to prove that an annual report (containing important information about the program) was sent to all employees of the organization, including documentation that it was sent to the plaintiff in a lawsuit. The ombuds office was also able to provide information to document that this person was also in attendance at a training program at which the ombuds spoke and presented key information about the program, including the fact that the ombuds was not authorized to receive notice of claims against the organization. There was even a record of the presentation used by the ombuds at this training program, and a copy of it still existed. For a litigator, having access to this kind of information is a dream come true.

3. Data Security

Ombuds have employed various ways to maintain the security of their confidential information. Typically, ombuds discourage the use of email for confidential communications because electronic communications are inherently insecure. While ombuds in programs that have a widely dispersed constituency may of necessity need to be contacted by email if only to schedule a time for a telephone call, even that presents some level of risk and for that reason usually is discouraged where possible. Other ombuds have found ways to use zip drives or not keep confidential data on servers maintained by their organizations, but because of the wide variation in types and scale of organizations with ombuds programs, there is no uniform practice. In this regard, IOA could provide a valuable service to its members by providing more current and sophisticated guidance on how ombuds programs can best ensure data security. Plans for doing just that are underway, but in the meantime, the best advice for ombuds programs and those planning to create ombuds programs is to work with internal IT resources to develop reasonable and appropriate ways to securely maintain confidential information and to create policies and practices that make this confidential information accessible by only the ombuds program. This should be an obligation shared by both the ombuds and the organization.

D. What Reports Should Ombuds Prepare and What Should Be Included?

Some aspects of ombuds' reporting are addressed in section B.2 of this chapter, Supervision and Evaluation. In essence, there are two audiences for any such reporting: the constituency served and the senior leadership of the organization. I have seen many reports by ombuds that treat each of these audiences as the same and provide only a statistical roll-up of the volume and types of issues presented. That is not sufficient. Ombuds should consider carefully the needs and objectives for each of these audiences to make sure that their reporting addresses those needs and objectives.

1. Reports to the Organization

An annual report sent to (or at least available to) the entire constituency served by the ombuds program is of great value. The main reason is that it serves to remind those who might want or need to consult with an ombuds that the ombuds program exists and to inform people how it works, how it can help them, and how to contact the ombuds. To accomplish this purpose, the best annual reports go beyond cataloging the volume and types of issues presented, though that clearly is a starting point. If the ombuds adds information about the level in the organization from which their visitors come or the years of service in the organization of their visitors, that information can be very powerful. For example, if a significant portion of visitors are drawn from longer-term employees or middle management (and even from senior management), as is often the case, it speaks volumes about the "acceptability" of going to the ombuds office.

Periodic reporting, along with brochures and FAQs that are available both in the office and on the office's website, are a good place to remind everyone of how to contact the office and key aspects of how it works (such as the promise of confidentiality, that it is not a place to file claims against the organization, and that ombuds have the ability to offer information, guidance, and options on virtually any organization-related topic). Good reports should include information on the Standards of Practice under which ombuds work and anonymous testimonial comments from people who have used the office. They can also include a description of the types of assistance an ombuds can provide, such as information only, coaching, referrals, facilitation, and mediation. Some annual reports have provided hypothetical or composite examples, similar to the actual ombuds examples in part II, to illustrate just how helpful an ombuds can be for people with conflicts or to address a concern that they have. For ombuds who do not have the experience or ability to prepare such examples without risking confidentiality, using an example or two from part II of this book for that purpose may be useful. And finally, if the report can be accompanied by a statement from the organization's most senior leader endorsing the program and validating the usefulness of providing people with a confidential and informal channel to address organization-related issues or to help resolve conflict, it strengthens the perception of the ombuds program and helps document its operations and effectiveness.

This last point about documenting the operations and effectiveness of the program should not be overlooked. As a lawyer who defended challenges to ombuds' programs and confidentiality, I can attest that good annual reports are also important evidence. They provide critical information about a program, and they also help establish that these program features were widely publicized.

2. Reports to Senior Leaders

Reports to senior leaders should go beyond the information typically made available in annual reports. The confidentiality of visitor information and communications must be maintained, but the challenge for ombuds is to provide a senior leader with insights drawn from the universe of issues with which the ombuds has dealt. If one of the responsibilities of an ombuds office is to provide an additional "listening post" for leaders of the organization, and if, as I believe, the ombuds will be consulted by people who are unwilling or afraid to resort to formal channels, then it follows that the ombuds will be privy to trends, insights, and warnings that will not come to a senior leader from other sources. It is incumbent on ombuds to make the often-limited time available for meeting with a senior leader count by mining statistical data available to the ombuds and the ombuds' own knowledge of the organization. The ombuds should come to these meetings having done the hard work of drilling down into the data to ascertain new and emerging trends, troublesome areas, and systemic issues.

Just identifying issues is rarely enough. Ombuds need to be able to offer practical suggestions for action on what the ombuds has identified or other recommendations to confirm the insights and information the ombuds has provided. One recommendation I have made to ombuds is that they mentally put themselves in the position of the senior leader and then ask themselves "What can and should I do with the information that the ombuds is giving me?" Being able to project one's insights into this leader role will often yield further insights into what might be able to be done to address a problem systemically.

Providing a senior leader with assurances that ombuds work hard to surface important issues is essential because the fear of what an ombuds might know that the organization does not know has been a major impediment in the creation of ombuds programs. One way to accomplish this without breaching confidentiality is to provide the senior leader with data on what ombuds typically do in the most serious cases. The IOA has prepared just such a report available to IOA members after distilling information from its practice surveys. This report responds to key questions, including "Why keep data about the most serious cases?", "What are the most serious issues reported by OOs [organizational ombuds]?", and "From whom did OOs first hear their most serious cases in the 2020 survey?"[2] It also includes information about how ombuds reported hearing about more complex cases and describes the way in which ombuds get information about the most serious cases to management. One of the findings, in particular, may come as a surprise to a senior manager: "Hearing [about a serious case] first from a *senior officer* was reported by nearly two fifths of the OOs, for at least one case, and hearing first from a *supervisor* by a quarter of OOs."[3]

Reports to senior leaders are best delivered in person with a minimum of documentation. There are three reasons for this advice. First, ombuds should be aware that it may not be in the organization's best interests to have detailed written reports that might later be misconstrued as putting the organization on notice of something discussed even if there is no disclosure of specific circumstances or confidential information. Second, if insights are offered with recommendations, it is a great opportunity for discussion. An interactive give-and-take about what might be done or whether a recommendation would be responsive to an issue is far more effective than merely a written report. Not only will an ombuds gain greater insight into the personality and approach of the senior leader, but this type of exchange will also help the ombuds going forward know what type of recommendations and insights will be most useful to the senior leader. And finally, the ombuds should always remain cognizant of the fact that it is the organization that created the program and that it is

---

[2] Mary Rowe, Timothy Hedeen, & Jennifer Schneider, International Ombudsman Association, Thinking about the Most Serious Cases Reported by Organizational Ombuds (2020).

[3] *Id.*, 1.

responsible for the program's continued operation. The embodiment of the "organization" in this sense *is* the senior leader. If the ombuds is perceived by a senior leader as not providing useful insights to him or her, it is only natural that support by that leader may wane. Although the decision to discontinue an ombuds program is always complex and usually involves many different reasons, a failure to provide meaningful insight and recommendations at the senior level, regardless of the effectiveness of the program in dealing with people, is usually a contributing factor.

E. What Is the Cost of an Ombuds Program?

This is one of the most common questions asked. While the answer obviously varies with the type of organization and the size and scope of a possible ombuds office, it is still a good question, and there is some guidance that can be offered in response to it.

The IOA conducts practice and compensation surveys in alternate years. The mean, median, and interquartile compensation for ombuds in various sectors is compiled from the responses to this survey and can be obtained from the IOA by its members and an organization wanting to create a new program. There will be additional regional variations in these compensation levels, for example to factor in high-cost metropolitan areas, so this data is not perfect, but it is a good place to start in assembling information for an ombuds program budget.

Moving beyond the compensation paid to an ombuds (and presumably any benefits), important cost considerations include whether support staff is provided, office operation expenses (including the cost of office space, printing and other marketing costs, as well as items such communications, technology, and translation services), travel expenses, and professional development and continuing education.

A few observations about these categories of expenses may be helpful. Because an ombuds can be expected to spend most of their time consulting with visitors—either on the telephone or in person—it is not a good use of their training and time to have them also be solely responsible for scheduling and arranging for appointments with visitors. Having an office assistant who can help triage inquiries, book appointments (and reschedule appointments), and follow up on some of the inevitable office operation matters can be extremely useful and maximize the time available for ombuds to do the work they are there to do. This additional person is typically an assistant who is paid at a much lower level than the ombuds but who increases the reach and effectiveness of the ombuds.

While in some cases there may be minimal travel expenses (as, for example, a single-location college or university), in other situations, travel expenses may be a significant cost. Even with the advent and use of online conferencing technology, large, multinational programs may have a need for travel for an in-person meeting with someone on a significant issue. Especially for programs that fit this profile and in non-COVID times, having an ombuds make a personal visit to facilities far distant from the organization's main offices to introduce the program or discuss it with local management is time and money well spent. It helps people, including managers, in the organization know about the program and how they can use or support it, particularly if they are in a country or culture where the concept of an organizational ombuds is not a familiar one.

An essential budget component for an ombuds program is the need for training and professional development. I have been going to the annual conference of the IOA for many years and have seen how truly necessary it is for ombuds. Many, if not most, work in single ombuds programs and have a limited ability to collaborate or interact with professional colleagues who do what they do and who understand the various challenges they face. The annual IOA conference is their main opportunity in the course of a year to touch base with often far distant colleagues or hear presentations on topics that advance their knowledge. For ombuds who work generally alone, these conferences also provide a substantial renewal, training, and energizing opportunity. To the extent that an ombuds is more junior in the profession, the need for a budget for this professional development and training is even greater.

A final observation about the cost of an ombuds program is necessary to put these costs in context. Most ombuds programs include only one or two people and it is rare for even large multinational organizations to have more than five or six ombuds. The all-in cost of an ombuds program (which includes compensation and benefits, office expenses, travel, and professional development) generally is extremely small in comparison with other (non–revenue-producing) support functions such compliance and HR. Even though the return on investment (ROI) on an ombuds program is hard to calculate, as discussed below, the nonquantifiable benefits are substantial, including improved culture and reduced conflict, expanding the reach and effectiveness of formal channels, and serving as a check on the organization and a feedback source for senior leaders as a component of good governance.

F. How Does an Ombuds Program Work Where the Organization Has a Unionized Workforce?

I have been neither a labor lawyer nor involved in negotiating with a union over terms and conditions of employment, including negotiations over whether an ombuds program can be implemented. I defer to others who have more knowledge and experience to provide advice on that topic. I have, however, had two experiences that provided me with some insight into how an ombuds program can function and be of assistance even when an organization has a unionized workforce.

As a general matter and under federal law, ombuds do not become involved in matters in which a union is recognized as the exclusive bargaining agent for a unionized workforce. That exception to the scope of ombuds services is usually specified in program descriptions, including charters, brochures, and FAQs on the ombuds website. For that reason, I was surprised when one very good corporate ombuds program that I represented once advised me that one of their best referral channels was the company's unions. When I pressed the ombuds for information about how this came about and worked, the ombuds explained that the ombuds office was not involved in any worker-management issues (because those were covered by the collective bargaining agreement), but when a dispute arose between or among union members themselves, the union would often refer those workers to the ombuds to see if there was a way to informally resolve the issue rather than having the union do nothing because its ability to take sides in favor of one union member against another was limited or nonexistent. In addition, there are many types of conflict between union members and supervisors that do not rise to the level suitable for a grievance. Not only is an ombuds a way for the union to help members with issues that would have been impossible or awkward for the union itself to try to address, but the union also found that this approach was quite effective.

The second experience involving unions was when I was contacted by a few representatives of the unions at an organization—not the organization itself—to speak with them about establishing an ombuds office at the organization. I met with them to explain what organizational ombuds do and how they work. In the course of these discussions, I am sure I also acknowledged that while an ombuds would not get involved or replace the union in connection with labor-management issues, it could be very helpful in helping to resolve conflict between union members. The union representatives candidly expressed their dissatisfaction with the HR resources available in the organization and stated that even with this limitation on the scope of an ombuds' scope of services, they were planning to push for the creation of an ombuds office. An ombuds office was subsequently created by that organization at the behest of its unions, and the office has continued to have their support.

Even though assistance to union members is not a major area of involvement for most ombuds in unionized workforces, I have received questions on this subject and thought that the issue should be addressed. The "Union Issues" category in part II includes actual ombuds examples to illustrate how beneficial ombuds can be in this context.

G. How Can the Effectiveness and Return on Investment of an Ombuds Program Be Evaluated?

Measuring the benefit of something that does not happen has bedeviled ombuds as well as other formal cost-prevention channels, including such well-established functions as compliance programs. The mere fact that disputes are resolved and not litigated or that issues find a way to be surfaced, albeit indirectly and generally without awareness of an ombuds' involvement, only compounds the challenge of producing a reliable calculation for determining ROI.[4] Even though it is hard to do, since managers of many organizations are conditioned to make management decisions based on data and performance metrics, an examination of how an ROI can be calculated is worth discussing.

Some of the insights into data that can be considered are included in the discussions earlier in this chapter (sections B.2, Supervision and Evaluation, and section D, What Reports Should Ombuds Prepare and What Should Be Included?). These sections, however, focus primarily on the information available from the ombuds program itself.

---

[4] Mary Rowe, *Identifying and Communicating the Usefulness of Organizational Ombuds With Ideas about OO Effectiveness and Cost-Effectiveness*, J. Int'l. Ombudsman Ass'n., v.3, no. 1 at 9 (2010).

But what about information available from other sources inside an organization and outside of it? Careful baseline studies of these other sources of data, along with industry standards or externally derived data, can be useful. For example, at the commencement of an ombuds program, a study of the nature and cost of an organization's litigation profile can be revealing. To what extent are there employment litigation cases or other types of lawsuits against the organization (Title IX or Title VII lawsuits, for example) involving an organization's policies or practices? What has been their cost, for both defense and payments for any settlements or damages? This type of litigation can be very expensive because outside counsel is typically retained. It would not be unusual for the cost avoided of even one of these types of cases to cover the cost of an ombuds for a year or more. In addition, what is required of personnel inside the organization for tending to such matters? While this cost is hard to assess, it is virtually never zero. Time and effort devoted to such matters almost always can be dedicated to other endeavors.

This same analysis can also be applied to other areas where the failure to address issues both costs money and diverts internal resources from other work that could be done. Grievance procedures, disciplinary proceedings, and employee attrition or turnover are three examples. As a result, those interested in determining an ROI for an ombuds program should be looking at data in those categories collected by people outside of an ombuds office to develop baseline data that might be of use later on to evaluate whether an ombuds office in any way affects the cost or nature of disputes that ultimately show up elsewhere and for which the organization incurs costs. This same baseline analysis also can be applied to an organization's risk management, compliance functions, and productivity in general.

In each of these areas, both the data and the calculation of any financial impact are outside of most ombuds' purview; yet this information, directly or indirectly, can be used by the organization to help calculate the impact of an ombuds program. The financial sophistication to undertake these calculations in a way that the organization respects, however, is beyond the expertise of most ombuds, whose primary skills are in dealing with people and assisting in conflict resolution.

In the absence of an organization-specific calculation, survey and industry sources of data may be an acceptable proxy for demonstrating a likely ROI to management. For example, an older ROI study for ombuds programs undertaken by John Zinsser, then of Pacifica Human

Communications LLC (and later an ombuds for the International Red Cross), revealed that for every dollar invested in an organizational ombuds program, the ROI was fourteen dollars, even without factoring in savings on legal fees for employment litigation.[5] Similarly, an article by David Bogoslaw, editor of *Corporate Secretary*, cited to another study reported by John Zinsser: a Fortune 200 company that carried out a full ROI study concluded that the return was twenty-two dollars for each dollar invested.[6]

Other reported calculations demonstrate the difficulty of properly accounting for all of the ways in which an ombuds program might have an impact on an organization, but which nevertheless provide insight into how significant the cost of employee conflict is and how beneficial highly engaged employees are to an organization. A study published in the *Harvard Business Review*, based on extensive interviews with eighty-three executives (87 percent of whom had more than ten years of work experience and 45 percent of whom had ten years or more in senior management roles), estimated the cost of wasted time in twenty categories, from "Hiring the wrong employees" to "Designing overly complex incentive schemes" and everything in between. The result:

> We expected our study to reveal significant waste. However, we were not ready for the magnitude of the results. In the course of a day, the executives estimated wasting an average of $7,227.07 per line item per day, for a total of $144,541.30 per day, summing the twenty points of waste. That's an astounding $52,757,574 of lost value and potential per year per organization on people problems. These are perceptions rather than scientific measures, but they reveal significant amount of lost value.[7]

---

[5] Jonathan E. McBride & James S. Hostetler, *Board Champions for the Ombudsman*, NACD DIRECTORS MONTHLY, May 2008, at 15.

[6] David Bogoslaw, *Ombuds Programs: Creating a Culture of Trust Rather Than Compliance*, CORPORATE SECRETARY, Summer 2015, at 9. *See also*, Andrea Schenck & John W. Zinsser, *Prepared to Be Valuable: Positioning Ombuds Programs*, J. INT'L. OMBUDSMAN ASS'N., vol 7, no. 1, at 23 (2014).

[7] Tanya Menon & Leigh G. Thompson, *Putting a Price on People Problems at Work*, HARV. BUS. REV., August 23, 2016, https://hbr.org/2016/08/putting-a-price-on-people-problems-at-work (last accessed March 15, 2019).

A more rigorous analysis methodology was used in another study and involved developing an Employment Engagement Scorecard (to grade companies on employee satisfaction, identification, commitment, loyalty, and performance) based on the authors' interviews with two hundred HR and marketing managers in fifty-two companies in North and South America, Asia, Africa, and Europe. After implementing this scorecard at seventy-five companies in India, China, Germany, Belgium, the Netherlands, Austria, and the United States, the authors went back a year later and studied thirty of those seventy-five companies. They concluded that:

> [a]fter controlling for other relevant factors including GDP level, marketing costs, the nature of the business and type of goods, we found that the **highest level of growth in profits (10% to 15%) occurred in the group of companies that were highly engaged**. (Emphasis added.)[8]

Several conclusions can be drawn from this brief discussion on measuring the ROI of ombuds programs. The first is that it is hard to do. Second, it is not an exact science because of the multiplicity of factors and assumptions that must be taken into account. Third, while data are often used to inform or drive management decision making, there is a dearth of comparative studies and data in this particular context. Even if more studies were available, the costs and assumptions relative to a specific organization may be sufficiently unique that they are of limited utility to another organization's analysis, other than possibly confirming or refuting assumptions. Finally, and this is perhaps the most important conclusion, because only a portion of the data that would be necessary for this analysis is available from inside the ombuds office, if an organization wants to calculate the ROI of an ombuds office, the organization and the ombuds need to work together to develop data and assumptions that are appropriate for that organization.

Because of these challenges, I believe that there has been a tendency on the part of both management and ombuds to ignore the ROI issue or hope that other measures or insights on effectiveness will

---

[8] V. Kumar & Anita Pansari, *Measuring the Benefits of Employee Engagement*, MIT Slone Mgmt. Rev., June 16, 2015, https://sloanreview.mit.edu/article/measuring-the-benefits-of-employee-engagement/ (last accessed March 15, 2019).

suffice. Accordingly, if an organization's management wants this type of data to confirm or measure the effectiveness of the ombuds program, the organization must be willing to commit to provide the management and financial expertise to produce a calculation that the organization's leaders will respect. An ombuds can certainly cooperate with this exercise and supply some key data, but it is not reasonable to expect that an ombuds can do this on their own.

H. Can Ombuds Programs Operate Internationally?

In a word, the answer to this question is "Yes." Multinational corporations have for many years successfully had ombuds programs that function around the world. In my former career as a lawyer for ombuds programs, I helped organizations establish programs in jurisdictions quite different from the United States, such as Japan and China. For one client, I retained counsel in almost twenty countries around the world to provide advice on local laws that might have an impact on ombuds programs, including such matters as mandatory reporting requirements, imputed notice, labor and employment laws, and how confidentiality could be protected, including by contract. We also explored what would be the procedures we could use to assert a claim of confidentiality in the courts of that country if it became necessary (but it never has become necessary). It was no surprise that we found some differences in law that had to be navigated, but we found nothing that would preclude the effective operation of a global ombuds program.

Before discussing some of the key issues that should be considered, I want to take a step back and look at the larger context of multinational organizations. In some ways, ensuring that an ombuds office can comply with local law around the world is the least of an organization's concerns. Presumably such organizations regularly obtain legal advice to make sure that their business operations, whatever and wherever they are, are fully compliant with the laws of every jurisdiction in which they operate. These organizations, and particularly the largest ones, are also in effect jurisdictions unto themselves, with their own rules and regulations, which cannot violate local law but, in many ways, exceed or go beyond local laws.

One of the statistics from *The Organizational Ombudsman* that made a deep impression on me and has been reverberating in my mind ever since is: "An analysis of the world's 100 largest economies in 2003 concluded that 53 of them were multinational corporations, 'which means that they are larger and wealthier on this index than 120–130 of the remaining nation-states.'"[9] That number has increased since then; according to research reported in 2018, more than two-thirds of the top one hundred economies in the world were corporations.[10]

A corollary to this observation on the economic size and scope of multinational corporations is that to be successful in their global operations, they must foster a global culture that transcends local laws and customs in some of the jurisdictions in which they operate. Ben W. Heineman Jr., longtime general counsel of one of the most well-known multinational corporations, best captured this concept by noting that multinational corporations that aspire to high performance and high integrity must create a culture of adherence to global ethical standards:

> [t]he high-performance-with-high-integrity culture must be strong and unyielding everywhere in the world. The core principles and practices that create that culture, therefore, must also be uniform and universal across business lines, different markets, and different regions. True, the transnational company must always be sensitive to local conditions. But variation on these fundamental cultural issues is hypocritical and confuses people. It is antithetical to integrity. It risks creating a cancer that can metastasize across a company, eating away at the culture.[11]

An ombuds program can be a valuable component of an organization's efforts to knit together a single high-integrity corporate culture for all the reasons previously discussed in this book, despite widely

---

9 The Organizational Ombudsman, *supra* note 1, at 105, *citing* Medard Gabel & Henry Bruner, Global Inc.: An Atlas of the Multinational Corporation, at vi (2003).

10 Ben Chapman, *A Majority of the World's Richest Entities Are Corporations, Not Governments, Figures Show,* Independent, October 17, 2018, https://www.independent.co.uk/news/business/news/companies-bigger-governments-un-human-rights-council-meeting-a8588676.html (last accessed July 25, 2021).

11 The Organizational Ombudsman, *supra* note 1, at 108–9, *citing* Ben W. Heineman Jr., High Performance with High Integrity: Memo to the CEO at 27 (2008).

disparate local cultures and customs around the world. While there are many examples that can be used to support this assertion, a simple one included in part II perfectly illustrates the valuable role that an ombuds program can have. The example relates to a young woman in a distant jurisdiction whose supervisor called her into his office and said, in effect, that he could see that she was pregnant and knew that she was unmarried and that if she were not married by the time the baby arrived, she would have to find a new job. This was absolutely counter to the worldwide employment policies of the multinational corporation but probably not illegal in the country in which it occurred. The supervisor's comments also reflected the prevailing local culture. Without a global ombuds office, where could this young woman have gone to raise the issue? Going to company leaders in her country (presumably the only ones she might have known) would likely have been unavailing, and her subsequent dismissal could have been brought about and documented in ways that would have escaped any higher or other review.

Aside from the terrible predicament that this young woman was in, this real vignette also presented a real threat to a high-integrity corporate culture in that it was a flaunting of company rules and policies in favor of local custom. After consulting with the ombuds and discussing various options for action, however, she authorized the ombuds to act on an option that involved informing her supervisor that his proposed action violated company policy and could result in his dismissal, not hers. The involvement of the ombuds was also a clear deterrent to possible retaliation against her for raising the issue.

Moreover, the ombuds helped put an anonymous Q&A on this topic in the company newsletter that was distributed to all employees around the world so that everyone in the company in all jurisdictions would be on notice that an attempt to discharge a female subordinate for being unmarried and pregnant constituted grounds for discipline and possible discharge of the supervisor involved. The young woman's identity was never disclosed in this newsletter piece or otherwise. What was the impact of having an ombuds program? An injustice was remedied, and the obligation to comply with worldwide company policies was reinforced.

With this larger context in mind, what are some of the issues an organization should consider in creating a global ombuds program? For starters, an organization should consider any potential legal restrictions. Such an exercise should include examining labor and employment requirements, compliance issues, mandatory reporting, imputed notice, and court processes and procedures that would be available to assert and protect confidentiality. This can be important because, for example, the labor laws in a jurisdiction may require giving notice or negotiating with unions or works councils before rolling out a program in a particular jurisdiction. While counsel for the organization can assist with some of this background research and certainly on issues affecting the organization itself, ombuds programs may also wish to consider retaining independent counsel in the relevant jurisdictions to obtain their own attorney-client privileged advice. Once this research has been conducted, it should also be considered in light of the fact that, in my experience of more than thirty years, challenges to ombuds operations in jurisdictions outside of the United States have been almost nonexistent.

Going into a detailed discussion on any of these issues is beyond the scope of this book and may not be helpful because laws change, but an additional legal issue should be flagged for consideration by counsel for the organization and the ombuds program: data security. In *The Organizational Ombudsman,* I included a section on the European Union Data Protection Directive,[12] but that provision has been superseded by the European Union's General Data Protection Regulation (GDPR), which became effective on May 25, 2018.[13] The GDPR has subsequently been used as a model for legislation in several non–European Union countries and even in California. Even though ombuds deal with only limited personal data, the provisions of the GDPR and other legislation modeled on it should be reviewed to make sure that an ombuds program is compliant with any restrictions on the transfer or use of personal data.

A final legal consideration for organizations considering a global ombuds program is to pay attention to corporate legal formalities. It is not unusual for corporations to have subsidiaries and affiliates that have a separate corporate identity, and possibly their own governing board,

---

12 The Organizational Ombudsman, *supra* note 1, at 406–24.

13 Regulation (EU) 2016/679 of the European Parliament and of the Council of 27 April 2016 on the protection of natural persons with regard to the processing of personal data and on the free movement of such data, and repealing Directive 95/46/EC (General Data Protection Regulation), https://ec.europa.eu/info/law/law-topic/data-protection/data-protection-eu_en (last accessed March 15, 2021).

through which the parent company operates in various jurisdictions. It is not likely that either the parent company or the ombuds wants a separate charter for an ombuds program for each of the entities that may be under the umbrella of the parent company. Accordingly, if the services of an ombuds program are provided in a jurisdiction that operates through one of these affiliates or subsidiaries, it may be advisable to document an understanding on a parent-subsidiary (or -affiliate) basis that the ombuds program operating under the aegis of the parent company is made available to employees and others of the corporate affiliate or subsidiary on the same terms and basis as provided in the charter approved by the parent company.

Beyond any legal matters, international ombuds programs should consider a variety of practical issues. Having an international program usually means that a single ombuds will not be sufficient. Hiring a diverse group of ombuds and basing them strategically around the world presents both opportunities and challenges. With global scale also comes the need for in-person visits to roll out the new program or periodically be available to people and leaders. This is particularly important as the concept of an organizational ombuds is not well understood or common in many parts of the world. Because there is generally greater familiarity with classical ombudsman programs, more effort may be necessary to explain just how an organizational ombuds program works and how it differs from any governmental or classical ombuds program.

A few other practical observations may be helpful. The first is translation and interpreter services. With a global program, it is virtually impossible to be able to employ ombuds who are fluent in all potential native languages of those served by the program. And yet, it is important for the ombuds to be able to communicate with a visitor in the visitor's native language. The good news is that there are services that can supply, even on short notice, interpreters to assist in oral communications. When arrangements for these services are made, ombuds should take care to make sure that all contracts with the service providers are with the ombuds program and have adequate protection for the confidentiality of the communications being translated. Similarly, there is a need to arrange for service providers to translate key documents (the charter, brochures, websites, FAQs, etc.) into local languages. As with any other translation project, care should be exercised to double check any translation to make sure that phrasing and idioms are either used or not used to avoid later confusion. For example, even the name "ombuds" may be difficult to translate or a translation may have unintended problems in conveying what it is. Some other name may be better to use instead of merely carrying forward the term "ombuds" in a language that has no familiarity with it. Note also that there may be restrictions on the use of the term "ombudsman," as is the case in New Zealand and possibly other jurisdictions.

I. How Should an Organization Address Allegations of Misconduct by an Ombuds?

This is one of those questions that is extremely difficult to answer since there are no reported cases or any other recognized guidance that answer this question. I hope that my suggested response will be only a hypothetical thought exercise for many years to come, but I suggest that an ombuds' confidentiality obligation makes an organization's response to an allegation of ombuds' misconduct somewhat different than would be the case for any other employee.

In the typical case in which an allegation of misconduct is alleged against an employee, most organizations respond in similar ways: they put the employee on (at least temporarily paid) administrative leave until they can investigate the allegations and determine what the relevant facts are. This information is then presented to the supervising authority or in a disciplinary hearing to determine what sanction, if any, is appropriate. That same overall approach can be applicable to an ombuds, but I suggest that an organization consider three additional steps to account for the fact that an ombuds typically has confidential information that should not be disclosed.

My first suggestion is that an investigation of the ombuds' office be undertaken by independent outside counsel (in other words, not the usual outside counsel for the organization) whose engagement would include an obligation to preserve the confidentiality of any confidential information shared with the ombuds (meaning not initially disclosed to the organization), except as described below. Investigating counsel should have full access to all information in the possession of the ombuds relevant to the claim of misconduct—whether confidential or not—in order to make their factual determinations on the alleged misconduct. This would require a confidentiality agreement between investigating counsel and the ombuds office that incorporates this obligation to maintain confidentiality along with the exceptions described here. If the conclusion is that the allegation is unsubstantiated, that conclusion should be reported to the organization. If, on the contrary, the conclusion is that there is a good-faith basis to conclude that some misconduct occurred, additional steps are needed.

If investigating counsel makes the good-faith determination that misconduct may have occurred, the second suggested step is that counsel be required to segregate any information relating to the matter under investigation from other confidential information relating to other matters. Counsel should then be required to take reasonable precautions to prevent disclosure of all such other confidential information (for example, other people who may have consulted with the ombuds on matters unrelated to the matter being investigated) in any subsequent disciplinary or other proceedings.

Only the information relevant to the allegation of misconduct, including any relevant confidential information, would then be disclosed to the organization for use in any disciplinary or other proceedings. In this regard, the decision to release information would be made by counsel, not the ombuds. I believe this shift in responsibility and partial disclosure is appropriate. Having had independent counsel first determine whether there is a good-faith basis for the allegation, the organization would have met a required threshold showing that justifies disclosure to the disciplinary authority in the organization—but only of the information relevant to the matter being investigated and not all matters. This is similar to requiring an initial showing of a good-faith basis that an attorney-client privileged communication has been used in furtherance of a crime or a fraud before compelling disclosure of attorney-client privileged communications.

The final additional step is an obligation of investigating counsel to seek protection in other venues, if appropriate, to prevent further disclosure beyond what is necessary in any hearing or disciplinary proceeding. Depending on the circumstances, this obligation may also involve moving for a protective order in connection with any subsequent litigation to limit disclosure to that case only or to only certain parties or witnesses.

Including these additional steps as part of any organizational investigation into allegations of misconduct should not present any substantial impairment to an organization's ability to ascertain the facts based on an allegation while still protecting confidential information where possible. Since no court to my knowledge has addressed this issue, this approach is only one suggested approach, but it tries to balance the legitimate interests of the organization in possibly needing access to confidential information with the ombuds' need to preserve confidentiality to the extent possible.

J. What Should an Organization Consider if It Decides to Terminate an Ombuds Program?

Unfortunately, I have had occasion to counsel ombuds whose programs have been eliminated by an organization, and there are some lessons for both ombuds and their organizations about how the shutdown of an ombuds office should best be accomplished.

The first lesson is that ombuds programs should only be terminated prospectively. An organization should understand that both the ombuds' visitors and the ombuds themself have relied on the promise of confidentiality arising from a properly structured ombuds programs. When that program has been documented with a charter employing terms-of-use contract language as described in chapter 4, both the ombuds and visitors will likely have at least third-party beneficiary rights to enforce the ombuds' confidentiality obligations against both the ombuds and the organization because of their reliance on the promise of confidentiality. To eliminate a program and also claim that any existing matters or communications are therefore no longer confidential is only to invite a court challenge to preserve the confidentiality of both the identities of those who have previously used the office and any confidential communications.

Accordingly, if there is to be a termination of an ombuds program, the effective date of the termination should be in the future and allow enough time for the ombuds to engage in various wind-up activities. Of immediate importance is making sure that a notice of the effective date of the termination is placed on the ombuds' webpage and other communications to give people fair notice. Those communications should encourage people who may not have otherwise heard about the termination to discuss with the ombuds options for any future action on their issue. And finally, it is important in this notice to reaffirm that the ombuds is committed to maintain confidentiality on all closed matters and on any current matters until the office is closed.

Meanwhile, the ombuds should also actively reach out to everyone with whom the ombuds is currently working to have them decide what they would like to have done. The organization should not merely assume, as I have seen before, that all issues being handled by an ombuds as of the termination will be forwarded to HR or some other formal channel. Because even consulting with an ombuds is not information that would be disclosed to anyone else in the organization without permission of the visitor and any action to be taken should be controlled by the visitor, an affirmative agreement to forward a matter to some other office needs to be made by each visitor with a current matter, not by the ombuds. If an ombuds has—and has complied with—a proper records destruction policy, there should be no records identifying previous visitors or their confidential communications. But, if for some reason, such documentation does still exist and the visitor does not provide consent to transfer this information to HR or some other entity, it should be destroyed if possible.

In addition to an outreach to visitors with current matters, the ombuds should be taking steps to eliminate emails, voicemails, and all other confidential data from any electronic files and backup equipment used by the ombuds. Similarly, any other confidential material not in electronic form should be destroyed unless prohibited by law.

The ombuds and the organization should discuss and decide how the ombuds' telephone, email, and mail will be handled or forwarded after the termination of the office, along with what messages should be included on transferred phone and email messages. Similarly, the ombuds and the organization should review any policies and procedures that previously referred to the ombuds office and decide whether those documents should be updated simply by eliminating the reference to the ombuds program or in some other way.

Once these steps are accomplished, the ombuds should arrange for the return or transfer of any nonconfidential data, reports, policies, and equipment. It is also a good idea for an ombuds to prepare a final report on the activities of the ombuds program and a summary of the steps taken to close the office and preserve the confidentiality of communications on which the office was based.

Now that important questions about how to create an ombuds office and how it should function have been answered, I hope it is clear why an ombuds needs to be a confidential and informal resource for the organization in order to be effective and to fill the gap that formal channels in the organization are unable to address. Because confidentiality is so essential to the work of an organizational ombuds, the next chapter is devoted solely to practical guidance on how to protect and maintain ombuds' confidentiality.

4

What Is Ombuds Confidentiality and How Does It Work?

Confidentiality is at the heart of what makes ombuds programs valuable. I think confidentiality is the ombuds' superpower, but this is such a paradox. Ombuds programs are based on the principle that they are an informal channel, meaning that they have no authority to accept notice of claims, to investigate or compel investigations, or to make business decisions or policy. They are expressly powerless, except for their ability to listen and confidentially to provide information, assistance, and help people with concerns and develop options for whatever action their visitor wants to take. And even when they report systemic issues to leaders of their organizations, ombuds have no power to compel those leaders to act on their observations and recommendations.

So where is the power? Simply put, ombuds can be approached by any visitor on any side of any divide on a no-barriers basis on conflict or other concerns that they might not otherwise take to formal channels, whether out of fear or uncertainty. And when ombuds help people or provide upward feedback, this power enables them to be of great assistance by providing a unique and invaluable service.

A. Why Is Confidentiality Necessary for Ombuds' Work?

As we discussed in the previous chapters, confidentiality is what makes the ombuds different from formal channels. Formal channels can legitimately represent to people that they will try to keep communications confidential, and on some occasions they actually can do so. But they are not confidential channels to raise issues. Their paramount obligation is to act in the best interests of the organization—not individuals—and if that means disclosing the name or communication of a person who raised an issue, then they must do so. Fear and uncertainty or both often keep people from reporting issues to formal channels, and these channels are not designed to provide counseling or coaching with regard to interpersonal conflict. The concern over "what will happen to me" by going to a formal channel does inhibit some people from going to these channels in the first place because they often view them as tantamount to the police. This is a key point because if a formal channel never learns of the issue, it is unable to do anything, much less try to protect confidentiality. Many people want to know what might happen, what the process involves, or what their options are **BEFORE** they are willing to take action or approach a formal channel. The defining benefit and power of an ombuds is the perception and reality that people can go to the ombuds with confidence that neither their identity nor their communications will be otherwise disclosed.

A related point flows from the independence of ombuds. Ombuds expressly are not part of management. They do not represent visitors or other employees and do not serve as their lawyers or advocates, but they do advocate for a fair process. In combination with a mandate to remain impartial, ombuds are, and are usually seen as, fair and helpful. This may not seem like a big thing. But as discussed earlier with regard to efforts to promote greater diversity and women, providing this kind of a resource to people on all sides of any divide is, in fact, a big thing. Perusing the examples in part II will make that point plain.

B. On What Legal Basis Are Communications Protected as Confidential?

Explaining why organizations should create ombuds offices may be an essential consideration but explaining how ombuds protect confidentiality is also a gauntlet that must be run because this is such a crucial issue. I applaud those leaders who raise this issue, and I welcome the opportunity to provide my response.

1. Privilege

My first introduction to the world of ombuds came in 1990 when my law firm and I were retained to represent the ombuds office of a multinational corporation in an employment discrimination matter in federal court in Connecticut. The plaintiff was an employee of the company who alleged that he had consulted with the company's ombuds and wanted to take the deposition of the ombuds, presumably because he thought it would help him prove his case. Both the ombuds office and the company believed that the ombuds should not be involved or a witness in the litigation, and so my assignment was to represent the ombuds office as counsel independent of the company's counsel and move for a protective order on behalf of the ombuds office to preclude the ombuds' deposition.

At that time, the development of law relating to ombuds was in its infancy, and we could find very little guidance on how to persuade a court to prevent the ombuds from being compelled to testify in a deposition. The only potentially relevant case we could find had been decided a few years earlier by a federal district court in Iowa.[1] That case involved efforts to obtain the testimony of a former prison ombuds whose office was created under a state statute that provided that ombuds could not be compelled to testify about matters within the scope of their official duties. Although that statute was not binding on a federal court, the court relied on its authority under Federal Rule of Evidence 501 to recognize a common law privilege to preclude this testimony. In particular, the court used a test (the Wigmore test) that previously had been recognized by the United States Court of Appeals for the Second Circuit. This test outlined the factors that a court should consider in recognizing a new privilege under Federal Rule of Evidence 501:

1. the communication must be one made in the belief that it will not be disclosed;
2. confidentiality must be essential to the maintenance of the relationship between the parties;

[1] Shabazz v. Scurr, 662 F. Supp. 90, 92 (S.D. Iowa 1987).

3. the relationship is one that society considers worthy of being fostered; and
4. the injury to the relationship incurred by disclosure must be greater than the benefit gained in the correct disposal of the litigation.[2]

With this guidance, we prepared affidavits with extensive exhibits to provide the evidence that demonstrated how the ombuds office in my case satisfied each of the elements of the Wigmore test. I was quite pleased when the district judge (who has since had a prominent career as a judge on the Second Circuit Court of Appeals) ruled in favor of the ombuds office on this point.

I have had other occasions to assert a common-law testimonial privilege for ombuds based on Federal Rule of Evidence 501 and have generally (but not entirely) been successful in doing so. However, no one should underestimate how hard it is to get a court to recognize a privilege that is neither based on a statute nor has a long history of judicial recognition (as is the case with the attorney-client privilege). It is one thing to say that a court might recognize a privilege in the right case; it is quite another to claim that ombuds' communications with visitors are privileged. The latter claim is overbroad and not likely to be true or accurate in many cases for several reasons.

First, recognition of a testimonial privilege flies in the face of a fundamental principle of our court system: that all evidence relevant to a matter should be available to the parties and to the court. In this sense, there is an invisible thumb on the scale opposing any restrictions to broad access to potential evidence. Only when a compelling case can be made, as in providing evidence to meet the requirements of the Wigmore test, does a court (sometimes reluctantly) recognize that evidence from an ombuds should be unavailable.

Second, not every jurisdiction has a rule that is the equivalent of Federal Rule of Evidence 501, by which federal courts can recognize new common-law privileges. Many states do not authorize their courts to

[2] *In re* Doe v. United States, 711 F.2d 1187 (2d Cir. 1983) (citing 8 WIGMORE EVIDENCE § 2285, at 527 (McNaughton rev. 1961)). Note that this case was decided before the United States Supreme Court applied a similar test (but without the balancing-of-interests prong) in *Jaffee v. Redmond*, 518 U.S. 1 (1996).

recognize *any* privileges beyond those found in state statutes, the state's constitution, or with an undisputed common law history. In those states, it would be impossible to assert any ombuds privilege in a state court.

Third, demonstrating entitlement to a privilege is very fact specific and requires marshaling facts to support a claim of privilege. Sadly, some who have tried to assert an ombuds privilege have failed to do this despite the fact that it is a basic rule of law that the party moving for a protective order has the burden of producing *evidence* to support the motion. When this has not been done, courts rightly have denied recognition of an ombuds privilege.

This failure has led to a fourth reason why reliance on an ombuds privilege alone is insufficient: the muddled record of prior court rulings. One of the leading cases in which an ombuds privilege was not recognized involved an ombuds office that had been eliminated by the time the case was heard by the appellate court.[3] The former ombuds office was not separately represented in the case and, given the prior elimination of the office, counsel for the defendant company was unfortunately unaware of important interests relating to the ombuds office. When counsel for the company moved for reconsideration of a discovery order that compelled the testimony of the ombuds, they failed to provide *any* evidence supporting the claim, relying only on citation to prior court rulings in the same district recognizing a privilege for that program. Although the district court ruled in favor of the company to preclude testimony from the ombuds, that ruling was appealed to the Eighth Circuit Court of Appeals, and there was no evidence in the record before that court about how the office was organized or operated. As a result, much of the Eighth Circuit's opinion reversing the lower court's ruling was based on supposition or facts assumed by the appellate court. Nevertheless, this court's ruling has been cited by subsequent courts—usually without any real analysis—as holding that there is no ombuds privilege, when the actual holding of the case was that the moving party had not demonstrated any entitlement to a privilege—a very different matter.

And finally, the court's opinion in that Eighth Circuit matter reveals another caution about too much reliance on a claim of privilege. Reliance on a privilege claim in the absence of a clear statute hinges on

---

[3] Carman v. McDonnell Douglas Corp., 114 F.3d 790 (8th Cir. 1997).

persuading a particular judge to rule in favor of the ombuds. Some judges may be more open to this type of argument than others, and they all have wide latitude to decide these matters. In addition, courts generally are unsophisticated in understanding that there are various types of ombuds functions. Instead, they have tended simply to refer to "ombudsman programs" as if all ombuds offices were the same, rather than consider the very different types of functions and how important compliance with structural features are to an organizational ombuds' claim of privilege. In large part, this is due to inadequate lawyering to explain the differences to the court and to provide documentation to support the claim of privilege. The effect of these failures in the past to appreciate differences among types of programs or to present adequate evidence is not limited to the case in which a claim is made. It also extends to how subsequent courts cite and use the rulings of prior courts. When a claim of privilege has not been granted, it is much more likely for some other court to seize upon that case to hold that there is no ombuds privilege.

Because of courts' and parties' unfamiliarity with a claim of ombuds privilege and courts' reluctance to recognize it, there has been confusion about how such a privilege would function in practice. A common assumption is that it would be like the attorney-client privilege and would be waivable by the "client," who is assumed to be the visitor to the ombuds. In the *Shabazz* case, however, the court permitted the ombuds office to assert the privilege. In the first case I handled, I also asserted that any privilege belonged to the ombuds office and could not be waived by a visitor. The court agreed. My reasoning was that the ombuds, unlike an attorney in the attorney-client privilege context, does not represent a "client." Ombuds are structured to be independent and neutral. The services offered by an ombuds are part of a program that serves an entire constituency, so the ombuds' actions affect more than just one particular visitor. The desire for evidence by one person who consulted with the ombuds should not be allowed to destroy the program's assurance of confidentiality for everyone else who may want to consult with the ombuds. The principal interest, therefore, transcends any particular visitor and belongs to the ombuds.

As a result, the proper analogy for analysis here is more like the mediation privilege, rather than the attorney-client privilege, and asserting a claim of privilege should be available to the ombuds and not unilaterally waivable by a single visitor. As this short discussion reveals, issues related to the recognition of an ombuds privilege have not been fully considered or well understood by both courts and the parties in prior lawsuits, and the result has been confusion over an ombuds privilege.

Is asserting a claim of ombuds privilege impossible? No. With the right set of facts, and in a jurisdiction in which a court has authority to recognize a nonstatutory privilege, a viable case can be made. But such a claim still requires marshaling evidence and persuading a court to rule that recognition of a privilege serves the public interest for reasons much like those articulated in the Wigmore test. So, while it is not impossible, the mere fact that it is not a certain thing means that ombuds should be prepared to rely in the main on other bases for protection of ombuds confidentiality.

2. Contractual Protection for Confidentiality

A far more reliable basis for asserting confidentiality is based on contract principles. This may not be as strong a claim as privilege protection, but it is far easier to document and prove and has been quite effective both in forestalling attempts to draw ombuds into legal proceedings to breach confidentiality and in providing an assurance of confidentiality that can be relied on. This is particularly true since, with rare exceptions, almost all of the challenges to ombuds confidentiality of which I am aware have come from those who have actually used the ombuds services.

In the same case in which I first asserted a claim of privilege, I also asserted a claim that conversations with the ombuds were protected by an implied contract. In essence, the contractual claim of confidentiality went like this: The company created the ombuds office and made it available to employees; its defining feature was that communications with the ombuds could be anonymous and confidential; no one was required to use it; but if they did, they should be required to abide by its programmatic features (including confidentiality) under which the office was made available to employees and should not be permitted to breach that promise of confidentiality and ruin the program for everyone else. The premise of this argument was that there would be no confidentiality if anyone could decide, after the fact, to compel the ombuds' testimony for their own purposes and in contravention of the design of the program. The court granted the ombuds office's motion for protective order on this ground as well.

As with the assertion of a claim of privilege, I have on subsequent occasions successfully asserted this implied contract claim of confidentiality. A major advantage of this basis for a claim of confidentiality is that it can be asserted in virtually all courts—even those in foreign jurisdictions—since all courts that I am aware of, even those not in common-law countries, have authority to recognize contractual and programmatic restrictions. This is also an easier argument for a court to entertain since it does not generally involve considering the fundamental principles of restricting the courts' and the parties' access to potentially relevant evidence. All the court has to do is evaluate the reasonable expectations of the parties with respect to the terms and conditions or programmatic features of the program when visitors availed themselves of the benefits of the program.

Over time, I realized that an implied contract argument was a good basis on which to assert confidentiality but that it could be even better if the organization and the ombuds could make it less "implied" and more "expressed." As a result, I suggested adding language to ombuds' charters (another good reason to have a charter). I have advised organizations and ombuds to state in the charter that the ombuds office was established by the organization on the basis of the four key principles recognized in the IOA Standards of Practice (independence, impartiality, informality, and confidentiality). The charter should provide a short explanation of each of the key principles and require the ombuds to adhere to these Standards of Practice. The charter should also contain language stating that the ombuds office is a purely voluntary resource and that no one is required to use it but that those who do avail themselves of it will be deemed to have agreed to abide by the terms, conditions, and principles upon which it was established and not call the ombuds to testify or produce documents with respect to confidential communications in any formal, legal, administrative, or other proceedings. It may even be possible to expand this language to provide that not calling an ombuds to testify or produce documents about confidential communications is one of the essential program design features and binding on everyone. I also have recommended that the "not calling the ombuds to testify or produce documents" language be paired with a similar commitment on behalf of the organization: because it has created the ombuds office on the basis of these principles, the organization also agrees that it will not call the ombuds to testify or produce documents with respect to confidential communications in any formal, legal, administrative, or other proceedings.

Adding language like this to an ombuds charter has had a twofold impact. It makes the argument for contractual protection much clearer and easier for a court in the event that there is an attempt to breach ombuds confidentiality by seeking testimony or documents from them. When the charter and other program literature, such as brochures and FAQs, are made widely accessible to constituents served by the office, it becomes much harder for those who used the office to try to claim after the fact that they were unaware of this important program feature. The combination of adding this language to the charter and widely publicizing this provision has also clearly had a prophylactic effect: the number of challenges to ombuds confidentiality where this has been done has dropped dramatically. And even if there were a serious challenge, a party seeking to compel a court to permit a deposition or trial testimony of an ombuds would have the burden of overcoming this express language. While not entirely eliminating a court's discretion, such language clearly limits it. The overall result has been both far fewer challenges to ombuds confidentiality and a stronger contract claim of confidentiality that can be enforced in virtually all courts.

3. Other Bases for Protecting Confidentiality

There are other bases on which an ombuds' claim of confidentiality can be asserted. Since this book is intended to be a practical guide, rather than a legal guide, I will not repeat here a full analysis of these bases.[4] It is important, however, to mention some of them here because, depending on the jurisdiction, they may be directly applicable to ombuds. Those who are skeptical about the ability to protect the confidentiality of communications with ombuds should be aware of this information. These other bases show why it is important for an ombuds charter always to indicate that protection of confidential communications may be asserted under any applicable privilege, mediation statute, or other

[4] See Charles L. Howard, The Organizational Ombudsman: Origins, Roles, and Operations—A Legal Guide (2010) at 255–77.

provision that protects the confidentiality of communications in connection with alternative dispute resolution.

Statutes dealing with the protection of mediation communications are a source of protection that can be of use to ombuds. As you can see in the compilation of examples in the "Facilitation/Mediation" category in part II, ombuds frequently are involved in assisting parties through mediation and facilitated discussions. Most states have statutes that permit a mediator and/or the parties to assert that these types of communications are protected as confidential, and ombuds may be able to invoke the protection of such a statute in their jurisdiction. While some of these statutes have procedural requirements that limit their applicability to ombuds (such as the requirement of a specific written mediation agreement, a practice that ombuds do not employ), the provisions of other statutes are broad enough to apply to ombuds' mediation activities.

The Uniform Mediation Act (UMA) is a perfect example. As of 2020, twelve states have adopted the Uniform Mediation Act, developed by the National Conference of Commissioners on Uniform State Laws in 2001. One of the provisions of the UMA creates a privilege against disclosure of "mediation communications" (a defined term) and makes them not subject to discovery. The official comment to the UMA articulates that this protection could include communications with ombuds who hold themselves out as mediators or engage in mediation: "There is not intent by the Drafters to exclude or include mediations conducted by ombuds a priori. The terms of the Act determine applicability, not a mediator's formal title."[5] Even if a state has not adopted the UMA, it may have adopted a mediation confidentiality statute with similar terms.

A similar statute that expressly refers to ombuds is the Administrative Dispute Resolution Act (ADRA). This law, originally passed by Congress in 1990 and reauthorized in 1996, encourages federal agencies to make greater use of alternative dispute resolution techniques.[6] The 1996 reauthorization amended the definition of "alternative means of dispute resolution" specifically to include the "use of ombuds."

[5] The Uniform Mediation Act (amended in 2003), https://www.uniformlaws.org/HigherLogic/System/DownloadDocumentFile.ashx?DocumentFileKey=9b244b42-269c-769e-9f89-590ce048d0dd&forceDialog=0 (last visited March 15, 2021), Official Comment on Section 3(a) at 10.

[6] Pub. L. No. 104-320, 110 Stat. 3870 (1996).

Although this statute applies only to federal agencies, its approach to protecting confidentiality offers a roadmap that could be used by analogy in other contexts. The confidentiality provisions of the ADRA, codified at 5 U.S.C. § 574, articulate the general rule that the neutral in an ADR proceeding should not disclose or be compelled to disclose dispute resolution communications provided in confidence unless the court makes findings that there would be "manifest injustice" or finds that there is a significant need for the information before compelling disclosure.

A court's inherent authority to supervise discovery and admit only proper and "relevant" evidence in a trial is yet another basis on which confidentiality of ombuds communications with visitors can be protected. This argument can be used by virtually all ombuds offices (not just those in federal agencies) in all courts and in all jurisdictions. Because almost everything that an ombuds may know about an issue is derived from communications with a visitor, in most cases any testimony of the ombuds about any underlying facts would be "hearsay" and not proper evidence to prove or disprove any those facts. I learned this lesson in a jurisdiction where courts were not permitted to recognize new common-law privileges and where the ombuds' program descriptions were not robust in setting forth a contract claim, but the court nevertheless granted my motion to exclude the ombuds testimony at trial because it would have been hearsay and therefore not relevant. As soon as the court issued this ruling, I immediately saw how beneficial the court's ruling was. The court refused to rule as a matter of law that the ombuds was entitled to confidentiality (which could have been reversed by an appellate court that disagreed with the ruling) and instead exercised its discretion to exclude the evidence as hearsay and not relevant (a decision that is reversible by an appellate court only if an opposing party could prove that the court had abused its discretion, a much harder burden of proof).

One area often overlooked by organizations that have ombuds programs is the protection of confidentiality in the context of arbitration proceedings. Arbitration is itself a contractual undertaking by or among the parties, and the power of the arbitrator is addressed in the arbitration agreement or in the arbitration rules incorporated by reference in the agreement. Most of those contracts and rules are silent on an arbitrator's authority to recognize privileges to limit discovery or evidence. Because arbitration has been used increasingly over the past two decades to resolve disputes of all types, including employment disputes, it is important that general counsel of organizations be aware that documents setting forth the authority of the arbitrator can be written to require an arbitrator to protect the confidentiality of communications with the ombuds. While the failure to take such steps may limit an arbitrator's ability to preclude discovery from or the testimony of an ombuds, the inclusion of a provision requiring an arbitrator to do so can be a safe and effective means of protecting confidentiality and yet another expression of an organization's commitment to ombuds confidentiality.

Two other bases for protection of ombuds confidentiality deserve only brief mention because they are of limited applicability. The first is a constitutional protection of communications under the California Constitution that was first recognized as a privacy right in *Garstang v. The Superior Court of Los Angeles County.*[7] Some lessons can be derived from the way in which the court reach this conclusion. Not only was a complete record of the facts and reasons for confidentiality made in the trial court and available for review on appeal, but the court's analysis also cited the Wigmore test and an early case that had recognized an ombuds privilege. This underscores the importance of always making a complete evidentiary record at the trial level whenever confidentiality is challenged. Furthermore, the court relied on the widespread publicity within the institution of the confidential nature of the ombuds function and evidence of reliance on those provisions. This type of evidence is also important for contractual claims of confidentiality.

The second is a federal mediation privilege, recognized by a federal district court in California in 1998.[8] This opinion has been cited and relied on by subsequent courts, but it has also been criticized. It is not universally accepted but may be of use in a case to support a claim of confidentiality for an ombuds' mediation activity.

As this brief discussion reveals, there is more to protecting confidentiality than just privilege. Confidentiality and privilege are not the same. Although recognition of a privilege would protect confidentiality,

---

[7] 39 Cal. App. 4th 526 (Cal. Ct. App. 1995).

[8] Folb v. Motion Picture Ind. Pension & Health Plans, 16 F. Supp. 2d 1164 (C.D. Cal. 1998), *aff'd without published opinion*, 216 F. 3d 1082 (9th Cir. 2000).

confidentiality can be protected despite an inability to establish a privilege. There is no substitute for knowing the mediation and other applicable statutes in a jurisdiction in which the ombuds office operates and clearly articulating the expectation of confidentiality in the ombuds' charter that must then be widely publicized internally.

C. Is Ombuds Confidentiality Absolute? If Not, What Are the Exceptions?

Before responding directly to this question, I want to point out that while a testimonial privilege is the strongest form of nonstatutory confidentiality protection available, no privilege is absolute. Even the attorney-client privilege, one of the most ancient and universally recognized privileges, is subject to a limitation that compels disclosure if it is used in connection with committing fraud or a crime. Another important limitation is the Sixth Amendment to the United States Constitution, which guarantees criminal defendants the right to confront and cross-examine their accusers.

It follows that if not even the attorney-client privilege is absolute, ombuds confidentiality is not and cannot be absolute. However, it does not follow that any such limitation based on the Constitution is a major impediment to maintaining confidentiality of ombuds communications. In more than thirty years of representing and dealing with ombuds confidentiality, I have never had a matter in which I had to address limitations embodied in the Sixth Amendment.

The most obvious exception to ombuds confidentiality is when a visitor grants permission to the ombuds to make some disclosure of information and the ombuds agrees that it would be appropriate to do so. This usually occurs when one of the options developed by the ombuds and a visitor is to permit the ombuds to help surface an issue by making a disclosure, which could range from a complete disclosure of the issue to revealing only some small part of it to protect the identity of the visitor but still prompt an investigation by a formal channel. The requirement of ombuds consent to this exception is important, as the ombuds may have other visitors or interests that may be implicated and may need to resist yielding completely to the wishes of a particular visitor.

Two other exceptions to confidentiality rest on a common public policy: that in some cases, the potential danger of nondisclosure is too great to allow anyone (including an ombuds) not to report matters when they become aware of them, notwithstanding concerns over confidentiality. Statutes that require reporting facts relating to child and elder abuse are two such categories of mandatory disclosures. Virtually all jurisdictions have such reporting requirements for certain categories of people or certain licensed professionals. An ombuds who becomes aware of such matters, and especially if they are a licensed social worker or an attorney, may have this obligation. Because the requirements vary from state to state, ombuds and their organizations need to be familiar with the requirements of these statutes in relevant jurisdictions in order to comply with the law.

A second broadly recognized exception to confidentiality of almost any type (including ombuds) is when someone learns of an imminent threat of serious harm to an identifiable third party. Sometimes this is embodied in a statutory requirement; other times it derives from prior precedent of courts in developing common law. Either way, this requirement is almost universally recognized and rightly so. If someone has the ability to prevent such imminent and serious harm, as a matter of public policy, one should be required to do so.

A final exception to confidentiality might be more accurately labeled possible and partial disclosure of confidential information. I have had a couple of matters over the years in which an ombuds was alleged to have been involved in or aware of misconduct of some sort by a plaintiff and either the plaintiff wanted discovery from the ombuds or the ombuds would have needed to make a disclosure of otherwise confidential communications in connection with a defense. Although to my knowledge there are no reported cases in this context, there is an analog that provides useful guidance on how such a situation can be addressed by the parties and the court: the crime fraud exception to the attorney-client privilege. That exception to the confidentiality of attorney-client communications is designed to keep the attorney-client privilege from being used in connection with obtaining advice for the commission of a crime or a fraud.

When there is an allegation that an attorney was a participant in such a fraud or crime, courts have developed a way to deal with this issue.[9] First, the party seeking to invoke the exception to the privilege

[9] U.S. v. Zolin, 491 U.S. 554, 564–72 (1989).

has an obligation to make a threshold showing of facts that demonstrate a good-faith basis for a belief that the exception to the privilege is applicable. Second, the confidential information in dispute is submitted to the court for an *in camera* inspection (meaning that only the court sees that information and not the other party). And finally, the court determines whether the exception applies, and if so, the court may order some disclosure. Using this procedure, a party seeking to obtain discovery from an ombuds concerning an allegation of an illegal act or some other violation would have to make such a threshold showing which, if sufficient, would require an ombuds to make an *in camera* disclosure for the court to evaluate. Likewise, if an ombuds needed to make a disclosure of confidential information as part of their defense, they could move to make the disclosure *in camera* for court review, and the court could then decide first whether to permit the filing of that material *in camera* and then after a review of it determine whether the ombuds confidentiality should be maintained or not.

Given these exceptions to confidentiality, does it still make sense to have an ombuds office? My view is that none of these exceptions to confidentiality have in the past or are likely in the future to impinge on the principal work of ombuds. Certainly, making a disclosure with permission of the visitor and making a disclosure on the basis of an imminent threat of serious harm (both of which are categories of actual ombuds examples in part II) enhance rather than undermine the value of an ombuds and demonstrate the value of the office. There may be situations in which ombuds may have had to report child or elder abuse, but to my knowledge this is rare. I cannot recall any ombuds ever consulting me on such a matter. An ombuds would likely be powerless to change the law on these matters in any event because they also are so deeply rooted in a societal obligation to avoid substantial injury to vulnerable segments of our population. Regardless, instances in which these limitations surface are insignificant in comparison to all of the contexts in which ombuds can provide substantial help to people and the organization precisely because they offer confidential services.

If the mandatory reporting obligations in connection with elder and child abuse have not substantially impaired the work of ombuds, we should also address the question of whether the same would be true if ombuds were made mandatory reporters on issues of discrimination and harassment. That is the subject of the next section.

D. Should Ombuds Be Made Mandatory Reporters on Issues of Discrimination and Harassment? If Not, Why Not?

Ombuds should **not** be made mandatory reporters for racial, sexual, or any other type of harassment or discrimination. While there have been attempts by the government to include ombuds as mandatory reporters on these issues (the topic of the next section), most of the situations in which ombuds have been required to report such matters have been ones where their organization required them to do so. In most cases, I think this is out of a fear that if situations are not reported up internally in the organization, the organization itself would be held liable (the topic of the section after that). Setting those two situations aside for the moment, I want to explain why an obligation to report elder and child abuse is fundamentally different from a requirement to report matters that may involve discrimination and harassment.

The principal justification for requiring mandatory reporting of child and elder abuse is that these segments of our society are vulnerable and often defenseless. It is quite possible for abuse of our very old and our very young to go undetected unless reported by those who are in a position to see some evidence of it occurring. We should all have an obligation to help protect these people since they may not be able to protect themselves. Because they are vulnerable, any such abuse might be life threatening (particularly with regard to elders) or result in lifetime psychological or physical disabilities (particularly with regard to children) if undetected and unreported.

Neither of these population groups is significantly represented among the populations of the types of organizations where ombuds programs generally exist, with the possible exception of hospitals and K-12 school systems, where there is typically an obligation to report child and elder abuse. By contrast, the groups that are most vulnerable to discrimination and harassment (women, minorities, and LGBTQ people, for example) represent a sizable cohort in our institutions of higher education and in our civic, governmental, and business organizations. Not only is this segment of potentially affected people substantially larger than that of children and elder groups, but its members are also not as vulnerable or defenseless as children and the elderly. The abuse of children and elders may go undiscovered in the absence of mandatory reporting laws, but people suffering from discrimination and harassment—whether in their teens or nearing retirement—are generally adults and able to report such misconduct on their own. As a result, they are better able to protect themselves. And finally, while discrimination and harassment unequivocally can be severe, such conduct is usually not as threatening to life as the potential harm caused by child and elder abuse. If an ombuds were to conclude from the facts in a specific case involving allegations of discrimination or harassment that the potential harm to a person was serious and imminent, the ombuds would be fully justified in breaking confidence on that basis, as is required by both the law and the IOA Standards of Practice. In effect, where intervention is necessary, it is best addressed as an imminent threat of serious harm rather than through mandatory reporting of discrimination and harassment.

Beyond the differences in population size and vulnerabilities among these groups in an organization, as well as the types of potential harm they face and their ability to protect themselves, there is another important difference. Mandatory reporting of child and elder abuse generally does not substantially interfere with the bulk of the work of ombuds. Most ombuds rarely have had to address this issue. That is not the case for discrimination and harassment. Ombuds routinely are consulted by visitors who have concerns about harassment and discrimination. Data from the 2017 IOA Practice Survey confirms this point. When asked to think of the most serious cases that ombuds had over the past year, "Harassment/discrimination based on sex/gender" and "Harassment/discrimination based on race/ethnicity" were two of the top six categories reported for ombuds' most serious cases.[10] To require ombuds to report each of these matters would have a huge negative impact on the work that ombuds do and limit their usefulness.

As demonstrated in chapter 2, sexual and racial discrimination and harassment remains a very significant problem, and many people want assistance in analyzing their options BEFORE they decide whether to make a report because they are afraid (and often with good reason) that they will be retaliated against if they do so. Deprived of a confidential resource with whom to consult and faced with the choice

[10] International Ombudsman Association, 2017 Practice Survey (Data collected Spring 2018), at 21, International Ombudsman Association.

of only reporting or not reporting this conduct, many simply will not report and suffer in silence until it is unbearable and then leave the organization or bring a lawsuit. To limit the effectiveness of this confidential resource in the hope of an increase in expected reporting is simply ill-considered and short sighted. I am aware of no data that shows that mandatory reporting requirements for ombuds in fact result in substantially increased reporting by the people affected by this conduct. Such a requirement would simply cause the ombuds to be seen as another function wearing a "blue uniform" and therefore inhibit people from seeking the ombuds' assistance on this as well as on other issues.

There are a few other reasons why ombuds should not be made mandatory reporters. First, apart from the fear of organizational liability addressed below, the premise behind the thinking that ombuds should be mandatory reporters is the assumption that ombuds are in a position to know whether discrimination and harassment actually occurred. But ombuds do not engage in fact finding, and they do not conduct investigations of what their visitors tell them. What they know is hearsay. They provide assistance based on what a visitor tells them and the experience they bring to their work. An ombuds may be able to provide assistance that helps a visitor see that an issue may not be discrimination or harassment or may provide coaching to enable the visitor to deal with it themselves or report it themselves. The ombuds may help the person report or resolve the concern in some other way. Ombuds are impartial but need not be passive. They have the ability to continue to work with visitors to find ways of resolving or reporting even discrimination and harassment issues without needing to be mandatory reporters and often without disclosing a visitor's identity or the fact that they were the one who raised the issue.

Simply put, the factual and policy reasons for making certain categories of people mandatory reporters of child and elder abuse are not applicable to ombuds in dealing with issues of discrimination and harassment. Much is lost when ombuds are required to be mandatory reporters in this context because there is a widely recognized need for confidential assistance for people who may be experiencing this form of misconduct. To require ombuds to be mandatory reporters also both misconstrues the information ombuds may possess and the effectiveness of other tools ombuds typically employ to assist people in surfacing or resolving these issues.

E. Shouldn't Ombuds Be Mandatory Reporters under Title IX and the Clery Act?

Many leaders of colleges and universities have sought to compel their ombuds to be mandatory reporters (and thus not remain confidential) on matters of sexual discrimination and discrimination under Title IX of the Education Amendments of 1972 (Title IX). Likewise, there has been pressure for ombuds to be classified as "campus security authorities" (CSAs) under the Jeanne Clery Disclosure of Campus Security Policy and Campus Crime Statistics Act (Clery Act). Although an institution has discretion to compel ombuds to be mandatory reporters under each of these federal statutes, neither statutory scheme compels an institution to do so. A properly structured organizational ombuds office does not meet the standards articulated in either of these statutes or their regulations. Government regulations and the guidance promulgated by the Department of Education on these topics have recently changed significantly, so let's address each of these statutory schemes in turn.

1. Title IX

The purpose of Title IX is to prohibit discrimination on the basis of sex in educational programs that receive federal financial assistance.[11] The penalty for noncompliance with Title IX is set forth in 20 U.S.C. §1682: termination of federal support for the institution but only after the appropriate person or persons in the institution (also referred to as the recipient) have been advised of the noncompliance and the Department of Education or the relevant agency has determined that compliance cannot be obtained by voluntary means. An early Supreme Court decision defined an "appropriate employee" under this section to be "at a minimum, an official of the recipient entity with authority to take corrective action to end the discrimination."[12] That court went on to hold that no private damages remedy would be available for a violation of Title IX "unless an official who at a minimum has authority to address the alleged discrimination and to institute corrective measures on the recipient's behalf has actual knowledge of the discrimination in the recipient's program and fails adequately to respond."[13]

---

[11] 20 U.S.C. § 1681.

[12] Gebser v. Lago Vista Indep. Sch. Dist., 524 U.S. 274 at 290 (1998).

[13] *Id.*

The Department of Education has issued a great deal of guidance and policy interpretation to educational institutions over the past twenty years on an institution's obligations and liability for sexual discrimination, and in so doing developed the concept of a "responsible employee" such that an institution could be liable if a "responsible employee" were aware of information relating to sexual discrimination and failed to take appropriate action. The knowledge of that "responsible employee" was then imputed to the institution to create institutional liability for failure to address the discrimination.

All of that guidance has been rescinded, and the Department of Education promulgated new final regulations for Title IX on May 6, 2020, that became effective on August 14, 2020.[14] These regulations, codified in 34 C.F.R Part 106, were accompanied by extensive analysis and commentary on the thousands of comments that the Department of Education had received on its proposed regulations.

A complete analysis of these new regulations is beyond the scope of this book, but a few key points about the new regulations are in order. First, the Department completely abandoned the "responsible employee" matrix for holding institutions liable for sexual discrimination and, relying expressly on foundational Supreme Court holdings, largely rejected imputed notice liability. Rather, it determined that a postsecondary institution would be liable for sexual discrimination if the Title IX Coordinator (whose job it is to deal with such matters) had knowledge of discrimination and the institution failed to institute corrective measures. Likewise, the institution could be liable if "any official of the recipient who has authority to institute corrective measures on behalf of the recipient" had actual knowledge and failed to institute corrective measures.[15] So, while knowledge of the Title IX Coordinator

[14] The 2020 Title IX regulations (effective August 14, 2020) are available at https://www.federalregister.gov/documents/2020/05/19/2020-10512/nondiscrimination-on-the-basis-of-sex-in-education-programs-or-activities-receiving-federal (last accessed March 15, 2021).

[15] The rules for elementary and secondary schools are different. In the commentary accompanying the rules the Department stated: "We note that with respect to elementary and secondary schools, notice to any employee, including an ombudsperson, triggers the recipient's response obligations." *Id.*, at 346.

is imputed to the institution, there must be actual knowledge of an official in the second category before the institution is liable.

In the commentary accompanying the final regulations, the Department of Education acknowledged that it had received a request (actually made by the IOA) that the final regulations not designate ombudspersons as "responsible employees":

> One commenter recommended adding to the final regulations a statement that meeting with confidential resources on campus, such as organizational ombudspersons who comply with industry standards of practice and codes of ethics, does not constitute notice conveying actual knowledge to the recipient. The commenter reasoned that the organizational ombudspersons are not "responsible employees" under the Department's current guidance, and that to ensure that organizational ombudspersons continue to be a valuable resource providing informal, confidential services to complainants and respondents, the final regulations should note that organizational ombudspersons are a confidential resource exempt from the categories of persons to whom notice charges a recipient with actual knowledge.[16]

In response, the Department specifically addressed this ombuds issue and both articulated the standard that would henceforth replace the "responsible employee" test and reiterated that postsecondary institutions have discretion to determine, on the basis of a fact-specific inquiry, who should be considered an "official of recipient who has authority to institute corrective measures on behalf of the recipient":

> The Department appreciates the opportunity to emphasize that whether a person affiliated with the recipient, such as an organizational ombudsperson, is or is not an "official with authority to institute corrective measures" requires a fact-specific inquiry, and understands the commenter's assertion that an organizational ombudsperson adhering to industry standards and codes of ethics should be deemed categorically a "confidential resource" and not an official with authority. ***The Department encourages postsecondary institution recipients to examine campus resources such***

[16] *Id.*, at 341–42.

> ***as organizational ombudspersons and determine whether, given how such ombudspersons work within a particular recipient's system, such ombudspersons are or are not officials with authority to take corrective measures so that students and employees know with greater certainty the persons to whom parties can discuss matters confidentially without such discussion triggering a recipient's obligation to respond to sexual harassment.*** (Emphasis added.)[17]

Even though the Department authorized each postsecondary institution to make this determination, it should be beyond dispute that an ombuds program properly structured to comply with the IOA Standards of Practice and Code of Ethics would not have authority to institute corrective measures for the institution. In keeping with the principles of independence and informality, an ombuds should not even be considered "an *official of* the institution" and should definitely have no authority to make management decisions on behalf of the institution.

Designating ombuds as mandatory reporters is not required by Title IX or its regulations and is inconsistent with the Department's regulatory standard (authority to take corrective measures). To make ombuds mandatory reporters for Title IX serves only to deprive people of a valuable confidential resource.

2. The Clery Act

The Clery Act requires colleges and universities to collect and disclose information relating to campus crime statistics and campus security policies. It requires disclosure of current policies of "the law enforcement authority of campus security personnel" and statistics for criminal offenses in enumerated crime categories "reported to campus security authorities or local police agencies."[18] The statute does not define the persons or entities who are "campus security authorities," but the regulations do. After first listing campus and police departments and campus security departments, the regulations provide that the definition also includes:

> (iv) An official of an institution who has **significant responsibility for student and campus activities**, including but not limited to,

---

[17] *Id.*, at 346.

[18] 20 U.S.C. § 1092 (f)(1)(C(i) and § 1092 (f)(1)(F)(i).

> student housing, student discipline, and campus judicial proceedings. If an official is a pastoral or professional counselor, as defined below, the official is not considered a campus security authority when acting as a pastoral or professional counselor. (Emphasis added.)[19]

Despite this statutory and regulatory framework, there has been a controversy for the past several years over whether an ombuds should be considered a "campus security official." In large part this was caused by the 2016 Edition of *The Handbook for Campus Safety and Security Reporting* published by the Department of Education. In a section captioned "How to Identify your Institution's CSAs," the Department correctly identified the regulatory test for this determination: "an official of the institution who has significant responsibility for students and campus activities."[20] The *Handbook* went on, correctly in my view, to provide that since job titles vary so widely, this analysis should not be based solely on a job title; it should be based on a functional analysis: **"If someone has significant responsibility for student and campus activities, he or she is a campus security authority."** (Emphasis in the original.)[21]

It is therefore astounding that, without any "functional" analysis at all, the Department in the following paragraph then listed examples of positions and entities that it said generally met these criteria and included "an ombudsperson (including student ombudsperson)."

Many attorneys for colleges and universities, as well as their leaders, followed the guidance in this provision of the *Handbook* to make ombuds offices mandatory reporters, fearful of their institution's liability if they failed to designate ombuds as campus security authorities. They did so even though the *Handbook* was only "guidance" issued by the Department, having no force of law, and the fact that there had been no change in the statute or regulations that compelled this overreaching conclusion.

---

[19] 34 C.F.R. § 668.46 (a) (iv).

[20] The Department of Education, Office of Post Secondary Education, The Handbook for Campus Safety and Security Reporting (2016 edition) at 4-2, https://clerycenter.org/wp-content/uploads/2017/01/handbook-2.pdf (last accessed March 15, 2021).

[21] *Id.*, at 4-3.

As it did with prior guidance issued for Title IX, the Department of Education rescinded the 2016 *Handbook* on October 9, 2020, and issued new guidance (also having no force of law). This new guidance, last updated on January 19, 2021, reverted back to the regulatory definition as the touchstone for determining who is a campus security authority. It attached a "Clery Act Appendix for FSA Handbook"[22] and made clear the reason for its revised guidance:

> The Appendix will strictly adhere to the definition of campus security authority (CSA) and will respect institutions' discretion in their reasonable determinations of who constitutes a CSA. The 2016 edition expanded the definition of a CSA to include individuals on campus that should likely not be designated so under a strict interpretation of the regulatory framework. The 2016 edition took an expansive view of the phrase "significant responsibility for student and campus activities" found at 34 CFR 668.46(a). As a result, it captured groups of individuals who did not have "significant responsibility." Even if the 2016 edition's guidance was drawn from Department experience, it was not applicable to every situation and may have resulted in creating more confusion than clarity. As a result, the Department's new guidance makes clear that it is up to an institution to identify which individuals are CSAs and it is beyond the Department's authority to disagree with that reasonable determination."[23]

Accordingly, institutions of higher education clearly have discretion not to compel ombuds to be "campus security authorities." A properly structured ombuds program that complies with the IOA Code of Ethics and Standards of Practice, however, does not have "significant responsibility for student and campus activities." For the same reasons that ombuds should not be designated as mandatory reporters under Title IX, doing

---

[22] Available at https://www2.ed.gov/admins/lead/safety/cleryappendixfinal.pdf (last accessed March 15, 2021).

[23] Rescission of and Replacement for the 2016 Handbook for Campus Safety and Security Reporting, U.S. Department of Education, October 9, 2020, Updated January 19, 2021, https://ifap.ed.gov/electronic-announcements/100920RescissionReplace2016HandbookForCampusSafetySecurityReporting (last accessed March 15, 2021).

so under the Clery Act would conflict with the standard articulated in the regulations and impair the ombuds' ability to be a valuable service to a significant class of people on important issues.

One way to eliminate any confusion in a college or university community about whether an ombuds is a mandatory reporter under Title IX and the Clery Act is to address this specifically in an ombuds charter. For example, there could be a provision in the charter that says that the ombuds is not designated as a mandatory reporter under either Title IX or the Clery Act because ombuds do not have authority to institute corrective measures on behalf of the institution and have no significant responsibilities for student and campus activities.

F. Isn't It a Liability Problem for an Organization if, Because of Confidentiality, an Ombuds Knows Information about Potential Claims or Issues that Senior Leaders Do Not Know?

When senior leaders are asked "What keeps you up at night?" one of the most common answers is "What I don't know. I worry about what may be happening that I do not know about." As someone who has been both a department chair and a general counsel in an organization, though on a much smaller scale than those in most companies and universities, I think I understand this concern. I have felt that way myself. Compounding this feeling is the fact that I also knew that, by virtue of my positions, it was very likely that no one would tell me some things that I really should have known about. Based on my own experience, I know this issue is a matter of deep concern.

The best place to start is to realize that, even in the best of circumstances, things happen in a large organization that a senior leader will not know and will never be told about. This is not just because people are reluctant to report things to a senior leader. It is also inherent in the scale of large organizations and their pyramidal management structure. With various tiers of management and specialized functions, many issues that arise can be addressed and resolved without the involvement of senior leaders—just as it should be. The role of a senior leader is to set policy, provide direction, and ensure follow through. The larger the organization, the more that can be dealt with by subordinates.

Another consequence of the scale of organizations is that the larger the organization, the greater the probability that there will be misconduct, mistakes, or failures of one type or another somewhere in the organization. This is also a function of scale and human nature. To repeat what I have said elsewhere, it is not a question of whether this will happen; it is only a question of when, where, and how. If anything, this only gives more credence to a concern about what one doesn't know. While most of these issues do ultimately get resolved or work their way to the top of the management structure if they are significant enough, the likelihood that some will not also increases with the size of an organization. Consequently, the risk of information "burial" also increases the larger an organization. This observation relates not only to issues of lesser significance but also to the more significant ones. As most leaders know, there is always a reluctance to surface the bad news up through the chain of command.

Adding an ombuds function to an organization may exacerbate this concern. Unlike other subordinates and middle managers, ombuds exist so that they can keep communications with visitors confidential. For this reason, it is hard to know how to supervise them (discussed in chapter 3). Even when an ombuds office is properly established, an ombuds has no ability to compel a visitor who might have important information that could impact the liability of the organization to report it to a formal channel. Just because some information disclosed by a visitor may pose a risk of liability does not mean that an ombuds is free to report that. Still, an issue left undisclosed could later explode into a liability. So, why isn't an ombuds office actually a liability risk for the organization?

The main reason for this concern about the unknown is that somehow information disclosed to an ombuds will be imputed to the organization itself so that the organization will be deemed to be "on notice" of an issue for which it may be liable but that, without actually knowing about it due to the ombuds' confidentiality obligations, the organization cannot correct or address. If liability is the root of the concern, an organization is not powerless to address that issue, and the best way to do so is to create an ombuds office that complies with the IOA Code of Ethics and Standards of Practice because they provide the best lines of defense to a claim of imputed notice.

To begin, the ombuds office should be created to be independent of the organization and operate pursuant to a charter that articulates all of the principles under which ombuds services are provided. The promise of confidentiality should be paired with clear statements on the limitations of the ombuds authority to ensure that it operates informally. The ombuds should have **no** authority to make business or policy decisions, investigate matters for the organization, and expressly not be given any authority to receive notice of claims against the organization. The provisions of the charter should be widely publicized to the constituents of the ombuds office so that no one could reasonably claim that in speaking with the ombuds they thought that they were notifying the organization of an issue.

If the response to this is to ask, "Why even have an ombuds office and take the risk," I submit that before reaching this conclusion the analysis should balance all of the relevant interests. The analysis should consider not only the potential risks but also the potential benefits of having an ombuds office. The reasons for having an ombuds office were discussed at length in chapter 2. There a real need for a confidential source of information, guidance and coaching, and help in developing options for action.

Going beyond need, the additional benefits of an ombuds program should be fully considered. First, an ombuds program is created not only to help people but also to help the organization. There is a duality to this role. While ombuds will not disclose who their visitors are or confidential communications with those visitors, they are obligated by the Standards of Practice to assist the organization by identifying systemic issues, gaps in policy, and similar matters. One reason for including so many different kinds of actual ombuds examples in part II of this book is to demonstrate that this does in fact happen on a regular basis.

Second, ombuds have a variety of tools available to them both to help people with their issues and to surface the issues to the organization. A perfect illustration of this is the example in the "Fear of Reporting or Retaliation" category in part II involving an executive assistant (EA) to a very senior executive who consulted with the ombuds. The EA, who worked only with that one executive, said it was an issue that could not be taken to *any* formal channel: it was a concern that the EA's boss was submitting fraudulent monthly expense reports and that, aside from the senior executive, the EA was the only other person with knowledge of that. She did not want to be fired or otherwise be retaliated against. Under normal circumstances, this issue would never surface.

Here though, the ombuds devised an option that involved suggesting to internal audit that it audit the expense reports of all senior executives at that same level in such a way that it would appear to be routine. No single senior executive was identified or singled out and no reason was given for the request. The audit was conducted, however, and discovered not only the fraud of the EA's boss, but also that of other senior executives. The problem was surfaced, and the company was able to take disciplinary action against all of them. The EA's identity or involvement was never compromised. The creative use of approaches such as this one expands the reach of formal channels and brings issues to them that probably never otherwise would have been raised.

Survey data from ombuds on their practices substantiate the conclusion that ombuds use a variety of tools to help surface issues that would be of concern to their organization. Ombuds were asked if, in the five (or fewer) most serious cases they had during the previous year, "you believed information needed to reach appropriate offices/authorities, what actions did you take?" The responses should be reassuring to even the most dubious that ombuds work hard to find ways to surface important issues:[24]

Received permission to convey the information (without identifying the source)	79.2%
Helped the visitor find some other way to get the information to where it needed to go	77.4%
Received permission to convey the information (identifying the source)	67.9%
Found another way for the information to get where it needed to go	43.4%
Found an effective way for manager or compliance office to find the information itself	24.5%
Breached confidentiality (because you perceived an imminent risk)	7.5%

And finally, from a senior leader's perspective there is a real benefit to having a listening post that can pick up on issues and problems that

[24] International Ombudsman Association, 2017 Practice Survey (Data collected Spring 2018) at 22, International Ombudsman Association.

are not, for all the reasons discussed above, likely to be raised with formal channels. In this way, not only are more issues brought to light, but they are also often raised before they can explode and become major problems. That is also a good reason why ombuds should have the ability to report to the highest levels in an organization, and even when necessary, to the organization's board of directors. In effect, this is an important governance principle, because the ombuds can be a useful check on an organization's failure to learn about or correct failures or misconduct.

An ombuds office will not entirely eliminate the concern over what may be happening in an organization that a senior leader does not know about. There is no guarantee that an ombuds will discover every problematic issue. Yet, when that concern is driven by a fear of organizational liability, there are steps that the organization can take to minimize or reduce that risk by properly structuring the ombuds office and limiting its authority. Weighed against any remaining risk are the substantial benefits resulting from helping people and helping the organization learn of issues that would likely never otherwise be raised through a formal channel. There are times when an ombuds office will be the only place that some problematic issues will be discovered. Ombuds can usually find some proactive way to surface a problem without disclosing identities and ombuds' communications with visitors. The superpower of confidentiality is what makes this possible. In this sense, the ombuds should be seen as a solution to—not a source of—the worry about what a senior leader does not know by helping them know more than they otherwise would know and by offering an independent perspective informed by deep listening and assistance to people across the entire organization.

G. When an Ombuds' Confidentiality Is Challenged, How Should an Organization and Its Counsel Respond?

Challenges to ombuds confidentiality can occur in many forms, but for simplicity, it is useful to divide them into two broad categories: those arising from within the organization and those arising from outside of it. Whether a challenge comes from the inside or the outside, however, a failure to handle it properly—at a time when the ombuds may not even know that there has been a challenge—could prove disastrous to the preservation of ombuds confidentiality.

When challenges arise from the inside of an organization, it is most likely—but not always—the result of well-meaning people in other business functions trying to do their job and not being familiar with the fact that ombuds are not just like everyone else. For example, I am aware of situations in which supervisors, HR representatives, the organization's internal counsel, compliance officers, and others ask people if they have consulted with the ombuds and, if so, what was said. Because communications with an ombuds, including the very fact that someone consulted with the ombuds, are confidential, this is not an appropriate line of inquiry. Formal channels should be trained that they should not inquire into such matters and all constituents served by the office should be trained that they need not answer such questions. In a similar vein, document searches by any of the other business functions should not target ombuds without a compelling reason and without approval of a senior manager who is familiar with the nature and functioning of the ombuds office. And, if some information with the identity of visitors or confidential communications is found, the ombuds office should be notified immediately. These educational and training issues underscore the point that it is not sufficient to just create an ombuds office; those in positions to interact with the ombuds or involved in management tasks that could impact it need to know what they should and should not do.

Challenges from outside the organization typically involve litigation or steps preliminary to litigation. Examples include receiving a litigation hold notice in a matter that either makes reference to or implicates an ombuds; receiving a copy of a complaint in a lawsuit that makes reference to involvement of the ombuds; or receiving a discovery notice or demand (such as a document request or a notice to depose the ombuds). At this point, there is a risk that dealing with such a matter in the same manner as other non-ombuds matters could destroy the confidentiality of even the best-documented program.

1. Independent Counsel

One of the first things to do is to alert the ombuds that they may be implicated in a legal matter and permit them to have access to independent counsel if appropriate. Keep in mind that properly structured ombuds offices should have a charter and that charter should address the independence of the office, including the right in appropriate matters to retain independent counsel. That acknowledgement of independence should be a signal to both inside and outside counsel for an organization that they might have a conflict of interest in trying to represent both the organization and the ombuds office in the litigation.

I know of two types of situations in which counsel for an organization failed to understand this point. The first, which has occurred on multiple occasions, is when the organization's counsel (regardless of whether inside or outside) compelled an ombuds to disclose the identity of visitors and the substance of conversations on the basis that they are "representing the organization and must know all the relevant facts." Once this compelled disclosure is made, any further claim of confidentiality (for example, with respect to the plaintiff) is lost because these actions belie the independence of the function and give the organization an unfair advantage over the other side. A second example is when counsel for a company filed a motion for a protective order on behalf of the ombuds office and the company. When this occurred, opposing counsel pointed out that either the office was not independent (and that the motion for a protective order should be denied) or that counsel for the company had a conflict of interest in trying to represent both the company and an independent ombuds office. Counsel for the company had no choice but to retain independent counsel for the ombuds to protect the ombuds' independence and confidentiality.

These kinds of issues can be avoided if, at the outset, ombuds are entitled to retain counsel to advise them on issues relating to confidential communications. The ombuds' counsel can then work cooperatively with the organization's counsel in a variety of ways to help the organization respond to the lawsuit. For example, a litigation hold notice relating to the ombuds could be sent to the ombuds' counsel, and the ombuds' counsel can assume the responsibility to ensure that documents coming within its scope are properly preserved and any document destruction activities appropriately suspended. In addition, the ombuds' counsel is able to have attorney-client communications with the ombuds to learn all the relevant facts and then cooperate with the organization's counsel to develop an appropriate strategy without disclosing confidential ombuds-visitor communications. Indeed, those joint strategy communications may be protected under the common interest doctrine.

Retaining independent counsel for the ombuds does not mean that there is no role for an organization's counsel to work with an ombuds. When there are legal issues that affect an ombuds as an employee or that involve company policies and procedures, there is no need for independent counsel to provide legal advice to the ombuds. The need for independent counsel relates to the ombuds' confidential communications, and when this is an issue, independent counsel should be provided to advise the ombuds.

Because an ombuds program is created as an independent office pursuant to the charter, if any motions or other proceedings are necessary to protect the ombuds' confidentiality, they should be filed by counsel for the ombuds, who may have to file an appearance with the court as representing just the ombuds. Counsel for the organization can join in support of any such motion, but as the party most affected by an attempt to compel a breach, the ombuds and the ombuds' counsel should take the lead.

2. The Organization's Counsel

There are several ways an organization's counsel can destroy an ombuds office's confidentiality.[25] Aside from compelling an ombuds to reveal confidential communications, as described earlier, a claim of confidentiality can be compromised by overly broad searches for electronic documents and possibly disclosing documents that implicate the ombuds office before advising the ombuds or retaining counsel for the ombuds. Even if inside counsel is trained and understands that an ombuds is not just another employee in the normal sense, outside counsel retained by an organization to represent its interests in the litigation may not be. Here, it is the obligation of inside counsel (or the ombuds' counsel, if one has been retained early enough) to work with the organization's outside counsel to keep them from taking actions that might otherwise be entirely proper and done in the normal course.

A good example of this involves the deposition of a plaintiff in a lawsuit. Defense counsel typically try to depose a plaintiff (examine

---

[25] Also note the discussion earlier in section B.3 of this chapter regarding ways counsel for the organization can help protect ombuds confidentiality in arbitration. The failure to take those precautions can jeopardize ombuds confidentiality.

them under oath) early in a lawsuit in order to lock them into their version of the facts. It is customary for counsel to first ask very open-ended questions, such as "What happened next?" If the plaintiff were to say that they went to the ombuds office, and the defense counsel were to then sharpen the questions to ask about what was said and by whom—something that would ordinarily be done—the counsel for the organization that created the ombuds office could have just blown any claim of confidentiality. Since this evidence would now have been disclosed by the plaintiff, the same fundamental concern of fairness mentioned above would make it highly unlikely that a court would grant a motion for a protective order to preclude the plaintiff's counsel from deposing the ombuds about the same facts and circumstances.

In contrast, consider how much stronger the ombuds' claim of confidentiality would be if counsel had said either at the beginning of the deposition or at the first mention of the ombuds: "The [organization] created the ombuds office so that [employees, students, others] would have an independent, impartial, and informal resource with which to have confidential communications. The ombuds' charter is clear that the ombuds is not a proper witness or source of documents relating to those communications. Accordingly, I will not ask you about any communications with the ombuds, and I am instructing you not to disclose them in this deposition. If there is a challenge to that confidentiality and the court rules otherwise, I reserve my right to inquire further into these issues, but for now, I won't ask you and I instruct you not to tell me about any communications with the ombuds." None of this results in prejudice to the organization and its ability to elicit this information if a court later rules that information must be disclosed, but proceeding this way greatly enhances the likelihood that the confidentiality claim will not be lost before it can be presented to a court.

This discussion about independent counsel and the organization's counsel may sound complicated, but it really is not for lawyers experienced in litigation. I mention these examples only to emphasize the point that preserving confidentiality involves more than just an ombuds and more than just the legal theory on which one can assert ombuds' communications are confidential. Failing to adequately educate and train other organization personnel and external lawyers that ombuds are created in this independent role to help preserve confidentiality can destroy all of the other good work that ombuds do.

In summary, confidentiality is the defining characteristic of an organizational ombuds. The discussions in earlier chapters demonstrate a need for this informal resource, and there are legal bases on which this confidentiality can be protected. While confidentiality is not absolute, not even the most ancient of privileges are absolute, so that fact should not be the basis for opposing the creation of an ombuds program. To concede that there are situations in which ombuds may be compelled to disclose confidential communications (child and elder abuse and where there is an imminent threat of serious harm, for example) is also not a sufficient basis to conclude that those exceptions should be expanded to areas, such as harassment and discrimination, where there is such a great need for a confidential resource. Expanding the areas that would be subject to mandatory reporting would seriously compromise the effectiveness of ombuds' assistance. While there is a risk that an ombuds may be aware of circumstances or situations that go unreported to the formal channels of an organization, organizations have it in their power to minimize any such risk to the organization by expressly specifying what ombuds are authorized and not authorized to do. Balanced against any such risk are the substantial benefits to people and the organization from having a confidential and informal channel of communication. An important ombuds role is to help the organization identify systemic issues and trends, and an ombuds can enhance the effectiveness of formal channels as they work cooperatively on an issue that an ombuds may identify. And finally, to preserve the superpower that derives from the ombuds' confidentiality, others involved in the organization—particularly other formal channels and counsel for the organization—need to learn that they also have an obligation to help protect ombuds confidentiality. This can be done, and when it is, both people and the organization will benefit from having a good ombuds program.

5

Conclusion to Part I

If I have accomplished what I set out to do, you should know why there is a need for organizational ombuds programs and how to avoid common pitfalls while setting up an organizational ombuds program. Importantly, you should also know why confidentiality is essential for ombuds to do their work and how ombuds confidentiality can be protected.

In concluding this discussion in part I, I want to emphasize three points discussed in the preceding chapters that I consider to be most important for your consideration.

First, we need organizations to model effective solutions for conflict resolution and to provide more support for their human capital. That need is all the greater because of the incredible pace of change and the social, technological, and political turmoil currently in our lives, coupled with the persistence of harassment and discrimination and the perception of inequality of opportunity for people of color and women. Recruiting more diverse people and women will never succeed if better support is not provided *from within* our organizations.

Second, the social, economic, and moral imperatives that are driving organizations to embrace diversity will not abate. So where will this support come from? An ombuds program can be a major part of the answer to that question because it provides an informal and confidential resource that supports an organization's diversity efforts, and also because it provides guidance and assistance to *all* people in an organization, including people at every level—even those at the very top.

An ombuds' ability to provide support for a particular person or group of people in no way limits his or her ability to provide similar help to other people or groups. People on both sides of any divide can benefit from ombuds services.

Third, IOA-compliant ombuds programs can be adapted to any size or type of organization in any field of endeavor, whether the programs operate on a full-time or part-time basis and use employee ombuds or contract service providers. Yet, as with most things in life, commitment is necessary for success. If an organization wants an ombuds program that is effective in helping people and providing important information about systemic issues and trends to senior leadership, the program must have a capable ombuds and support from and access to senior leadership. Leadership must work with the ombuds to let the organization's constituents know that the program exists and that it can provide help when people do not know where to go or are afraid or unwilling to go to a formal reporting channel.

I hope you find the examples in part II illuminating.

PART II
Actual Ombuds Examples

INTRODUCTION

There is nothing like a story to illustrate a point and transform knowing into understanding. Having provided my answers to some of the most difficult questions, it is time to review actual ombuds examples to bring the work of ombuds to life—real life—so you can see the kinds of issues they deal with and how they do so. The desire to collect and present more examples (I included some in my first book) was one of the primary motivations for writing for this book.

Collecting these examples to pull back the curtain on what ombuds do and how they do it has not been easy. Because of their obligation to preserve the confidentiality of communications with inquirers, ombuds in virtually all organizations are able only rarely to disclose when or how they have been involved in a matter. I can tell their stories because I am not an ombuds or part of any ombuds office. My deal with the ombuds was this: if they would send me actual examples of matters they had handled, I would present them here in such a way as to demonstrate what the issue was, how it was handled, and what the result was, but no one would be able to identify the people or organizations involved. The one absolute requirement that I had of ombuds was that any example they sent to me had to be absolutely true; no composite or hypothetical examples were allowed. This is also why I cannot specifically name and thank the ombuds who shared their stories with me.

Even a cursory review of the examples collected from around the world and in many different types of organizations reveals a universality to both the need for this resource and the helpful ways ombuds can assist individuals and organizations with the issues involved. Not only do the issues raised have a universal quality, the reasons people do not go to existing resources and functions in the organization to address their issues have universal roots: formal channels failing to act, a fear of reporting and retaliation, uncertainty, a concern over possible misconduct but a desire not to be a whistleblower, an overwhelming desire to learn options for action in a safe and confidential space *before* deciding whether or how to take action, and a need for help from a skilled conflict resolution specialist to help resolve interpersonal conflict.

Before you review them, I would like to remind you of a few caveats.

First, the space limitations of this printed book precluded having more than a sampling of examples in the pages that follow. A much larger compilation of examples is available as PDF downloads using the URL at the end of this introduction to part II. While I understand that it may be cumbersome to take this additional step to fully access all of the examples I collected and categorized, I realistically had no other choice because I thought collecting as many of them as possible was important and the resulting collection comprises more than six hundred pages. I hope that reviewing the examples that are printed in the book will whet your appetite for a fuller exploration of all of the examples.

Second, many of the examples that I received relate to more than one category. Since my purpose in putting them in categories was to make them easy to locate by someone looking for an example on a particular topic or category, I thought it best to include some of them in more than one category. This no doubt expanded the size of the collection of the examples, but I trust that the convenience of finding a relevant example in a category outweighs any inconvenience in seeing an example appear more than once.

And finally, please don't be put off by a failure to find a specific kind of example in a specific category. For example, the number of examples in the "Federal Agencies" category are relatively few. That is not because they don't exist. Rather, examples from federal agencies that involved middle management, for example, or other issues where the context of a federal agency was irrelevant were also collected in another category. For that reason, only those issues that uniquely dealt with federal agencies will be found in that category. The same principle applies in many other contexts because for many issues, there is no fundamental difference in how corporate ombuds, government ombuds, or university ombuds handle counseling, mediation, fraud, upward feedback, and many other issues. For that reason, I added an Author's Note at the beginning of some categories to remind the reader that other relevant examples may be found in other categories and in the PDF downloads.

Before proceeding to the categories of examples, please pause to review the following questions. I hope that reflecting on these questions will deepen your understanding of the examples.

Questions to Consider

This book is intended to respond to questions about ombuds programs. In part I, I provided my answers to questions often asked of ombuds and me. Part II has real-life examples of what ombuds do without any commentary from me, but I do ask that you consider my questions to you as you review the examples.

The questions below are intended to help you understand why organizations should have an organizational ombuds program apart from anything I have said in part I. Not all of the examples are responsive to each of these questions but thinking about these questions in the context of actual issues that have been brought to an ombuds and how the ombuds then dealt with them demonstrates the range of assistance provided by ombuds. They also show why ombuds are uniquely positioned both to help individuals and improve an organization's culture and functioning.

- Where else could the issue have been brought?
- Why was the issue brought to the ombuds instead of a formal channel?
- If it were not for the ombuds, how likely would it have been for the visitor to have:
  - raised the issue with a formal channel?
  - left the organization?
  - filed a lawsuit?
- What other outcomes would have been possible or likely had the ombuds not been involved in the matter?
- What would have been the reputational or relationship impact on people and/or the organization if the issue had not been raised or resolved with the help of the ombuds?
- How important was the independence of the ombuds and/or the promise of confidentiality to the visitor's willingness to bring forward the issue?
- How important was it to the visitor to be able to obtain information, guidance, or learn about options BEFORE the visitor had to decide what else to do?
- Was the ombuds able to provide information, referrals, coaching, or other assistance to help the visitor take action themselves?
- Was the ombuds able to provide options to surface the issue without disclosing the identity of the visitor?
- Was the ombuds able to help resolve a conflict or resolve the issue expeditiously and cost effectively?
- Did the actions of the ombuds benefit the organization; and if so, how?
- Did the visitor's issue raise questions about conduct or action that, if true, was contrary to the expressed values of the organization?
- Were the ombuds' actions in keeping with the expressed values of the organization?
- Did the work of the ombuds help make the organization a better place?

- Did the actions of the ombuds promote fair process?
- Was the ombuds able to provide an impetus for systemic change that helped people and the organization?
- Was information the ombuds provided to senior management meaningful?
- Did the ability to raise issues with the ombuds help address inappropriate activity in the organization?
- What would have been the probable costs to the organization and individuals if the matter had not been raised or resolved with the help of the ombuds?
- What were the benefits to the organization and individuals because the matter was raised or resolved with the help of the ombuds?

Link for Digital Download of Full Compilation of Actual Ombuds Examples

Those wishing to access the full collection of examples may do so at http://ambar.org/Howard-ombuds-examples.

Categories of Ombuds Examples

PROVIDING INFORMATION/ SERVING AS A SOUNDING BOARD

An Ombuds Is Especially Helpful for Middle Management

Many people assume that ombuds exist in organizations primarily to help lower-level employees understand and deal with workplace conflict and how to most effectively surface issues of concern to them. The reality is that most experienced ombuds report that people at all levels in their organization consult with them. What is most surprising to people, however, is the typically large number of "middle managers" and "team leaders" who approach an ombuds on their own to have confidential conversations.

One experienced ombuds reported that these folks describe themselves as "stuck in the middle" or disrespected and bypassed by upper management. Mostly what they want is someone to listen and validate them. Many times, the ombuds can provide them coaching on communicating more effectively with their bosses. The ombuds also serves as a valuable sounding board for these middle managers as they try to implement directives from upper management or address conflict and other issues among the team members they supervise. Even though the options offered by the ombuds often include a willingness to participate in a facilitated conversation between a middle manager and his or her boss, in most instances this offer is rejected. Middle managers fear a confrontation with the boss and the perception that they need help. Because they are part of management, they often are not comfortable taking issues to HR or other formal channels. On some occasions the ombuds, at the request of a middle management visitor, is able to take an issue (without attribution) to upper management with suggestions on how to promote better conflict management and communication training but this is not common.

The Importance of Confidentially Discussing the Process BEFORE Raising Sexual Harassment Complaint

An employee came to the ombuds with concerns about sexual harassment the employee was experiencing from a supervisor. The employee wanted the harassment to stop and yet was uncertain about reporting it for fear that her issues might not be taken seriously. The employee was also afraid that reporting her concerns could result in victim blaming, shaming, retaliation, and a ruined career. Yet, she also was concerned that not coming forward would leave others vulnerable to the same or similar conduct by the supervisor.

The ombuds talked through with the visitor the pros and cons of both reporting and not reporting her issues. After an extensive conversation about these issues, the employee gave the ombuds permission to consult with HR leadership in the region where she worked (but without disclosing any information that might identify her or her supervisor) to find out exactly what would happen if a sexual harassment case were reported.

After finding out this information from the regional HR office, the ombuds reported back to the employee that the alleged perpetrator would be placed on paid administrative leave while an investigation into the claims was conducted and that an independent professional investigator would be used to fully investigate the claims. The employee was relieved to learn this process and thought that having the supervisor out of the workplace on administrative leave while the investigation occurred would allow her to be in a safe environment.

With this information, the employee decided to come forward and report. The process transpired exactly as promised, which the employee appreciated tremendously. The investigation resulted in her allegations being substantiated. The employee and her supervisor had no further professional interactions.

Referral to an Internal Resource Helps Avoid a Lawsuit and Resolve a Pension Issue

A former employee who had recently accepted a voluntary separation package during a restructuring program contacted the ombuds. They were having difficulty resolving issues with their pension and were very frustrated with the way the company had been responding to their questions and concerns. They were about to engage the services of legal counsel to pursue their issues.

The ombuds listened to the concerns of the former employee and provided them with them with direct contact information for an internal pension advocate, who the ombuds said was there to assist employees and former employees with just such issues.

The pension advocate worked with and on behalf of the former employee and was able resolve all of their issues without the necessity of their having to retain a lawyer or bring suit. Clearly, the company also benefited from the resolution of this dispute without a lawsuit.

Information from the Ombuds Makes a Difference

A post-doctoral fellow came into the ombuds office worried that her boss was going to fire her. She was from another country, and she did not want to go home in disgrace. She said her boss yelled at her and always criticized her written work. She also reported having no friends and feeling lonely. She said she didn't know how to make friends and missed her family.

The ombuds talked with her about ways to get suggestions before she wrote a paper and discussed resources on campus such as clubs that she could join to meet others. The ombuds also mentioned the Employee Assistance Program in order to deal with her depression and perhaps to talk about assertiveness (in response to her statement about it being difficult being a woman in science.)

The visitor was very excited about the idea of getting help with assertiveness and effusively thanked the ombuds for her various suggestions.

The university could have lost a post-doctoral fellow, and the student was able to build her confidence. Upon follow-up, the fellow reported that she was now getting along with her professor and publishing a paper.

A Probationary Employee Clarifies a Policy Without Hurting his Career

The organization president issued a policy statement to all employees mandating a furlough. The policy stated that all employees had to take a certain amount of time off without pay and that they could do so when they chose, in partial day increments, one day at a time, or in multiple day blocks up to five consecutive days.

An employee still in probationary status (having worked for the organization for less than one year) contacted the ombuds office because, contrary to the directive from the president, his supervisor had dictated when employees had to take the unpaid days off. Because he was still in his probationary period, the employee was unwilling to raise the issue directly out of fear that doing so would hurt his chances for employment when his probationary period ended.

After discussing various options, the employee gave the ombuds permission to contact the HR office to raise the issue generically. Once HR became aware of the issue, it revised the FAQs on its website to address the issue with a question on whether a department or division could mandate when furlough is taken. The answer to this question given by HR was "No. A department should not dictate when the required furlough days must be taken by an employee or a department." This information was disseminated to all departments, including the department in which the employee worked, and the problem was eliminated.

The Need for a Truly Confidential Discussion and Help from the Ombuds

An employee contacted the ombuds, relying on the promise of confidentiality, to discuss possible implications of a serious health problem that the employee had involving a chronic and deteriorating (but noncommunicable) disease. He wanted to know the benefits that would be available to his wife when he died. The employee indicated that he is able to function well at present but did not trust HR to keep such an inquiry confidential. He also did not want to inform his supervisor because he did not believe he would be incapacitated anytime soon and was afraid that he would not be taken seriously for promotions or new responsibilities if others know about his life-threatening illness.

The ombuds helped him research all of the applicable company policies to answer his questions on death benefit policies. The ombuds also raised with him a concern over the fact that because no one else in the organization knew about his condition, it could be a problem for the organization if he were to be incapacitated or die suddenly. The ombuds and the employee discussed several options, and the employee decided to prepare a sealed envelope with instructions that it only be opened in the event that a medical crisis occurs while he is at work.

CONFIDENTIAL COACHING AND GUIDANCE

Restoring Morale and Improving Communication

When the COVID-19 stay-at-home directives were put in place, not all teams embraced the required changes. The ombuds heard from staff across the university that, in many units, there was no plan and leaders were dropping the ball. Some visitors had not heard from their supervisors in weeks. The ombuds provided communication coaching to empower visitors to initiate and frame conversations with their supervisors to address remote team communication and other issues resulting from the stay-at-home directives.

In one case, the visitor was new to their position and fearful of raising their concerns. They were also not comfortable giving the ombuds permission to speak directly with their supervisor. Rather, they gave the ombuds permission to reach out to others in the university who could possibly help discreetly address the situation systemically. The ombuds reached out to those offices to share the visitor's concerns—but without disclosing the identity of the visitor—and helped devise a plan to intervene and support the team without the supervisor knowing the impetus.

Assistance Provided to a Senior Leader Outside of the United States

In an emerging markets region, due to rapid business growth and employee turnover, some talented employees were promoted to senior positions before they had received sufficient supervisory or leadership training. One such employee came to the ombuds for advice because she was feeling overwhelmed. She was very capable and had demonstrated excellent performance in her previous technical role, but after she was promoted, she began managing a large team (more than one thousand employees) and multiple projects across different countries.

She was confident in her substantive abilities and learning quickly in her new role. She wanted to know how other leaders had handled situations similar to those she was encountering and wanted to benefit from understanding best practices for managing and motivating large teams. She said she considered the ombuds a trusted coach and discussed with the ombuds alternatives in a variety of situations with which she was dealing.

One example she shared involved a member of her leadership team who had taken a lead role at a new site. At the beginning of the assignment, he was quite engaged and passionate. After a few months, however, his performance declined significantly. He expressed to her that, due to the COVID-19 impact and personal challenges he was facing with relocating his family, he would like to return to a role in his home city.

Unfortunately, there were no available jobs for him there at this time. The new manager asked the ombuds whether she should approach this from a performance management perspective or a leadership development dimension to take the best approach for both this highly talented employee and the organization. The ombuds inquired about the background of the site, her expectations for the employee, and any performance gaps. Together with the new manager, the ombuds reviewed the pros and cons of each option for approaching this issue. The new manager ultimately sought other candidates for the site lead role and searched for other jobs for the current site lead in a more suitable position closer to his home base.

The ombuds also advised the new manager about her further development as a leader and encouraged her to leverage her supervisor and shared company training options for additional skill building. The ombuds suggested that she register in the company's mentorship program to identify a senior leader outside of her work group who might provide regular guidance to her.

Counseling a Manager who Received Performance Coaching

A manager reached out to the ombuds office after receiving a disciplinary coaching memo. The memo was the outcome of an investigation into allegations made by one of his direct reports that he had been refusing to conduct one-to-one meetings with subordinates and demonstrated an abrasive communication style. The manager felt that this disciplinary action was unfair because there were rumors that the direct report who raised the issue had complained about others in the past. The manager feared that this would ruin his reputation. For the last couple of weeks—since the investigation—the manager reported that he and the direct report had avoided each other.

The ombuds acknowledged to the manager how difficult it is to go through an investigation and more so when the subject of the investigation and the complainant must continue working together. The ombuds explained that, irrespective of whether the employee had lodged prior complaints against others, this particular issue had been investigated by the company and disciplinary action had been decided upon. This was something that the manager needed to accept.

The ombuds also explored with him the opportunities that the advice in this coaching memo might bring to help him improve as a manager and to ultimately advance his career. The ombuds suggested that he make regular one-to-one meetings with direct reports a priority, articulate his desire to change any behaviors that were making them uncomfortable, and encourage them to let him know if they were troubled at any time by his actions—without fear of retaliation. The ombuds helped the manager to understand that avoiding the direct report who had raised the issue was not a viable or productive option and would appear to be retaliatory because he did not treat other subordinates in that manner.

The manager indicated that he would move forward with the advice received and that he understood the importance of changing some of his behaviors.

Guidance for a Foreign Student on Dealing with Professorial and Peer Pressure

An undergraduate student in a political science class addressing politics and academic freedom came to the ombuds to discuss how to deal with pressures from his professor and classmates that he participate in a demonstration that he feared, as an international student, could adversely affect his visa status.

The student said that the class had been encouraged by their professor to take part in a peaceful demonstration at the state capitol to raise awareness about climate change. Because he was an international student, he was reluctant to attend the demonstration for fear of jeopardizing his visa status. Nevertheless, he felt a great deal of peer pressure and consternation and was even called out in class by another student as being a "climate denier." He said that he was concerned that his refusal to participate may affect his grade, particularly because the professor did not intervene when he was shamed in class. The student wondered whether he should take the risk and attend the demonstration in order to avoid both social and academic consequences.

The ombuds and the student explored various options. He could attend the demonstration, but he quickly ruled that out because the risk was too great. He could soldier on and hope that once the demonstration had come and gone the class would move on, although there was no assurance that the issue would blow over. He could also request a mediated conversation with the professor to share what he was experiencing in the hope that she would back down. The option selected by the student was to have the ombuds reach out to the professor, hear what she had to say, and if both were in agreement, facilitate a conversation between the two of them.

When the ombuds met with the professor, it became apparent that she was not aware of the student's full story and, in particular, the visa concern. Regarding the in-class shaming, she stated that she did hear an exchange among students and the use of the phrase "climate denier" but did not know the context so let it go. She also stated that it was her intention to let the students decide for themselves if they wanted to attend the demonstration. However, because it required cancelling class the day of the demonstration, those who were not going would be required to write a short paper on climate change.

The professor acknowledged that her manner of delivery regarding those factors may not have been sufficiently clear. In sum, she felt sorry about how events unfolded for the student and wanted very much to meet with him to say so directly. Additionally, she stated that she planned to emphasize to the class that every individual could choose whether to attend and reinforce that not participating in the demonstration could be for a whole host of reasons and did not equate to climate-denying.

The ombuds hosted the facilitated conversation soon thereafter. The professor listened intently to the student's account; and when he was done, she apologized for her lack of awareness, particularly with respect to the reaction of some of the class members regarding the student's decision not to attend the demonstration. She asked the student whether he would be comfortable with her making a statement to the class about these points, and after some discussion, he agreed provided she did not single him out or refer to him personally. She agreed to the caveat, and they both left the meeting having a much better understanding of each other. It also resulted in a teachable moment for the class regarding mutual respect and recognition of diversity of thought.

Difficult Boss and Policy Guidance Regarding Annual Reviews

A faculty member came to the ombuds with a myriad of issues regarding her department chair. One of the issues involved the chair's practices around the annual review process. The faculty member explained that at annual review time, her department chair would expect her to read, digest, and sign her review in front of him. He essentially would give her no time to respond or clarify the review before expecting her to sign it.

In the ombuds' discussion with the faculty member, the ombuds explained that Faculty Handbook policy allowed a faculty member to compose and submit a written response to a review if they so desired. The ombuds also explained that the policy provided that signing a review did not necessarily mean that a faculty member agreed with it; it simply meant that one had read it.

The ombuds helped the visitor consider various options for how to proceed and, ultimately, the visitor decided that she would like the ombuds to contact the dean (the department chair's supervisor) to inquire as to her expectations regarding how chairs should conduct annual reviews with their own supervisees. The understanding was that the ombuds would not identify the faculty member or department in question.

When the ombuds spoke with the dean, the dean explained that she expected the annual review to be a conversation and that that conversation should be seen as an opportunity to make any reasonable edits to the review. As a result of the conversation with the ombuds, the dean agreed to remind all chairs of her view of how the process should work, as well as of the policies regarding faculty's right to submit a response.

The faculty member's improved understanding of her rights in the process, along with the dean's reminder to all chairs, allowed the faculty member to have a more productive conversation regarding her performance and made the process fairer for all, without compromising confidentiality.

POLICY QUESTIONS/OMBUDS ACTING ON OWN INITIATIVE

Unpaid Labor

Through a series of visitor consultations, the ombuds identified a pattern of unpaid labor for graduate students. Because this issue appeared to be a systemic issue involving multiple locations in the university, the ombuds brought this issue to the university's legal counsel without providing any identifying information relating to any of the visitors who had raised the issue with the ombuds. As a result, the university's counsel was able to investigate the issue and then develop a resolution of the matter campus-wide.

Addressing the Need for More Communication During a Pandemic

A hospital ombuds noticed that with all the rapid changes happening at the hospital after the outbreak of the COVID-19 pandemic, as the hospital was trying to respond to the many challenges of COVID-19, communication with hospital staff was generally becoming confusing about various initiatives.

In particular, the ombuds noticed that several employees were asking various questions about reassignments. The ombuds office gathered the questions and made a recommendation to a leader in HR that preparation of an FAQ could help address employee concerns and improve communications. The feedback was accepted, and an FAQ addressing these questions was subsequently posted on the website.

Manager Violating Company Policy

Multiple sales representatives reached out to the ombuds office to discuss what they believed was a violation of company policy. The visitors shared that they feared reprisal from their manager.

The concerns raised involved the district manager (DM) to whom they reported. They discovered that she had been recording virtual sales calls between employees and customers without their knowledge. She did not provide any prior notice of her intent to record sales calls with customers, and no consent or disclosure was made to employees or the customers that their meetings were being recorded. When one of the sales reps learned that this was happening, she confronted the DM.

The DM explained that the purpose of the recordings was to provide the sales reps with feedback on their communication style and marketing techniques. During normal times, this type of feedback would have been provided during ride-alongs with her. Because of the pandemic, however, all sales calls were virtual. So, she came up with this idea to accomplish that purpose. The sales reps remained uncomfortable with this practice but were afraid to raise this concern to senior leadership because they were unsure if it had been endorsed by upper management. They decided to seek guidance from the ombuds office.

The ombuds was able to share with the visitors that company policy prohibited unauthorized recording of communications. They discussed the sales reps' obligation as employees to report the DM's behavior and to ensure that they do not participate in any further recorded calls. The ombuds encouraged them to report the concern via the compliance hotline which could be done anonymously.

In addition, because multiple visitors had come forward to the ombuds office with the same issue, the ombuds was able to separately take the issue forward as a trend to local HR and compliance departments for investigation. During the inquiry, additional privacy law concerns about this practice were identified. The organization ultimately communicated to the entire sales force that the unauthorized recording of calls was strictly prohibited.

Systemic Issue Report Results in Policy Change

To control costs, the finance and HR departments of the company changed the company's travel policy. Under the new policy, reimbursement rates for domestic travel accommodations were reduced to half the amount previously allowed.

The new policy had an immediate and national impact, resulted in dozens of employees contacting the ombuds office to complain about the changes. Because they had not been involved in developing the new policy, these employees did not believe they could approach management directly to discuss their concerns. Yet, they all believed that the new reduced reimbursement limits were unacceptable and disrespectful because the only hotels or motels available to them at rates within amounts specified by the new policy were of very low quality, dirty, and unsafe. The employees expressed both their personal concerns and the concerns of their families about the health implications of the new policy. As a result, the impact on morale was great; the employees thought the company was not treating them like human beings and that the company only cared about the money that could be saved by the new policy.

After speaking with the employees who raised this issue, the ombuds concluded that it was a systemic issue that needed to be raised directly with management. The ombuds reviewed both the old policy and the new policy and then met with the HR director. The ombuds presented information on the reality of possible accommodation options under the new budget, which corroborated the employees' concern. As a result of this intervention by the ombuds, the policy was changed to increase the amounts that could be reimbursed to employees for accommodation costs.

Some of the employees expressed their gratitude to the ombuds that the policy was changed and said if they had not been able to consult with the ombuds, they would not have known how or where to raise their concerns. Just as importantly, the HR director thanked the ombuds for bringing the issue forward to give the company an opportunity to review the implications of the new policy and to make changes.

Benefits and Inclusion for Same-Sex Marriages

A female employee in a same-sex marriage contacted the ombuds to express her frustration about a limitation in the company-provided insurance benefits. In this discussion, the ombuds learned that the employee and her wife had been preparing over the past few years to start a family of their own, with the employee being the one to carry the child. At first, they assumed that IVF (in vitro fertilization) was the only option, a procedure where the woman's egg is stimulated, retrieved, fertilized, and transferred back to the female. But upon researching further, they found IUI (intrauterine insemination) was the best option for them. This is a procedure where sperm is simply injected into a uterus. IUI is a lower-cost option and a much more practical avenue for same-sex female couples who do not require additional fertilization techniques to conceive.

The employee stated that she had made several calls to the company's insurance provider for information and was told IUI was only covered after the couple "tries to conceive" for one year and that they would need to prove their "exposure to semen" in order to be covered. The inquirer indicated that she thought the company's insurance coverage was antiquated and unfair; although it provided extensive, often expensive, coverage for women in heterosexual relationships facing infertility issues, the plan did not consider being in a same-sex marriage (and a very healthy individual) to be a valid reason for fertility benefits coverage.

The employee also strongly felt that the company's public statements conflicted with the coverages in the plan it provided for employees. The company continued to raise flags in celebration of PRIDE month and had discussions of inclusion, but this lack of coverage for same-sex couples was not consistent with that message. The employee also felt that it would be humiliating to try to address this with her local management, as the terms of coverage in company insurance policies is determined at the corporate headquarters level.

After this discussion with the ombuds, the inquirer agreed that since this was a companywide topic and if the Ombuds were to raise this issue it would not necessarily be linked to her in particular, the employee granted the ombuds permission to share the concern with the global benefits vice president and their team for review. As a result, the company's policies were changed to allow all employees equal access to fertility benefits: the criteria of needing a diagnosis of infertility to access infertility benefits was removed; the cost of donor sperm would be covered by the plan; and cryopreservation would be covered for both eggs and sperm for up to 12 months.

The ombuds also made sure these changes would be mentioned in various LGBTQ communications materials that the company put together each year.

Help for Pregnant Employee and in Enforcement of Global Policies

An employee from a location outside of the United States contacted the Ombuds to say that her boss had called her into his office to tell her that he noticed that she was pregnant and that he knew she was unmarried. She said that the boss had told her that if she were not married by the time the baby was delivered, she would be fired. Such conduct was not illegal in the country where she worked but violated the company's policies. She was uncertain what to do, afraid of losing her job, and feared retaliation by management of the company in her country, who she felt would support her manager.

The ombuds discussed various options on how to proceed and assured her that such action would violate company policy. With her permission, the ombuds forwarded her issue to a formal channel at the company headquarters, which intervened with local management to reinforce the company's policies and reiterated to local management that retaliation against her for bringing this issue to the attention of the company would not be tolerated.

The ombuds also worked with those responsible for the company's newsletter, which was sent to tens of thousands of employees around the world, to address the issue prospectively and generically (no reference to any names or locations) in a question-and-answer format to advise everyone in the company that it would violate the company's policies for a supervisor to discipline a female subordinate for being pregnant and unmarried and that attempting to do so would subject the supervisor to discipline, including possible dismissal. Such clear and direct guidance not only helped reinforce the company's global policies but may have spared other women throughout the world and in these circumstances from having to deal with the threat of termination and/or retaliation.

A Policy Recommendation Addresses the Performance Review Concerns of an Employee (and Possibly Many Others)

In the ombuds' organization, annual performance evaluations were typically communicated to employees by November. When an employee contacted the ombuds in mid-April to complain that the employee's performance evaluation had not been completed, the ombuds discussed various options the employee could take to address the problem directly, and the employee then took action to do so. Unfortunately, none of the steps taken by the employee were successful, and the employee came back to the ombuds for further guidance.

At this point the ombuds understood that the problem this employee had experienced was a systemic issue that also could be adversely affecting other employees. The ombuds also concluded that the solution to the problem likely was to raise the issue at the level of senior management. After discussing this option with the employee and receiving permission to raise the issue generally (and without identifying the employee who had raised the issue), the ombuds recommended to senior leaders that there was a need for them to develop procedures for following up on the annual evaluation process to ensure there were no outstanding annual appraisals in the organization.

Ultimately a change was made to the software system that allowed for better monitoring. Thereafter, HR was able to print more detailed reports and follow up with specific supervisors missing performance management deadlines, and the problem was resolved.

Prompt Action by Ombuds Assists Leadership on Control Issues

A visitor scheduled an appointment with the ombuds to discuss a stressful work environment that focused on results over quality. At the start of the meeting, the visitor communicated that this was their last day with the organization.

The visitor presented the ombuds with a lengthy document detailing instances where the work climate had resulted in policy breaches over the past few months. As the ombuds questioned the visitor about each item, the ombuds learned that the visitor and colleagues had spoken up as each issue occurred and line management had, in fact, addressed them. However, the ombuds also learned that employees now felt pressured about continuing to speak up and, in some cases, were told specifically not to discuss anything with HR or the ombuds.

When the ombuds asked if there were any open issues that hadn't been reported, the visitor pointed to the final item and said, "That's why I'm here. I wanted to put it on the record, confidentially, before

I leave today," and then proceeded to communicate a recent breach of controls that, if left unchecked, could take the organization out of regulatory compliance.

As the ombuds reiterated that speaking with this office did not constitute "putting it on the record," the visitor began to back off, stating that they'd done their job and weren't willing to do more. Then the visitor stood up to leave, and the ombuds quickly asked, "What if I were able to arrange for the head of compliance to speak with you right now, assuming they are available? Would you be willing to repeat what you've just told me?" The visitor was hesitant and didn't fully believe that would happen but gave permission for the ombuds to try. The ombuds then immediately got the head of compliance on the phone to speak with the visitor and stepped out of earshot, so as not to be part of the notice chain as the visitor made their report.

A few days later, the ombuds learned that the internal audit team had been engaged to investigate the visitor's allegation. They identified a control issue, as described by the visitor. The head of the business was notified, and appropriate controls were restored, just days before a regulatory audit began. New processes were put in place to shore up both the control environment and the climate in this group, freeing individuals to continue to speak up before any issue became significant.

Ombuds Identifies Need for a New Policy to Address Serious Accidents or Death

The ombuds at a public sector organization learned of an incident in which one of its personnel was injured in a foreign country in a car accident on a weekend. While the other people in the car suffered only minor injuries, the person in question had a major injury that was not immediately visible and thus her supervisor did not take it seriously and thought she was faking it. The injured person felt abandoned by the organization and that she was being discriminated against because of her national origin.

By the time the ombuds learned about the matter, the injured person had been med-evacuated back to the United States and was facing serious surgery. Once the seriousness of her injury had become apparent, representations had been made by others in the organization to her that could not have been acted on. Also, even though the injured person did finally receive proper medical treatment, the ombuds realized that the organization did not have a policy in place to deal with serious injuries or death of people in such circumstances and brought the issue of a lack of an appropriate policy to the attention of senior leadership in the organization.

Senior leadership agreed that such a policy was needed and developed just such a policy in the event that similar events occurred in the future.

An Observant Ombuds Addresses a Needed Accommodation

The ombuds of a large organization usually used the north entrance to the building where she worked. From time to time, the ombuds saw an employee using a walker and moving very slowly to approach the same north entrance to the building. When they both arrived at the entrance at about the same time, the ombuds would usually say hello and, if possible, hold the door for the employee to enter. Although the north entrance had a ramp to the entrance, it did not have a button to push for the door to open automatically.

On one of these occasions, the ombuds also inquired whether the employee had thought of using use the south entrance to the building, which did have a button to push to open the door automatically. In response, the employee said that the south entrance was not an option because of the greater distance to the elevator and the location of the employee's office.

Soon thereafter, it occurred to the ombuds that as an advocate for fair process, she may be able to address the need for an accommodation. Without disclosing that the inquiry was based on her own direct observation and without seeking or receiving permission to raise the issue on behalf of the employee with the walker, the ombuds merely inquired of the head of facilities if anyone had ever thought to add a button on the north entrance to automatically open the door. The ombuds also made the same inquiry to the local HR representative. Within a month, the ombuds noticed that an automatic opening button had been added to the north entrance door and that the employee with the walker no longer struggled to open the door or needed assistance from a coworker to open it. Rather, the employer had provided an accommodation to assist employees. The employee with the walker—and any others with a disability—no longer would have to struggle to get in the building to go to work.

Relocation and Reimbursement Process

The ombuds was contacted by several visitors with questions about the organization's relocation payment policy. This case was particularly complex as it involved multiple components of the policy and application of the policy to different situations.

Because of the larger policy issues implicated, the Ombuds brought these concerns to management with the permission of the visitors but without disclosing who they were. The ombuds also provided additional input to help management clarify the process, identify the decision-makers, articulate expected timelines for making a decision, and describe what appeal processes were available. The resulting revised policy was much clearer and addressed the issues that visitors had brought to the ombuds.

FEAR OF REPORTING OR RETALIATION

Fear of Retaliation Is So Great That Employee Will Trust Only Ombuds

An employee was concerned that a supervisor was misappropriating funds by submitting false entertainment vouchers. The employee was extremely concerned about possible retaliation and the consequences of raising these issues about her supervisor. She said that she was not prepared to submit any documents or to speak to anyone other than the ombuds because the ombuds' communications were confidential.

After several rounds of conversation with the ombuds during which they discussed options for raising the issue, she finally agreed to speak with an internal auditor but only anonymously. The ombuds arranged for an anonymous call between her and internal audit. The employee, communicating through the ombuds as an intermediary, was also able to provide internal audit with other information they needed to commence the investigation, but the employee's identity was never disclosed.

The audit revealed misconduct and the supervisor was terminated.

Ombuds Helps an Employee Experiencing Bullying Resolve a Hostile Work Environment Claim and the Company Avoid a Lawsuit

An employee contacted the ombuds about an abusive manager. The employee described how the manager bullied the employee and also a number of coworkers. The employee told the ombuds that they had been the only person to raise the matter with their local HR team. In fact, they had twice gone to the local HR team, but no action had been taken in connection with the abusive manager. Compounding the abusive behaviors and bullying from the manager, the employee also reported being subjected to retaliation for having made the reports to HR. The employee was on the verge of leaving the company and retaining counsel to bring suit against the company. Under these circumstances, it was clear that a confidential conversation with the ombuds was extremely important to the employee.

The ombuds and the employee explored various other internal options available to the employee before the drastic action of leaving the company and filing suit against it. One of the options was for the employee to collect evidence of the manager's abusive and retaliatory conduct and then to contact the ethics and compliance office (ECO) with a request to conduct an investigation. The ombuds coached the employee on how to collect and collate their evidence and also how to then discuss the matter with the ECO.

The employee took this option, collected the relevant evidence, and contacted the ECO. The ECO investigated the issue and found that the employee had been subjected to a hostile work environment and retaliation. The manager involved was disciplined and removed from the company. The employee was able to continue working for the company in a greatly improved work environment.

Local Management Misconduct and Fear of Retaliation

Employees at one unit of the company had been using company products and equipment to create their own personal business, resulting in a loss of customers and revenues for the company. Some of the people involved in the scheme were members of the local management. As a result, employees who knew about this misconduct felt that they could not report it to local management and were afraid to raise it through formal channels. They were not sure how to contact or approach higher levels of management or if higher management might also be involved.

Some of the employees who knew about the scheme came to the ombuds office because they understood that it was independent and confidential. After discussing the issue with the ombuds, the ombuds, at their request, facilitated contact with the compliance office, which investigated and eventually terminated the employment of those involved in the scheme. The employees who came to the ombuds office stated that the experience made them more comfortable raising issues with the company's compliance office.

Where Does a Vice President Go with Concerns About the President?

The ombuds of a multinational organization received a call from a regional vice president with concerns about an international region president. The inquirer expressed concerns that the regional president was acting strangely and making improper comments about people at an offsite meeting where over a dozen other vice president–level organization officials were present, together with several outside counsel, professionals, and other consultants to the organization. The inquirer was concerned that the regional president could have a drug problem, as the strange behavior had been evident for at least the preceding few months. The vice president making the call, however, was also obviously concerned that he may be wrong and was worried about the possible impact on his own career.

The ombuds discussed various ways this issue could be surfaced and investigated. The inquirer gave the ombuds permission to convey information about the regional president's conduct at the off-site meeting (but not the inquirer's identity) to the top levels of the organization at its international headquarters. When this information was relayed to the president of the entire organization and the head of HR, they instigated an investigation almost immediately by having many of the attendees of the offsite meeting interviewed. The regional president was also interviewed.

As a result of this investigation, they made the decision to remove the regional president from his position and announced that he was relocating back to the organization headquarters. He retired from the organization not long thereafter.

Ombuds Arranges for an Anonymous Call to a Formal Channel

Multiple employees on a regional sales team had been talking among themselves about the disrespectful, abusive, unsupportive behavior of their mutual supervisor. The employees all worked in different states and were connected only by way of a virtual network, so that their interaction with each other, their supervisor, and potential resources was entirely by phone and email. They expressed great fear of retribution from the supervisor if they spoke up. They also did not trust other resources in the organization. With frustration mounting and many of them finding it increasingly difficult to focus on their jobs, a representative of the employees contacted the ombuds in search of a way to anonymously raise their concerns.

After listening to the concerns expressed and understanding what the employees had already attempted to do to resolve the problem, the ombuds discussed various options. The option selected was for the ombuds to contact HR to arrange for an anonymous telephone call between a regional HR director and some of the employees. The understanding was that the ombuds would coordinate the conference call and that four employees would participate in it with the HR director but that the employees would not identify themselves. The ombuds coordinated the call and once all participants were connected, the ombuds dropped off so as not to be part of a formal, but unusual, teleconference.

As a result of the conversation, an investigation was begun into the leadership behavior of the supervisor in question. In the end, the supervisor was switched to a nonleadership role in the organization.

First a Test, and Then the Real Issue

An ombuds who works outside of the United States received a call from an inquirer who lived in a Middle Eastern country and worked for a unit of the organization located in that country. The ombuds and the inquirer were of different nationalities and worked in different countries. The inquirer, who wished to remain anonymous, presented the ombuds with what appeared to be a relatively minor issue dealing with a business process within the organization. The ombuds was given permission to raise the issue, which the ombuds did. The issue was resolved and that appeared to be the end of the matter.

Approximately three months later, the same inquirer called the ombuds again, but this time it was with a concern over what later was determined to be a major fraud. In the course of dealing with the inquirer on the second matter, the inquirer disclosed his identity, and it came out that he had been the person who had raised the first issue. The inquirer indicated that while his real concern all along had been the fraud issue, he raised the first issue to test the ombuds to make sure that his identity would be protected and to see if there would be any attempt by management to identify him and retaliate against him. He said that since the handling of the minor matter had shown that the ombuds could be trusted to keep information confidential, he felt comfortable raising the fraud issue with the ombuds.

After discussing options on how to deal with the fraud issue, the inquirer had a greater understanding of the process and indicated that he would be willing to disclose his identity and meet with investigators for the organization. The fraud was investigated, uncovered, and resolved.

Ombuds Helps Avert Retaliation

During discussions with the ombuds, a visitor revealed explicit employment-related actions their manager had threatened if the visitor were to report errors for which the manager was accountable. Fearing reputational damage, loss of employment, and difficulties in securing a new job in a somewhat closed field, the visitor was reluctant to make a formal report.

The ombuds reviewed the organization's antiretaliation policy and coached the employee to speak up in formal channels. Feeling relieved about the organization's stance on retaliation, the visitor spoke up, an investigation ensued, corrective actions were taken, and the visitor's reporting structure was eventually changed.

While satisfied with the new structure, the visitor began to feel uncomfortable—as though the new manager was "walking on eggshells." In a follow-up visit with the ombuds, the visitor stated that they "couldn't put their finger on it," but they felt there was something looming that made the new manager act this way. The ombuds asked for permission to check in with the formal channel to whom the visitor had made the report.

The ombuds learned that the senior department head—who had never been informed of the former manager's threats—believed the visitor was complicit in the issue, by not reporting it more quickly. He was in the process of working with HR to issue a warning letter. The ombuds explained how the manager's threats had impeded the visitor's decision to report quickly and further explained that issuing a warning letter would be tantamount to retaliation.

Given the new information, the senior leader and HR agreed not to issue the warning and the relationship between the visitor and the new manager improved and progressed well.

Suspicions of Misconduct But a Fear of Reporting

An employee believed his supervisor had a falsified resume, including on it advanced degrees that the supervisor never earned. He thought this was wrong and wanted it reported but only if his name could be separated from the report. The employee was not willing to allow any action to be taken unless he could be assured that his identity would be protected.

After hearing various options explained by the ombuds, the employee decided that he would use the organization's hotline option since he now understood that information communicated to the hotline was passed directly to the chief of HR, who had responsibility for conducting an investigation. The ombuds coached the employee on the process of calling the organization's hotline and advised the employee how to include enough information in the report to allow the investigators to assess and investigate the allegation.

Once the information was disclosed, the investigation revealed that the information was correct, and the supervisor was disciplined.

FRAUD AND COMPLIANCE

Ombuds Helps a Visitor Surface a Fraud Issue Through the Whistleblower Hotline

A visitor asked the ombuds for assistance with a case she was afraid could get her fired. She was a research assistant and she thought that her boss, a grant primary investigator, was asking her to use grant funds illegally. He was basically asking her to move monies from one account to another in a way that was in direct violation of the applicable federal guidelines.

As the research assistant, it was her job to keep the grant operating within the guidelines, so she was worried she could either get fired by the supervising federal agency for not following protocol or by her boss if she didn't follow his instructions.

The ombuds discussed options, such as filing a grievance, making a report to the federal agency, or transferring to another research project. The ombuds also discussed the possibility of talking with another senior research assistant who might know a legal way to reach the primary investigator's goals while staying within applicable rules.

Of course, the ombuds also pointed out that she could quit her job, but the visitor said she needed it to support her family and for the medical benefits. She did not want to report the primary investigator in any way that would allow him to identify her involvement. Given these concerns, the ombuds mentioned the possibility of filing an anonymous comment on the Whistleblower Hotline. That option helped the visitor feel safe from retaliation, so she agreed to do that as well as start her job search as a backup plan because she no longer wanted to continue to work with that investigator. She was committed to not breaking the rules regardless of the pressure to do so.

Proceeding in this way could bring the issue to the attention of the university, which could conduct an investigation. The university and its reputation would be protected from the unethical acts of the primary investigator if they responded to the report on the hotline and the visitor's concerns were validated. Regardless, the employee was relieved to have options so she could live according to her conscience.

An Ombuds' Careful Listening Helps Spot Possible Financial Abuse

A woman came to the ombuds for help on how to deal with what she perceived as discrimination in her work group. The visitor felt that women with children were being given more flexibility in work schedules than women without children. As a single woman, the visitor wanted to have flexibility for vacation time or flex hours to either go to school herself or take care of relatives. She claimed her supervisor always considered her requests behind those of women with children and their associated needs.

During the discussion with the ombuds, the visitor mentioned some financial behaviors she attributed to her supervisor and coworkers that, if true, could be breaches of the financial practices of the company. The ombuds tucked that information away and focused on coaching the visitor on how to advocate for her own needs.

At the end of the conversation with the visitor, the ombuds asked if she could ask a bit more about the financial behaviors the visitor had mentioned earlier. The visitor agreed to share more details with the ombuds and then described expensive meals, travel, and unapproved use of car services. The visitor later gave the ombuds permission to alert the internal audit group to these potential abuses.

The ombuds did alert internal audit to the possibility of financial abuse in this unit without disclosing the identity of the visitor, and an investigation was initiated. After several weeks, the ombuds learned that the investigation had uncovered vast fraud and abuse. Three people in the unit were terminated and disciplinary action was taken against others. The head of internal audit expressed great appreciation to the ombuds for bringing this issue to their attention. The discrimination issue first raised by the visitor became moot in light of the terminations and other disciplinary action that was taken.

An Ombuds Helps Raise Systemic Financial Manipulation of Foreign Graduate Students by Professor

A visitor came to the ombuds to inquire about how they might address their concerns with the conduct of a professor. The visitor was an international graduate student from the Middle East in a renowned campus program. They were taking a class with their professor advisor who was also the program director. The visitor stated that they needed an internship over the summer months and that the professor knew they were returning to their Farsi-speaking country for the next semester. The professor was also aware that a previously arranged internship had fallen through at the last minute. The visitor said that the professor indicated that she could use support on a book she was presently writing. She proposed that if the student was willing to translate the book into Farsi and ascertain if there was a market in their country for the book, the professor would help the student obtain internship credit and consider hiring them as a teaching assistant in the fall semester when they returned (to offer them some remuneration for their work). The visitor shared that they saw this as an excellent opportunity.

The visitor undertook the translation and helped market the professor's material. The visitor also connected the professor to a network of future opportunities to utilize when the book was completed. Upon their return to the campus, the student met with the professor but was told that she had already hired her teaching assistant for the fall semester. The visitor reported that the professor was adamant that she had never promised anything to the student in the way of compensation for their work and insisted that internship credit should have been viewed as substantial value to the student.

The visitor told the ombuds they were aware of similar conduct by the professor in the past from alumni of the program and two other current students. In addition, the visitor said that they had contacted an administrative assistant to the professor and urged the assistant to contact the ombuds about the professor's conduct. The administrative assistant visited the ombuds and confirmed much of what the student had told the ombuds, describing their own experiences as well. The ombuds asked if the administrative assistant and the visitor would ask if the other current students might be interested in contacting the ombuds office.

Eventually, several alumni, a few other students, and a couple of other administrative assistants contacted the ombuds office and shared similar stories of misrepresentations by the professor and manipulation of staff and students. The administrative assistants also shared that they were told to issue funds from specific budgets and grants to pay a few of the students, and that the professor had used students to translate her personal writings into several different languages but never gave the students any credit in the published books, papers, and articles.

The ombuds helped the individuals consider all of their options individually and in a small group. Everyone agreed it was best to share the information with campus leaders, including:

- the Equal Rights Director
- the Human Resource Director
- the Departmental Dean
- the Provost
- the University Legal Counsel

The ombuds was asked to act as a neutral facilitator for the discussion.

The ombuds helped the students and administrative assistants prepare for this meeting by considering how best to share the information. The ombuds urged them to try role-playing the situation acting as themselves and as university leaders hearing and responding to this information. During this discussion the individuals raised concerns about retaliation by the professor, who remained the director of the program.

The students contacted the campus leadership, asking each of them if they would participate in this meeting and if they'd object to having the ombuds act as a neutral facilitator. No one objected to the process. The discussion went very well, lasting more than three hours, with the leaders asking many questions and thanking the individuals for coming forward with their concerns. They assured the students and staff that if any retaliation occurred, they should immediately contact the Equal Rights Director as it would not be tolerated.

Cooperation Between Audit and Ombuds

Internal audit received a report that a member of the research and development staff of twenty had been conducting a personal real estate business from his office computer. Two auditors arrived at the department one morning. They announced to the entire department that they were there to conduct an audit and then began at the office at the south end of the corridor.

An employee in the department, who or may not have been the whistleblower in the first place, realized that the office of the person with the personal business was on the north end of the corridor and that the auditors would not get there for several hours, giving the employee plenty of time to erase files. He immediately called the ombuds to describe the situation and gave only the office number of the suspected employee. He never disclosed who he was or any other individual information. It then took the ombuds less than a minute to reach the chief of audit to relay the information. The chief of audit then immediately called the auditors in the field to inform them that they should begin in a specified office number at the north end of the corridor.

The audit discovered evidence of the employee's personal business on the company computer. Both the audit chief and the ombuds felt that the cooperation between the ombuds and audit worked well. Doubtless the employee making the call to the ombuds would agree.

CONCERNS OVER SUSPECTED MISCONDUCT

Concern About a Possible Misrepresentation by a Former Coworker

An employee contacted the ombuds with concerns over possible misrepresentations by a former coworker who had been rehired in a different job in a different region of the same organization. The employee contacting the ombuds thought that the employment of the former coworker had been terminated because of sexual harassment. The employee was not sure about the reason for the coworker's departure but feared that, if true, employees in the new location might be exposed to inappropriate behaviors. The employee wanted to speak with the ombuds confidentially about how such a concern might be surfaced.

After discussing various options with the ombuds, the employee gave the ombuds permission to speak with the coworker's previous supervisor without disclosing any information about the employee raising the issue. The previous supervisor confirmed that the employee had indeed been terminated for inappropriate behavior.

The ombuds then put the previous supervisor in touch with an HR specialist and the employee's current supervisor. HR discovered that the employee had not been truthful in several employment applications by not disclosing that he was previously terminated for sexual harassment. The organization promptly terminated the employee's employment. The ombuds also noted that this case underscored the need for the organization to consider establishing a common HR data system that would include all of the organization's locations.

Ombuds Helps an Employee Use the Hotline

An employee came to the ombuds because she was concerned that a colleague in her office was tampering with time sheets. She said that she would normally have reported this to her supervisor but could not do so in this situation because she was one of the few people who knew that the colleague and their supervisor were having an affair. She felt that, under the circumstances, the supervisor would not be an appropriate person to whom to make the report, and she was afraid that if she tried to report this to someone else, she would be asked why she had not reported it to the supervisor. She did not want to have to lie or answer that question.

The employee and the ombuds discussed various options to surface the issue, including speaking with her supervisor's supervisor, an anonymous letter sent through intraoffice mail, and an anonymous call to the organization's hotline. She still was uncomfortable raising the issue with a formal channel or the supervisor's supervisor directly. Since hotline calls were received by an off-site independent company, she felt that was a better option than sending an anonymous letter to someone at the company. She decided to raise the issue that way. The ombuds worked with her by explaining how to include in the hotline call sufficient hard facts to adequately describe the problem for the investigators.

Ombuds Helps the Organization Avoid a Class Action Lawsuit

A female professional staff member contacted the ombuds office with concerns over actions by the predominantly male staff in her group. She had only been with the organization for a few years but was highly educated and at the cutting edge of her scientific field. She had also received high ratings as an employee. She related that she and other women in her group had experienced demeaning, disrespectful, and dishonest treatment by the male professional staff in her group. She thought one of the worst offenders was her former mentor, who was also a highly valued staff member responsible for bringing in millions of dollars of new business. She and the other female scientists and technical staff had been ignoring the demeaning behavior by him and the other male colleagues because they needed his skill and research projects.

The female staff member also mentioned an episode six months earlier in which a male staff member had created a dangerous condition in the lab with only women present. While the incident had been investigated and the male staff member transferred to another group, a verbal threat on her life had been made to her to prevent her from speaking about the episode. That event clearly had traumatized her, and she had not reported the threat. Since that time, however, she had been keeping a record of the incidents and comments. In addition, the women in the group had been advising potential new recruits to the organization that they could not recommend working at the organization.

The ombuds discussed various options with her on several occasions. During this time, the staff member urged other women in her group also to speak with the ombuds. The ombuds thought that the facts outlined by the women created a real possibility of a class action lawsuit against the organization and was trying to find a way to help get the issue to senior management. While most of the women insisted on anonymity, two of the women with whom the ombuds spoke were willing to speak about their concerns with management.

The ombuds helped coordinate a meeting between those two women and the CEO. As a result of those conversations, an investigation was undertaken to deal with the issues in that group. In addition, senior management engaged workplace consultants to work with staff throughout the organization to raise awareness and deal with gender-related communication and interaction.

Only After Extended Conversations with Ombuds Does an Employee Come Forward

A long-term employee nearing retirement contacted the ombuds office anonymously to discuss concerns over possible ethics violations by management in vendor contracts. Being so close to retirement and fearing retaliation, the employee refused to reveal, even to the ombuds, his name, location, or anything else that he felt could reveal his identity. The employee, however, was willing to discuss generically the behaviors that he felt were unethical.

The ombuds presented various options to the employee. The ombuds and the employee then discussed and considered the possible ramifications of each option to the employee if he were to reveal his identity. After several conversations, the employee agreed to let the ombuds contact HR with a scenario that he and the ombuds had developed to ascertain what HR's response and process would be if he chose to reveal his identity and participate in an investigation.

The ombuds spoke with HR and then with the employee on several occasions thereafter as they tried to work through how to proceed. Although it took some time, the employee gradually came to trust both the ombuds and HR as resources that were available to him. Finally, he agreed to meet with HR based on the repeated promise that retaliation would not be tolerated.

As a result of the information that the employee provided, an investigation was conducted, resulting in the termination of high-level personnel. The employee felt supported not only by the ombuds office, but also by HR and the organization. He retired soon thereafter and expressed his appreciation to the ombuds for helping him work through the decision to come forward on the ethical violations that had bothered him.

Job Protection and Fear Above All Else

The ombuds received an anonymous call from an employee in a multinational organization through an overseas operating center. The caller was extremely nervous about calling but was put at ease when the ombuds first explained how the ombuds office works (confirming confidentiality, neutrality, informality, and independence) and was able to speak in the person's first language. The caller explained that he worked in a unit that had high security, separate badge access, and security cameras because the unit dealt with valuable assets and financial information. He also explained that his supervisor had been harassing his unit for more than a year with veiled threats about employees losing their jobs, asking for personal errands, bullying them, and instigating rough-play games (such as hitting, boxing, wearing blindfolds, tying people with a rope). The so-called "games" were played in an area with no security camera coverage and supposedly were to have "fun" and break the monotony in the work area.

Even though there were at least twenty employees in the unit who had been subjected to these practices and an HR office and higher supervisors located in the same building, there was so much fear of potential job loss that no one spoke up for a year. Finally, when a coworker had to leave work discreetly to go to the hospital because he broke several ribs in one of the "games" and did not report the incident, the caller decided to call the ombuds in the United States since he had heard that it was confidential and had seen announcements about the ombuds when the ombuds had visited his location several months earlier.

The ombuds and the caller discussed various ways that the issue could be raised. The caller decided to give the ombuds permission to contact HR and security, but he was too fearful to give permission for the ombuds to contact the higher-up supervisor (a vice president of the organization) because he believed that his immediate supervisor was extremely well regarded by that person. The ombuds, without revealing the identity of the employee who had made the call, passed along information to HR and security concerning the type of activity that had apparently been occurring. They then investigated the matter by interviewing many of the employees separately at an outside location.

The investigation corroborated the allegations, and the immediate supervisor and a higher-ranking supervisor were terminated from the organization.

Limited Disclosure Solves the Problem and Protects the Informant

An employee came to the ombuds to report that he suspected that one of the subcontractors working on plant renovations at the facility where he worked was not doing the work to code. The employee felt that this should be brought to the attention of the company for safety reasons but because he was a union member in the same trade as the subcontractor, he was unwilling to be the one to raise the issue with a formal channel. He was certain that he would suffer retaliation by other members of the union if it became known that he had been the person who reported the issue.

After discussing various options, the employee agreed to permit the ombuds to contact the facility manager to suggest to him that it would be advisable to have an inspection of the construction work by the local building inspector, but not reveal any other information. The manager arranged for the inspection, which uncovered the defective work, and the company required the subcontractor to correct it. Since the inspection appeared to be a routine inspection by the building inspector, the identity of the employee who came to the ombuds was protected.

An Alert from the Ombuds Helps the Organization Avoid Committing Illegal Acts

Information was conveyed to the ombuds that the organization may have been skirting the law in hiring foreign nationals, but the source of this information was unwilling to come forward directly or to permit disclosure of his identity. The inquirer was willing, however, to permit the ombuds to alert the COO of the organization that this type of activity might be occurring.

With the alert from the ombuds, policies and procedures were tightened to eliminate the potential for misconduct. In the process, the COO was able to reinforce to those responsible for hiring what the law and the organization required and that violations would not be tolerated.

No further concerns on this issue were brought to the ombuds.

SEXUAL HARASSMENT/ DISCRIMINATION/MISCONDUCT

Author's Note:* Additional examples in this category are included in the PDF downloads as well as in the 2021 Special Issue of the *Journal of the International Ombudsman Association on Sexual Harassment and Discrimination, JIOA SI 2021.

Ombuds Helps Clinical Fellow Stop Unwanted Attention from a Senior Colleague

A new female clinical fellow contacted the ombuds to discuss her discomfort with attention she was receiving from a senior male clinician. The senior clinician, an internationally recognized physician and author of a popular medical textbook, had been contacting the fellow repeatedly by phone and text, complimenting her appearance, and offering her a valuable collaborative clinical research opportunity during her fellowship. The fellow did not wish to make a formal complaint because of the impact on her career, the embarrassment it would cause the senior clinician, and because the senior clinician had not asked her out, touched her, or said anything exceedingly inappropriate. However, she had a clear sense he was interested in her romantically and may cross those boundaries in the future. She said she only wanted a professional relationship and to be able to complete the fellowship. She indicated that she had not talked to anyone else affiliated with the hospital about the situation and presently had no intention to do so.

The fellow and the ombuds discussed keeping a record of the texts and a journal of the inordinate contact as a backup measure and then began exploring ways the fellow could more clearly communicate her discomfort to the senior clinician either directly or through an intermediary. She decided that, as a first step, it would be most appropriate for her to respond to a text message she received that she's noticing he's contacting her quite a bit and that it makes her somewhat uncomfortable, and that she'd prefer to communicate with people with whom she had professional relationships by email only. As a secondary measure if the excessive contact persisted, she indicated that she may ask the ombuds to speak to the clinician confidentially on her behalf. Several weeks later the fellow returned to ask the ombuds to speak to the senior clinician so he would stop.

The ombuds subsequently asked the senior clinician to meet and explained the "off the record" nature of the ombuds office. When they met, the ombuds simply said that the ombuds had been asked by a fellow if he, the senior clinician, would honor a request made of him about communicating by email. The senior clinician, understanding the confidentiality and informality of the ombuds office, expressed gratitude for the message.

The fellow reported back to the ombuds a few months later that the excessive contact from the senior clinician had stopped and she was now more comfortable dealing with her colleague.

Ombuds Helps New Director Receive Additional Training

A department that supports hospital operations had recently gone through several leadership changes and was being managed by a new director. One of the employees of the department shared with the ombuds her concerns that she was being micromanaged, that her manager was abusive toward her, and that some duties were being arbitrarily removed from her area of responsibility. The visitor also alleged that the director was discriminating against her on the basis of sexual orientation. The employee said she had asked the director to participate in a facilitated discussion on these issues, but the director had declined to do so.

Over the course of the next few months, several other employees in the department approached the ombuds office with similar concerns about the director and their fear that they would be retaliated against if they were identified as persons bringing concerns forward to formal channels. The employees gave the ombuds permission to discuss their concerns with the associate vice president but without sharing their identities. The associate vice president also wanted to loop in an HR director to provide guidance and consultation on addressing the concerns. Working together with the ombuds and HR, the associate vice president developed a training and development plan for the director, and the director was also assigned an external coach with which to work on a regular basis. The concerns were discussed with the director, as well as expectations going forward.

The visitors were made aware of this and were asked to update the ombuds on their interactions with the director and to bring further concerns forward confidentially to the ombuds. To date the coaching and additional training appear to be working well.

Sexual Harassment and Complaint with Investigation

A female employee reached out to the ombuds after a terrible experience she'd had with a coworker at a social hour that followed a meeting. While she was sitting at a table with two other employees, another coworker joined them at the table. The coworker had been drinking and moved his hand over her leg and knee under the table. This wasn't the first time he had made advances towards her that she had rebuffed. With this second incident, where the coworker had touched her in an inappropriate and unwelcome way, she was ready to take action.

She called the ombuds not only to understand what her options were, but also to learn what an investigative scenario would look like once it unfolded. She had never been part of an investigation before and was anxious about it. The ombuds was able to identify for her the appropriate investigative resource and also explain the investigative process and what her role and experience would likely be. The ombuds encouraged her to share her questions and concerns with the investigator so that she could be reassured about how things would be handled. The ombuds explained to her that while participants in an investigation are instructed that they must not discuss the investigation with anyone, consulting the ombuds was considered an exception to that requirement. Consequently, she could stay in touch with the ombuds during the process if she wanted to.

This employee again called the ombuds at the conclusion of the formal investigation and described her mixed experience with it. Her allegations about the coworker had been validated and she was assured that he had been disciplined but was also told that he was not being terminated. This in itself did not trouble her. She had not necessarily wanted him to be fired. Initially, she just wanted his conduct to be addressed and for him to stop behaving inappropriately toward her or anyone else. However, once she was told that he was going to remain employed, she began to consider the practical implications. There would be future meetings at hotels and social gatherings with alcohol served. Thinking about seeing him in those scenarios made her anxious and fearful. She had expressed her anxiety to the investigator and asked for guidance for both of them. The investigator replied with a response that she found insensitive: "Now that the decision had been made to retain him, the focus should be on business continuity. Everyone should just resume all normal work activities."

She wanted the ombuds' perspective on the response from the investigator. The ombuds helped her understand that the response from the investigator, despite being a formal channel, was not consistent with the organization's values. With her permission, the ombuds connected her with a senior leader in the business unit's HR organization. The senior HR leader was extremely supportive of her. The senior HR leader took action to make it clear that her coworker, because of his inappropriate behaviors, was no longer permitted to attend the meetings where she would be present. The investigator was also coached and reprimanded for the misguided response to her request for post-investigation assistance. She was also informed that her experience helped to inform the way the organization was going to address similar matters in the future.

OTHER TYPES OF UNFAIR TREATMENT

"Failed" Mediation Led to Good Result

A junior faculty member approached the ombuds with a concern about the culture of an academic and clinical department, what he considered "toxic" interactions during faculty meetings, and a performance evaluation from his department chair that he deemed unbalanced, unfair, and not reflective of his work and contributions to the department.

After sharing these concerns with the ombuds and discussing options during a consultation and coaching initial meeting, the junior faculty member requested that the ombuds facilitate a discussion so that he could share the concerns more fully with the chair via mediated discussion. The ombuds agreed to do so and then met with the chair to briefly discuss the nature of some of the concerns and to ask if he would consider participating in the discussion as requested. The chair agreed, and a meeting was held.

Though the chair had initially referred the junior faculty to the ombuds and had subsequently agreed to participation, during the meeting he seemed agitated and questioned several times, "Why are we here?" Sensing that this may have been intimidating for the junior faculty member, the ombuds interjected, reminding the chair that he had referred the faculty member, was made aware of the process, and had agreed to be present and listen in an effort to address the concerns. The ombuds also reminded the participants of the ombuds' role as a neutral and described the training and experience that had prepared the ombuds to facilitate such a process. The meeting continued and concluded awkwardly. There was further discussion about the concerns, and the chair agreed to reconsider some of the language in the evaluation. However, the chair did not take responsibility for the alleged "toxic" environment in the department and believed that faculty should be able to freely express themselves in meetings even if some were offended.

Several months later, the ombuds had a chance encounter with the junior faculty member who asked if the ombuds remembered his case. The junior faculty member expressed profuse thanks to the ombuds for the assistance and explained that sometime after the mediated discussion he was able to change departments at his request and with the support of both department chairs. He reported that he was now in a much more collegial and supportive professional environment. Though the ombuds had recalled the intervention as unsuccessful, the faculty member reported that he believed that the assistance of the ombuds was helpful during a very difficult time, and that the coaching and intervention was the catalyst for a resolution to his situation.

Coaching to Improve Communication Skills

A male employee found an image ridiculing him stored in a shared folder on the company computer system that had been posted by a female team member. The employee thought that the image was offensive and did not think it should have been posted in the shared folder. When he brought this issue to his manager, the manager's response was that it was just a lighthearted joke. The male employee, however, felt that he had never been close to that female coworker and did not have a joking rapport with her. He remained upset about the continued presence of this image on the shared folder and was frustrated by the fact that his manager had not taken his concerns seriously. The male worker also believed that he had been the victim of a double standard—had he posted a similar image about the female coworker, the manager would have responded very differently.

Having tried to raise this issue with his manager without success, the male employee wanted to speak with the ombuds confidentially about how further to address the issue. The ombuds listened to the employee to understand why the image upset him and discussed his expectations on how this should have been handled. They also discussed his working relationship with his coworker and what the implications might be from different approaches he might take on his and her future interactions at work. The employee decided not to take any further formal action but asked the ombuds to coach him (which the ombuds did) on how to engage in conversation with his supervisor and his coworker to better express his reaction to this posting and to have better communication in the future.

Inappropriate Conduct by Senior Leader

During a site visit in Latin America, several employees visited the ombuds with concerns involving a senior leader who was providing inappropriate directives to their team as well as violating company policy by making inappropriate "agreements" with government officials.

The employees who came to the ombuds were extremely fearful of retaliation. They did not trust their leadership chain, because they were unsure whether more senior leadership was aware of and supported the senior leader's conduct. Most of the employees who came to the ombuds for guidance had tried to advise the senior leader directly of their concerns. He responded, however, in a threatening manner and told them that he was their supervisor—they needed to abide by what he was telling them to do.

The ombuds discussed with each visitor the options they had for notifying the company of their concerns and how they could go about doing so. However, each felt that, because they had already expressed concerns to the supervisor in the past, he would know who it was that was complaining. The ombuds also had explained to the employees at the outset of each of their meetings with the ombuds that part of the ombuds office charter required that where three or more visitors approached the office with the same issue, the ombuds must raise that systemic issue to leadership for action.

In this situation, because the ombuds had had multiple employees come to the office with the same concerns, the ombuds was able to raise this "trend" to the most senior leader of the business unit for action. The ombuds also advised the visitors that it was important to document and gather any communications that they had with their supervisor on this topic so that they would be prepared to answer questions once the investigation was underway. They discussed how best to manage through the current environment, such as seeking clarity from the supervisor if he made additional similar requests so that conduct and guidance would also be documented.

After raising this "trend" to the most senior business leader, the matter was investigated. The investigation determined that the supervisor was indeed violating company policy, thereby placing the company at risk. The supervisor's employment was terminated, and the employees moved forward with performing their jobs in a manner consistent with company policy without fear of retaliation. Having the ombuds office bring forward this trend allowed the company to take corrective action and avoid a potentially major impact to the organization.

Healing a Rift

The ombuds had received a significant number of cases from members of a department in the organization who expressed concerns about how the department was being managed. Visitors shared that they were frustrated, furious, or outraged, and some said that they might seek legal counsel to address the matter. Low morale was widespread across the department.

As more details emerged, it became clear that visitors were describing a rift within the department, with essentially two disciplines in the department having been pitted against one another. Visitors described examples of infighting and poor professionalism. Visitors suggested that the rift had been created by the department's leadership when leadership encouraged people to choose sides using a heavy-handed approach. Others described apathy on the part of some members of the department's leadership. Overall, the department's internal warring resulted in confusion, unrest, and disorganization, which negatively affected people individually and may have also resulted in losses both in employee retention and in the department's productivity.

Visitors said that numerous complaints about these concerns had been made to the organization's HR and compliance offices but had not produced results. This only increased their frustration and confusion.

Visitors wanted to be sure that the organization was made aware of their concerns. Their objectives included improved communication, response to concerns, clarity in work roles, and fairness in schedules, treatment, and pay. They wanted to be freed up to do their jobs effectively and feel good about working as one cohesive team again.

When the visitors came to the ombuds individually, the ombuds listened to each person actively and provided a safe, confidential space for them to share all that was on their mind. In a very real way, the assurance of privacy and commitment by the ombuds not to share with anyone that they were meeting with the ombuds gave them the opportunity to fully open up and express their concerns. The ombuds met with many of these visitors on a recurring basis and offered suggestions on how they might better handle the situation themselves immediately and provided individual coaching and support. As a result, visitors gained confidence in themselves, even though their work situation hadn't changed.

Because the many individual concerns also represented a significant systemic dysfunction within the department, with the permission of the visitors the ombuds engaged in a series of facilitated discussions that included members of the organization's senior leadership. These discussions with senior leadership raised their overall awareness and understanding of the broad and complex nature of the concerns in the department. Ultimately, significant changes were made, including structural improvements, leadership changes, communications plans, and changes in workflow.

After these changes, the department was functioning cohesively as one unified whole. Communications and morale also improved. The changes were so pronounced that visitors reported back to the ombuds to let the ombuds know how much better things had become, describing the difference before and after the ombuds involvement as the difference between "night and day."

Mediated Discussion about Racist Comments Leads to a "Mountaintop Experience"

The ombuds received a call from two Black women employees who were offended by comments made by a white male employee who had called their office for assistance. At the end of the call, the White male employee had made some racist comments. The two women were quite disturbed by the man's comments and decided that they wanted to address the issue with him. They called the ombuds for guidance on what they might do.

After listening to the women and discussing various options, including a possible mediation, the two women indicated that they would like the ombuds to explore whether a mediation was possible. When the ombuds contacted the male employee about a possible mediation, he agreed to participate.

Both women and the man came to the ombuds office on the day of the mediation willing to engage in a mediation process. The result was heartfelt reconciliation. The women were most forgiving. The man sincerely apologized. The process was such a powerful and poignant "mountain top" experience that it has remained one of the most significant experiences in the long career of the ombuds involved and inspired the ombuds to develop resources on the power of apologies and use an anonymous version of this matter as an example in discussing mediation as an option with subsequent visitors.

Confidential Conflict Coaching Enables an Employee to Act on His Own to Discuss Concerns with Management

An employee came to the ombuds because he wanted to discuss in confidence the retaliation he felt he was experiencing after returning from military reserve duty. Specifically, the employee said that he felt that he was not receiving opportunities being given to other employees and that, as a result, he had received a lower than usual performance evaluation. The employee felt that fulfilling reservist obligations should not be seen in a negative light or result in adverse consequences. The employee was looking for guidance on how to raise these concerns.

The ombuds provided various options to the employee on how he might try to raise this issue. The option selected by the employee was to have the ombuds help him raise the issue himself. Through conflict coaching and help preparing an outline of talking points, the ombuds helped the employee raise the issue himself directly with management in an appropriate, professional manner.

After speaking with management about his concerns, the employee contacted the ombuds to express appreciation for the guidance and said that he was confident that management would give this matter due attention.

MIDDLE MANAGERS

Author's Note: **Included in this category are examples that uniquely involve middle managers. Examples in other categories may involve middle managers but were placed there because they were also relevant to that topic and due to space limitations. Please review other categories and the PDF downloads for additional examples involving middle managers.**

Ombuds Helps New Director Receive Additional Training

A department that supports hospital operations had recently gone through several leadership changes and was being managed by a new Director. One of the employees of the department shared with the ombuds her concerns that she was being micromanaged, that her manager was abusive towards her, and that some duties were being arbitrarily removed from her area of responsibility. The visitor also alleged that the director was discriminating against her on the basis of sexual orientation. The employee said she had asked the director to participate in a facilitated discussion to discuss these issues, but the director had declined to do so.

Over the course of the next few months, several other employees in the department approached the ombuds office with similar concerns about the director and their fear that they would be retaliated against if they were identified as persons bringing concerns forward to formal channels. The employees gave the ombuds permission to discuss their concerns with the associate vice president but without sharing their identities. The associate vice president also wanted to loop in an HR director to provide guidance and consultation on addressing the concerns. Working together with the ombuds and HR, the associate vice president developed a training and development plan for the director, and the director was also assigned an external coach with which to work on a regular basis. The concerns were discussed with the director, as well as expectations going forward.

The visitors were made aware of this and were asked to update the ombuds on their interactions with the director and to bring further concerns forward confidentially to the ombuds. To date the coaching and additional training appear to be working well.

Merged Unit with New Manager Resolves Conflict Issues with Ombuds' Help

The visitor, a new mid-level manager, was concerned about the lack of respectful communication within their group. The new manager was hired approximately one month after two teams were merged into one group. They believed that the conflict and backbiting was mostly due to differences in the culture of the two teams and how they each had previously communicated. The manager requested that the ombuds train the combined group on a personality inventory tool (DiSC®) to help them understand their differences and to improve communication.

While exploring options with the ombuds and clarifying what they hoped to see as a result of the DiSC or similar training, the manager related the hope that the conflict would subside because of improved communication. After the ombuds explained how it might be beneficial to understand the problems from the perspective of individual group members, the manager decided to inform the group about voluntarily sharing their point of view with the ombuds. They were all given the ombuds' contact information, including an anonymous line for those who did not want to be identified in any way. Several individuals did speak with the ombuds, both on the phone and in person.

Based on the input provided to the ombuds, individuals from one team revealed resentment toward the other team due to a perception of having to slow down to train the other team while already working many hours to get things done. The other team expressed frustration about not having enough guidance and feeling undervalued. This input also revealed that prior to the merger of the teams into one group one team was predominantly programmatic and the other team was predominantly support staff. The support staff team had previously been available to several groups in the division to provide cost estimates and purchasing. The programmatic staff team had been in charge of scheduling and execution of the work. In sum, three underlying issues were identified: who was trained to do what, the lack of understanding of roles and responsibilities, and lack of clear expectations and timelines.

The manager found it tricky to navigate the conflict because the manager had been assigned to the group a month after the groups were combined without much discussion or preparation. As a result of the lack of clear guidance and communication around expectations, the two teams did not really understand the new roles and responsibilities in their new group, and the manager had received little or no guidance from their higher-level supervisor.

After the key issues were identified by the ombuds and discussed with the manager, the manager decided to develop roles and responsibilities based on the individuals' skill sets and the overall needs of the group. The manager outlined a process that would clarify expectations, how the work would be done by specific people or teams in the group, and what technical and other training might be needed. At the same time that the process was being revisited by the manager, the ombuds provided several communication classes for the group. The manager then met with the group to share a vision for the group, including specific tasks and deliverables, and how they would communicate with input from the group before implementing the process.

The group's manager expressed great appreciation to the ombuds because the manager had benefited from clarifying the underlying issues leading to interpersonal discord and from the guidance the ombuds had provided on creating clear and specific expectations for the group. Those group members who spoke to the ombuds benefited from being heard about what was of concern to them, and all group members benefited from participating in the communication skills classes that the ombuds had provided. The organization benefited from the group having developed a shared understanding of roles and responsibilities, identifying training needs for staff, a more efficient process, and improved communication skills.

People Manager Issue

A female manager, who had been recently promoted into that role, reached out to the ombuds to discuss an issue with an employee on her team who was struggling to keep up with the work assigned. The manager did not want to go to her manager for advice because she felt that he would not tolerate the underperformance and would demand that she take formal action. The manager wanted to try to address the matter more informally to see if the performance could be turned around without moving to a performance improvement plan.

The underperforming employee was a tenured employee over 60 years of age. She had been missing things and not completing work assigned in a timely manner. This was requiring the manager and others to pick up the slack and was also causing a delay in the group's output. The manager was concerned because, up until the past six months, the employee had been performing very well. Now, her whole team was focused on the lack of performance and the amount of work and pressure there was on everyone else to deliver results. The manager knew she needed to do something but wasn't sure how to approach the employee and the situation in a way that was fair and appropriate.

The ombuds discussed with the manager the performance management process at the company. They also discussed the negative impact of inaction on the manager's part for both the employee and the manager's team. The ombuds made clear that it is the manager's responsibility to coach employees and address underperformance. In addition, the ombuds explained that it is the responsibility of the employee to address identified areas of deficient performance.

They agreed that the manager would have a candid discussion with the employee about the areas in which her performance was not meeting expectations, with specific examples. She needed to hear the employee's perspective on her level of performance and ask whether there was anything that the employee wanted to share that may be causing her performance to deteriorate in such a short period of time. If the employee identified anything medical that might be having an impact, the manager would then need to refer her to the occupational health group, where she would learn of the benefits available to her, such as short-term disability leave or a reasonable accommodation, if appropriate. If the employee did not raise any medical issue, the manager needed to clearly set forth the performance expectations with milestones and timelines. She would schedule consistent one-to-one meetings to review the employee's performance and provide regular feedback.

To that end, the manager met with the employee and then followed up with an email, documenting their discussion. The manager's plan was to monitor the situation closely to determine whether the employee's performance improved, while continuing to coach and document any continuing performance concerns. Her hope was that, by working closely with the employee, they could bring her performance to an acceptable level. However, if the performance did not improve, the manager would be in a good position to bring the matter forward to HR and her manager for formal action.

Facilitated Discussion Helps Employees Resolve their Workplace Issues

A supervisor in the business and accounting department called the ombuds concerned about conflict in his department. There were more than twenty-five women working in cubicles in the same large room, and they were complaining about room temperature, cooking odors, allergies, etc. The supervisor asked if the ombuds could help with this type of problem. He didn't know where else to turn.

The ombuds presented the supervisor with some options, including an offer to meet with the group and create a subcommittee that could work on a plan to address the complaints. The supervisor was thrilled with that offer and immediately scheduled a meeting time for the group.

The ombuds met with the large group and listened to their concerns and then created a subgroup of volunteers. Over the next six weeks, the subgroup met with the ombuds to formulate their plan. At the end, they presented it to the larger group and asked for feedback. A few alterations were made, and the department adopted the plan.

The ombuds checked in with the supervisor periodically over the next three months and all seemed to be working fine. The supervisor was greatly relieved.

This was a large department, and all the conflict was impacting productivity. The individual workers previously had been very uncomfortable at work every day. One pregnant employee had been considering suing the university for having an unhealthy work environment. The employees were much happier about their work environment and having had their concerns heard and a role in recommending the changes that were implemented.

SENIOR MANAGEMENT

Author's Note:* Included in this category are examples that uniquely involve senior management. Examples in other categories may involve senior management but were placed there because they were also relevant to that topic and due to space limitations. Please review other categories and the PDF downloads for additional examples involving senior management.

Senior Leader Seeks Interpersonal Relationship Advice

A male business unit president reached out to the ombuds office because he wanted some confidential guidance on how he might address an uncomfortable situation. A lower-level female employee was pursuing a relationship with him. He stated that he is not interested in a romantic relationship with her. However, he was concerned for her well-being because she had shared with him that she had experienced suicidal thoughts in the past. He said that he feared raising this with his manager or HR, because he thought they would jump to the conclusion that there did exist a romantic relationship between them, and he had no real way to prove that one did not exist.

The ombuds explored with him why he felt HR and his manager would believe that there was a relationship between them. He shared that he had been friends with her for many years and that, before he became president of the business unit, he and she would often get together outside of work. Their relationship was never sexual although she expressed that she did want a romantic relationship with him. In most cases, there were other employees present when they were together after work, but there were times when they were alone. On one of these occasions, she shared that she struggled with mental health issues due to abusive relationships in the past.

He also shared that when she first expressed that she wanted a relationship, he said that he was not interested because he was happy in a committed relationship already. She continued over the years to raise the possibility and—while he was flattered at first—he became uncomfortable over time. He eventually told his then-manager about her pursuing him and that he had told her he was not interested. His manager said that, even though she did not report to him, it would be a good idea to stop spending time outside of work with her. He thought that was a little harsh and would be upsetting to her. So, he did continue to see her outside of work but tried to include others in their outings. He asked his manager not to do anything and said that he could handle the situation. Since he had been promoted to the position as president, he had not raised the situation with his new manager.

Through several sessions, the ombuds discussed the president's actions with him, and he came to realize that he was sending a mixed message to the female employee by continuing to socialize with her after she had expressed her desire to move their relationship in a romantic direction. They discussed an action plan where he would clearly communicate to her that theirs would only ever be a professional relationship. He would also express empathy for her mental health struggles—which she continued to raise with him—and suggest that she reach out to the company's Employee Assistance Program (EAP).

They also explored asking his prior manager if he would be willing to go with the president to HR or his current manager, to share the discussion they previously had to establish that he had previously reported her unwelcome overtures. The president expressed his fear that if he clearly drew a line with her, she might retaliate by filing a claim against him. After all, it was his word against hers. The ombuds pointed out that having him make a new formal report to the company would be important to make a record that she was pursuing him, not the other way around.

The president ultimately decided to first clearly communicate to the female employee verbally, followed in writing, that theirs is and would only ever be a professional relationship. He would also provide EAP contact information to provide support to her. Additionally, he decided to ask his prior manager to go with him to speak with his current manager and HR to raise this concern, while accepting that perhaps he should have distanced himself from her, and even more so after he became a senior leader. He would stress to them that there was not now, nor had there ever been, a romantic relationship between them. The president had the difficult discussion with the female employee and promptly took the other steps upon which he had decided.

She expressed great upset, and a week later she raised allegations of sexual harassment against him. The report by the president to HR and his manager, prior to her claim being raised, allowed for his side of the story to be heard. The matter was investigated, and she received coaching along the lines that she would refrain from pursuing the personal relationship with him and behave in a professional manner toward him at all times. She was also provided with a list of resources and benefits available to her, including EAP and short-term disability leave. He also received coaching from the organization to ensure that in the future, he clearly separated his personal and professional relationships, particularly in the very senior role he now held.

When a Senior Leader Is the Problem

Over a period of months, a number of people in a department individually consulted with the ombuds. The visitors had roles at varying levels in the hierarchy and in a variety of disciplines, but they all shared concerns about the same senior member of the organization's leadership. Visitors expressed confusion or concern about the senior leader's quick ascension in the organization and about the appropriateness or justness of his promotions and power.

The visitors also described the senior leader's conduct, including insulting or publicly disparaging people, interfering with projects or work, character assassinations, attacking professional reputations, and terminating people unfairly or unjustly. Some considered this conduct as bullying. Others perceived the behavior as antithetical to the organization's code of conduct or other policies. Some questioned the legality of the leader's conduct. Given the overall perception of the senior leader's power in the organization, visitors expressed a variety of fears. In particular, visitors were afraid that if it were discovered that they sought help from the ombuds, they would become the next target or otherwise suffer retaliation for speaking up. Many of these individuals were at such a loss that they said they were considering leaving the organization.

Trusting that the ombuds office was strictly confidential, visitors met with the ombuds—often more than once—to share their concerns and to obtain guidance and support in addressing them in a meaningful way. In every session, the ombuds provided support and advice, including on how to address individual communications as they were evolving. (On request, the ombuds provided direct, individual, real-time, one-on-one coaching.)

The ombuds and visitors talked about words the visitor might use directly with the senior leader, meetings that they might hold with others, emails they might write to document plans, other senior leaders who could lend assistance, and policies that were at play. The ombuds and visitors also discussed the organization's resources for support, including persons higher in their chain of command, the Human Resources department, the ethics and compliance hotline, and of course the ombuds office.

In addition to serving as coach to individual visitors, an option that the ombuds offered was for the ombuds to serve as a conduit to improve communications, to serve as a mediator to open and improve direct dialogue, and to raise the pattern of concerns to other senior leadership who were well placed to hear and address the concerns. While a systemic pattern of concerns had clearly emerged, the ombuds continued to work with visitors individually to help them work through their individual goals or needs but the ombuds eventually sought permission to bring the matter forward as a pattern while preserving the confidentiality of all visitors.

Ultimately, the ombuds took the pattern of concerns to senior leadership, which engaged the organization's formal investigation processes. The investigation uncovered conduct that was in violation of the organization's policies, and appropriate corrective action was taken.

The ombuds was thus able to help to provide direct and immediate help to each of the individual visitors while working with them to find an effective way to bring the existence of the systemic issue to the attention of senior leaders who could order an investigation and take corrective action. As a result, none of the visitors left the organization and many of them have expressed their appreciation to the ombuds and how much happier they are.

Assistance Provided to a Senior Leader Outside of the United States

In an emerging markets region, due to rapid business growth and employee turnover, some talented employees were promoted to senior positions prior to receiving sufficient supervisory or leadership training. One such employee came to the ombuds for advice because she was feeling overwhelmed. She was very capable and had demonstrated excellent performance in her previous technical role, but after she was promoted, she began managing a large team (more than one thousand employees) and multiple projects across different countries.

She was confident in her substantive abilities and learning quickly in her new role. She wanted to know how other leaders had handled situations similar to those she was encountering and wanted to benefit from understanding best practices for managing and motivating large teams. She said she considered the ombuds a trusted coach and discussed with the ombuds alternatives in a variety of situations with which she was dealing.

One example she shared involved a member of her leadership team who had taken a lead role at a new site. At the beginning of the assignment, he was quite engaged and passionate. After a few months, however, his performance declined significantly. He expressed to her that, due to the COVID-19 impact and personal challenges he was facing with relocating his family, he would like to return to a role in his home city.

Unfortunately, there were no available jobs for him there at this time. The new manager asked the ombuds whether she should approach this from a performance management perspective or a leadership development dimension in order to take the best approach for both this highly talented employee and the organization. The ombuds inquired about the background of the site, her expectations for the employee, and any performance gaps. Together with the new manager, the ombuds reviewed the pros and cons of each option for approaching this issue. The new manager ultimately sought other candidates for the site lead role and searched for other jobs for the current site lead in a more suitable position closer to his home base.

The ombuds also advised the new manager about her further development as a leader and encouraged her to leverage her supervisor and shared company training options for additional skill building. The ombuds suggested that she register in the company's mentorship program to identify a senior leader outside of her work group who might provide regular guidance to her.

Coaching from the Ombuds Helps a High-Level Leader Resolve a Compensation Issue

A high-level leader approached the ombuds after a committee meeting to ask if the ombuds had a few minutes. The employee had been told three times by her manager that she was going to get a considerable salary increase after she had agreed to take on an additional role as interim in addition to her original role. She had now been waiting three months for this increase to take place, and when she checked in with HR, she was told that her boss had yet to complete the needed paperwork. This visitor was particularly nervous as her boss was known to be a difficult woman who played favorites, sidelined people who challenged her, and wielded a lot of power.

This visitor and the ombuds spent considerable time talking about how the previous three conversations went with her manager, whether or not there was a written record of the conversation to obtain an increase in salary, and what the organizational policy and procedure for short-term pay increases looked like. After ninety minutes, the visitor said she was ready to approach her manager again. One month later the visitor reported happily that the salary increase had gone through.

Sometimes It Is Necessary to Take an Issue to the CEO

Several employees and leaders expressed concern to the ombuds about a very senior leader's bad temper. His behavior was intimidating and caused his direct reports to be afraid to approach him, provide information, or seek guidance from him. Nevertheless, there was an imminent possibility that this leader would be elevated to the next-higher level despite his behavior. All of the employees who came to the ombuds were afraid to be identified as someone who had complained about him, but some of them requested the ombuds raise the issue with higher management without identifying them as the source.

The ombuds met with the CEO of the organization and indicated that concerns had been expressed about the conduct of this senior manager and provided some examples of his conduct that could have been easily observed by many people but did not reveal the identity of any person who had come to the ombuds.

The CEO expressed appreciation for the information and arranged for an executive coach to assist the leader.

UNION ISSUES

Union Leadership Referral about Director Behavior

The background for this case involved a highly regarded director who supervised twelve union members in a high-functioning unit. The unit had been acknowledged as one of the most productive in the organization, and the director had been a protégé of the CEO when the CEO was a vice president. Several of the union members in the unit had previously complained to the union leadership about the director's abrasive and bullying behavior and the culture of fear in the unit that he instilled. The union members had evidence of demanding email exchanges where members were asked to repeat already completed tasks, hearing disparaging comments about line supervisors, and were told by the director that mistakes, even minor errors such as typos in draft documents, were being documented. The members indicated that the supervisors who report to the director were sympathetic and tried to act as a buffer, but "are in a tough spot because they are suffering the same abuse." The supervisors, also union members, were unwilling to share their perspective with union leaders or participate in any type of complaint process.

Though none of the individual incidents were specific contract violations, the union leadership had the ability to assert an "on behalf of" grievance regarding the director's behavior. Based on prior experience this type of grievance action, which is similar to a class action claim, involves a protracted and labor-intensive series of hearings, interviews, and collection of evidence. In most cases, it fails to result in a resolution since no specific policy or contract violation can be identified. While a few members in this case felt they had nothing to lose, the majority of the complaining union members were adamantly opposed to filing such a grievance for fear their work environment and reputations would suffer further. Most of the union members were petrified that the director would find out they had even spoken to the union.

The union leadership contacted the ombuds to describe the situation and see if, given this background, an informal and confidential channel to the director or senior leadership could be established. The union leaders then recommended that the members meet with the ombuds individually or in small groups. After consulting with the union members over several weeks, the ombuds reached out to the supervisors to see if they would also be willing to have a confidential and informal conversation with the ombuds. The supervisors agreed and, when they met with the ombuds, confirmed the treatment described by the union members as well as their own personal difficulties with the director.

The ombuds then scheduled a meeting with the CEO to discuss the concerns brought to the ombuds office (without attribution to any individual). The CEO was initially surprised to hear the concerns but was alarmed by the breadth of discontent within the unit. The CEO decided to schedule a meeting with the director and the supervising vice president to alert them to concerns the CEO had heard about the way people were being treated in the unit, to reinforce the need to comply with the code of management conduct, and to encourage the director to meet with the ombuds to discuss ways to improve the culture in the unit. The ombuds agreed that this was a good plan and agreed to meet with the director if the director were to call the ombuds.

The director subsequently met with the ombuds on several occasions. Though frustrated with what the director referred to as the staff's incompetence, the director agreed to make changes in the approach and tone of email communications, to delegate more to the line supervisors, and to refrain from threats about documenting mistakes. Several weeks later, the union leadership contacted the ombuds to relay that members reported that things had improved somewhat but that they had doubts the director could sustain the improvements.

After a couple of months, the union leaders again contacted the ombuds to report the director had returned to many of the same behaviors, including disparaging one of the supervisors in a team meeting with another unit. Many of the members had now agreed to the class action–type grievance over the recent events, while several members had met with the ombuds to provide an update on the team meeting episode. The ombuds, however, requested the union to hold off on filing the grievance for a week and then followed up with the CEO on the recent events. At this point, the CEO removed the director from supervising the unit and placed one of the supervisors in the role of interim director while a search could be conducted for a new director. The former director was reassigned to another role without supervision of employees and the grievance process was avoided.

The union leadership members were notified of the change in director and cooperated with the transition in leadership. The CEO later expressed appreciation to the union for using the ombuds channel rather than initiating an arduous grievance process and affirmed the institution's commitment to responsible management. Over the ensuing months, several of the union members contacted the ombuds office to relay their appreciation and their satisfaction with the work environment in the unit. The former director remains an asset to the institution in the new role without direct supervisory responsibility.

Labor and Management Unaware of Gap in Contract

A professional union had among its members a small subset of technicians who worked in research labs at an off-site location and who had minimal contact with colleagues at the main facility location. Several technicians independently contacted the ombuds to seek to discuss various workplace issues. Though not the reason for any of the visits over a two-year period, the ombuds noticed that the off-site technicians were not receiving performance appraisals according to the same practices used for union employees at the main facility. When asked, the technicians commented that the lack of evaluations was similar to other jobs they had previously had and assumed that the practice for their current positions was the same.

The ombuds, however, reviewed the union contract and noticed that an addendum to the contract contained a section on working conditions for the technician classification. Unlike the main contract, the addendum language in this section on technician positions was vague and did not reference procedures for performance evaluations, only mentioning that merit increases were based on job performance.

The ombuds contacted the union leadership to inquire about the different language for the technician positions in the addendum. The union leadership was unaware that the technicians were not receiving performance evaluations. Upon reviewing the language, the union leader recalled that the creation of technician positions was being contemplated during the last contract negotiations and, because no one then held those positions, the language was added as an addendum at the request of management in the event that the organization were to hire for these positions. Due to ongoing negotiations over other matters that were occurring at the time, the union was hesitant to appear to be asking for a concession from the organization by requesting a revision of the addendum. The ombuds offered to serve as an intermediary between the union and the organization solely for the purpose of finding a remedy for the technician performance evaluation issue.

After obtaining permission from the union, the ombuds contacted the organization's general counsel's office to recommend the union and general counsel agree to revise the technician position addendum and make it compatible with performance evaluation practices for other union employees. The counsel's office also recalled the evolution of the addendum and agreed the technicians were now in an unfair position as employees. The ombuds and general counsel discussed the framework of remedies that appeared acceptable to the union leadership and the importance to separate the addendum from the ongoing negotiations of other matters. The ombuds reported back to the union leaders there was agreement on setting a separate meeting to revise the addendum.

Later that month, the general counsel and union leadership met and jointly produced a memorandum of understanding (MOU) revising the addendum for the balance of the current contract and aligning the performance evaluation process for technicians with the contractual practices of other unionized employees at the main facility.

After the MOU was signed, the general counsel and union leader independently contacted the ombuds to inform the ombuds of the resolution of the technician performance evaluations issue, share the MOU, and to express their gratitude for the ombuds' assistance.

Union and Labor Relations Referral to the Ombuds

A union representative went to the labor relations office with a grievance involving a claim by one union member against his coworker, also a member of the union. The first worker was complaining that his coworker was bullying him and that it was creating a "hostile work environment." There was no implication of a protected class to warrant a claim of harassment. The supervisor was at a loss about what to do, stating that the first worker would often cry, but also indicated that the coworker had been there for many years, worked very hard, and had no problems working with anyone else. The union rep and labor relations thought that perhaps the ombuds could help.

The ombuds met with both of the workers individually. The first worker stated that the coworker was always yelling and threatening him with tools and equipment. The coworker stated that he just happens to have a loud voice, that he gestures emphatically, and that he usually has tools in his hand. He admitted that he is often frustrated by the first worker's poor progress in covering the shared workload.

The ombuds suggested to both workers that one option was that they have a facilitated conversation with the ombuds, but the first worker was too afraid. In fact, the first worker was afraid to be in the same room with the coworker. With permission from each worker, the ombuds shared each worker's perspective with the other worker. The first worker did not think that he could ever have a working relationship with the coworker. (Incidentally, the ombuds also referred the first worker to the Employee Assistance Program to deal with what appeared to be an irrational fear). The coworker felt that he had done everything he could to be kind and gentle.

In separate conversations with each worker, the ombuds asked them what outcome they would like to see and told them that this was their opportunity to come up with a solution since the union and the supervisor couldn't fix the situation.

After a number of conversations, by way of the ombuds' shuttle diplomacy, the workers agreed that they would split the work area so that each had a separate, specific area to cover, and would time their shifts so that they wouldn't run into each other. They agreed to share the plan with management, and the first worker—and the union—dropped the grievance.

The ombuds subsequently ran into each of them periodically, and they both have indicated that they are happy with the arrangement.

Union Member's Request to Confirm Benefits Eligibility and Coverage

A female staff member, who was also a union member, came to the ombuds indicating that she was uncomfortable making direct inquiries regarding her eligibility for parental leave benefits and the requirements of providing notice to her supervisor or to the organization's human resources department. Based on past experiences, she also said that she was worried about reaching out to the union with her questions. She said that she was concerned about providing too much advance notice and then being perceived or treated differently due to her pregnancy status.

Without disclosing the identity of the visitor or any facts pertaining to her specific circumstances, the ombuds obtained clarification with human resources and benefits staff regarding her eligibility for leave and other benefits coverage, as well as applicable procedural information. Based on the information the ombuds provided, the staff member indicated she had received the answers to her questions, understood the process and procedural requirements, and felt comfortable with how and when she would provide notice regarding her request for a leave.

NEW HIRES

How Does a New Senior Manager Deal with a Lack of Support?

A senior manager scheduled a meeting after a lengthy phone conversation about how the ombuds office conducts its business (confidentiality, neutrality, informality, and independence). When he then met with the ombuds, he disclosed that he was new to the organization and had been hired after a national search. He said that both during the search process and after his accepting the position, he had had many discussions with the people above him about how his unit had not been performing well for many years. He said that he was told that his predecessor had been in the position for many years and was popular with employees but regarded as entrenched and resistant to change. The new manager believed he was given a "mandate" to make systemic changes within his unit.

After he accepted the job and began work, the manager experienced a great deal of resistance (covertly and overtly) from employees at various levels in the organization. Not fully appreciating the culture of the unit or the broader organization, he admitted to having made some tactical missteps that compromised his legitimacy and the respect of the employees. He felt unsupported by those above him and undermined by those below. Though given a mandate to make significant systemic changes because of the unit's history of poor performance, that mandate was never articulated to the employees in the unit. Rather, senior officials in public speeches praised the "wonderful work" that previously had been done by his unit. This created a perception that the changes were unnecessary. As a result, his initiatives were perceived by the employees in his unit as being motivated by his need to "reinvent the wheel" and to put his stamp on the unit. He felt very isolated and was seriously considering resigning. He said that he felt he could not discuss these issues either with those to whom he reported or those who reported to him (directly or indirectly).

During the course of many meetings to discuss options, strategy, and implementation, he and the ombuds also addressed the organization's culture, how to develop "buy-in," rebuild his reputation, and how to nudge those to whom he reported. While there continue to be challenges with his position, the manager did not resign and has reported that his situation has improved immensely.

Organizational Culture Can Be a Barrier to New Employees

The organization reorganized its sales force and brought in several new employees with no background or understanding of the organizational culture, terminology, and philosophy. They were also not given any background on the reasons for the reorganization. Unfortunately, the prevailing culture in this organization was to let new employees learn on the job and not to provide them with training or orientation.

The new employees' excitement with being a new and reenergized part of the organization soon gave way to confusion and frustration, as management and the new employees were not communicating effectively with each other. Some of the new employees reached out to the ombuds and were coached on various aspects of the organization and the history of the reorganization that led to their hiring. The ombuds also presented then with options for how to raise the issue of the need for better communications going forward.

The employees chose the option of requesting an opportunity to sit down with management and discuss their frustration over the lack of training and communication. The ombuds was given permission to make this request to management. Management agreed to the meeting, and as a result of it, management recognized that it needed to provide a better understanding of the organization and reorganization to these new employees. Roles were clarified, training implemented, and the employees gained a better understanding of the organization's needs, style, and expectation.

Help for a New Manager

A newly promoted manager came to the ombuds with a concern about an employee who was described as volatile and intemperate but also a good friend and former peer and coworker of the new manager. The manager expressed the desire to preserve the friendship but also that he wanted to do a good job as manager. Because he was so new in the job, the manager was unwilling to reveal to higher management that he needed help in resolving this issue. Being able to have a confidential discussion of the problem was critical to him.

After exploring various options, the manager had the ombuds coach him on how to speak directly with the employee. The ombuds and the manager engaged in role playing, and the ombuds helped the manager craft language about the impact of the employee's problematic behavior and the manager's predicament as the "boss." The ombuds helped the manager finds ways to articulate his desire both to preserve the friendship and to be a good boss, but that he would have to be a good manager if the two roles conflicted and could not be reconciled.

In a follow up discussion much later, the manager reported that he had had the conversation and that it had been a very difficult one but that there had been no more incidents of volatility. The manager also expressed more comfort in being able to impose discipline if it became necessary.

New Employee's Religious Concerns Accommodated

A new hospital tech employee was required, as part of her orientation, to scrub into an operating room to observe a surgery. She subsequently learned that the scrub uniform she would have to wear included pants. Her religious tenets prohibited her from wearing pants—normally she wore long uniform skirts that did not interfere with her work. She came to the ombuds because, as a new employee, she felt vulnerable and did not want to cause a problem. Confidentiality was important because she wanted to discuss available options before taking any action with a supervisor or the hospital itself.

After speaking with the ombuds, she gave the ombuds permission to make inquiries in other areas of the hospital, including surgery, the intensive care unit, and the hospital laundry. The ombuds learned that disposable (and sterile) long-sleeve skirt-like garments were used for patients in the ICU. The ombuds was also able to arrange for the tech (whose identity still had not been disclosed) to wear that garment in the operating room, provided that she wore regular scrubs under it. That solution satisfied everyone, and the problem was resolved.

DIFFICULT BOSSES

***Author's Note:* Included in this category are examples that uniquely involve difficult bosses. Examples in other categories may involve difficult bosses but were placed there because they were also relevant to that topic and due to space limitations. Please review other categories and the PDF downloads for additional examples involving difficult bosses.**

Ombuds Helps Resolve Staff Issues with Difficult Director

A high-level director had a reputation for being abrasive and sometimes unprofessional with her staff. Throughout the years, most staff members reporting to her feared retaliation and would not come forward to report her conduct. A couple of them who had come forward to file complaints had their complaints dismissed and ended up leaving the organization.

Over time, however, complaints to the ombuds about this director became more frequent. The principal issues involved bullying, overwork, and even alcohol use on the premises. The complainants still feared retaliation, even those who were more senior managers. The ombuds asked the complainants if they would be willing to come forward if others did. Some of them responded that they would, but only to a particular administrator whom they trusted and only in the presence of the ombuds. The ombuds arranged a meeting with the staff and administrator. The staff all told their stories.

The administrator subsequently informed the director of the issues that had been raised by her staff. The administrator also suggested that the director seek guidance from the ombuds, who could mediate between the director and the staff. When the director declined to engage with the ombuds, the director and administrator negotiated a new role for the director where she would not need to supervise staff.

Some members of the staff in her former unit reported back to the ombuds that they felt like a great weight had been lifted and noted that attrition in the unit had dropped.

Conflict with Manager

An employee reached out to the ombuds office because he wanted to explore his options on how to deal with his manager. The employee felt his manager had been retaliating against him after he had a straight talk with the manager regarding the manager's dictatorial management style and his confrontational comments during meetings.

The employee had raised his concerns of retaliation with both HR and his second-level manager, and, to date, his manager's conduct had not changed. Most recently, in the employee's mid-year review, a number of comments were made by the manager that were not accurate, and the manager had also provided feedback that the employee was disrespectful, too outspoken, and failed to follow the "chain of command." The employee felt that his manager's comments were contrary to the organization's open-door policy.

The employee was convinced that his only option was to leave the company. After discussing the pros and cons of that possibility, the ombuds suggested a number of other avenues for him to consider.

First, they discussed the possibility that the manager's cultural background (Asian) might be playing a role here. The ombuds pointed out that respect for and deference to those considered senior was an integral part of the manager's Asian culture and that while this would not excuse behaviors that violate company policy, it might explain and provide context for the manner in which the manager was acting. The ombuds noted that it was not the employee's role to address this potential cultural gap—that was the role of the company's formal channels. Next, they moved to a discussion of his options. These included following up with the second-level manager (in writing) to ask what the next steps would be based on the allegations of retaliation that he had raised. Another option was for him to escalate the concerns beyond local HR and his second-level manager—possibly to corporate employee relations—which would allow independent eyes to review the situation.

They also discussed the impact if he chose not to follow up or raise this to another formal channel: the opportunity would be lost to possibly see a change in the manager's behavior. Moreover, the employee could possibly feel compelled to leave the organization. In addition, advancing the concern would perhaps help others who report to this manager even if he did leave the company.

After considering all these options, the employee decided to both follow up with the second-level manager and then raise his concerns to the employee relations team, while simultaneously looking externally for a new job.

Facilitated Discussion Helps with Training of Difficult Manager and Addresses Concerns in Unit

A director at a large academic health center requested to consult with the ombuds regarding complaints she had been receiving from phlebotomists in a unit that served outpatient areas. The staff had reported that their manager had difficult interactions with them, information and expectations were not communicated consistently and clearly, and there seemed to be favoritism in the unit (e.g., concerning granting vacation, overtime, etc.). Also, they perceived that they would be subject to retaliation if they spoke up regarding concerns, and their unit was treated much differently (a less than positive work climate) than phlebotomists who worked in the inpatient units. The director also reported to the ombuds that there were also conflicts between the staff themselves, particularly the group that was viewed to be "favored" and the ones who were not. The director believed that the unit would benefit from assistance from the ombuds, and the employees were asked to contact the ombuds if they would like to further discuss concerns. The director requested that all the employees in the outpatient unit (even those who had not previously discussed any concerns) schedule individual, confidential meetings to share their work experiences with the ombuds, as well as their perspectives on the communication and interactions in the unit.

In addition to meeting with the employees in the unit, the ombuds also met with the manager on the same confidential basis. Based on these meetings, the ombuds recommended to the director that the entire group participate in a dialogue session with the ombuds that would provide a forum for raising concerns openly, an opportunity for the group to generate recommendations to address their concerns, and an opportunity for training in conflict resolution, effective communication, personality styles, and civility.

The Director agreed to this and agreed to hold an all-day session facilitated by the ombuds. (Because of scheduling challenges, this was held on a weekend, and treated as a paid workday for employees.) Attendance was not required, but it was strongly suggested that staff attend so that resolutions could be jointly developed by the group. Most of the staff attended the session and participated throughout the day, including the director and the manager.

Using an appreciative inquiry approach, the ombuds asked all participants to answer a series of questions about what was working well, what should be improved, what an ideal working environment would look like, and each person's individual commitment to addressing the issue and improving the team dynamics. The session included discussion of their responses to these initial questions, along with a facilitated discussion of the issues that had been raised in the earlier individual meetings. During these discussions, the ombuds was also able to provide the training components mentioned above. The session resulted in a resolution plan developed by those in attendance that included recommendations for how concerns should be addressed, agreements about group behavior moving forward, and individual commitments from each staff member. Privately with the ombuds, the director agreed to more closely oversee the performance of the manager and address further concerns via the performance management and coaching and development process.

What to Do with a Bullying Boss?

Several employees from one department in an organization came to the ombuds with concerns about the behavior of the department head. Most came separately, but a few came as a small group. The department head was described by them all as being defensive, belittling, and absent from daily tasks.

After discussing various options, the visitors gave the ombuds permission to raise the concern with the head of the business but not to identify them. In the discussion between the business head and the ombuds, they concluded that more information was needed. The ombuds was asked by the head of business to conduct a confidential "climate survey" to determine more about the department head's behaviors and the impact on employees.

To conduct the climate survey, the ombuds sent out an email to all people in the department inviting them to participate. The ombuds then met with each person individually and solicited comments and conversation around three questions: What is your leader doing well? In what areas could your leader improve? How could you help improve the work environment?

The ombuds verbally shared a summary of the high-level themes from this climate survey with the business head, without disclosing the identities of any of the people who had visited the ombuds or who had responded to the survey. With this information, the business head determined that a warning letter should be issued to the department head along with an offer to provide coaching to help him change his behaviors. Ultimately, the department head decided on his own to move to a new assignment after he completed the coaching. The business head expressed appreciation to the ombuds for bringing this matter to his attention, remarking that he would not have been aware of it had the ombuds not brought it to him.

Resolution Process

An employee with a previously exceptional performance record came to the ombuds with concerns over treatment by his new boss. His former boss had been promoted, resulting in the employee being reassigned to another director who had not been consulted or given any say in the reassignment. The employee said that his new boss had indicated that there were problems with his work and work ethic and had given him a poor performance rating.

At the same time, the employee told the ombuds that a terminally ill parent was living with him and had to be cared for daily, including being delivered to and from an adult care facility while the employee worked. The employee had used vacation time and sick leave for the extra time that this required, but he had recently learned that he may be eligible under the Family and Medical Leave Act (FMLA) for additional time off. His director, however, had told him that he could not leave early or arrive late; and when he did apply for FMLA leave, the director denied his request without explanation. The employee was distraught by this situation and did not know where else to go. He himself was also experiencing stress and other health-related concerns as a result of the situation.

In the course of consultations with the ombuds, the ombuds was able to help the employee first consult with medical services to attend to his own health problems while they worked on the other issues. They discussed various options to try to address the continuing issues with the director. The option selected by the employee was to use the organization's dispute resolution process to appeal the performance rating that he had been given by the director.

As a result of the dispute resolution process, the employee's performance rating was changed, the FMLA request was granted, and the director was reprimanded for his actions.

DIFFICULT EMPLOYEES AND COWORKER CONFLICT

Facilitated Conversation with Ombuds Addresses Abusive Colleague's Behavior

Nearly all residents in a highly respected training program complained about a second-year resident to faculty clinicians, including the program chair of residency training. The complaints centered on abrasive peer interactions, shirking of clinical duties, prioritizing moonlighting over clinic responsibilities, and speculation that the resident was more abrasive toward women and minority peers. The resident was among the least favorite among attending clinicians and was considered arrogant, though his clinical performance was considered slightly above average. The residency program chair had spoken to the resident on several occasions about these perceptions but had not issued discipline as there was no evidence of clinical or academic deficiencies. The chief resident, who had also tried to coach the resident, informed the program chair that the second-year resident's negative behavior had become more frequent and that it was time for the program chair to drop the resident from the program. The other residents felt that the program leadership was demonstrating a lack of care for their well-being and a lack of follow through about expectations of professional standards. Several residents indicated that they were considering submitting a formal complaint about discrimination to the EEO office; others were circulating a draft of a letter to the ACGME (Accreditation Council for Graduate Medical Education).

The program chair contacted the ombuds to seek assistance, understanding the informal, confidential, and neutral posture of the office. Several options were discussed, including more aggressive intervention by the chair, referral to a hospital-wide review committee, and facilitative intervention process organized by the ombuds. The chair wished to pursue the voluntary facilitative process before attempting more formal options and a plan was agreed upon whereby the chair would ask if the chief resident and the second-year resident would be willing to talk individually with the ombuds about the situation. Both were willing to participate.

The second-year resident was adamant that he believed there was no basis for the complaints but was willing to participate in a dialogue with the other residents if they thought it would help. The ombuds met with the chief resident and asked for background and the chief resident agreed to arrange several small meetings between the ombuds and the other residents. The residents agreed to abstain from submitting any formal complaints or letters until the facilitative process had an opportunity to proceed. After hearing from the residents and the second-year resident, the ombuds began serving as a go between, shuttling preliminary requests to and from the second-year resident, the Program Chair, and the other residents. Ultimately, the ombuds facilitated a group meeting that included the program chair, chief resident, and all other residents to discuss "ground rules" for behavior and a three-step protocol on how to respond to violation of those ground rules by any member. The entire process took place over six to eight weeks.

A Restorative Justice Approach Helps Address What Were Perceived to Be Racist Comments

A visitor came to the ombuds looking for help with a sensitive situation. She felt she had been humiliated and that the motivation had been racism when a colleague challenged her in a large meeting. She wasn't sure whether she wanted the other person to pay in some way, but she did want to address the problem and not sweep it under the rug.

The ombuds, who was trained in restorative justice practices, thought this might be a perfect opportunity to help people deal with the sensitive issue of racism in a way that leads to empathy and understanding rather than accusations and punishment.

When the ombuds described the circle process and discussed with the visitor why it is used, the visitor was receptive to the idea. Since the woman who insulted her was a colleague with whom she needed to continue to work, she decided her goal was to seek understanding and behavior change.

The ombuds asked the visitor who she would like to have in the meeting, and she selected the person who she thought had made the insulting comments and both of their supervisors. She wanted all of the other three to understand how the situation impacted her.

All three of the other parties agreed to participate in the circle. Two parties were Black and two were White. The discussion lasted two hours. There were tears and promises that all would be sensitive to how they talk to others and especially in front of others.

This is the kind of situation that many people do not address. Their feelings are hurt, and the other person is not held accountable or given a chance to learn from the situation. By having the ombuds suggest and help with this restorative justice process, hopefully both the individuals and their supervisors benefited by their new understanding of how they should treat others in the future. And, by helping to resolve the conflict in this manner, the university and its culture were also beneficiaries.

The Ombuds Helps Address Both Individual and Systemic Issues Involving Racial Aggression in the Workplace

An African American laboratory technician visited the ombuds to talk about a recent race discrimination complaint that he had brought to HR. The matter involved the use of the "N" word in the visitor's presence by a White coworker. According to the visitor, an investigation by a White HR professional involving the three levels of management for both colleagues (all of whom were White), resulted in no finding of violation of the racial harassment policy. Despite the fact that the subject of the investigation admitted to using the offensive language, his behavior was found not to be a violation of the policy because the coworker had not known that the African American visitor was present.

The ombuds provided a confidential and safe space for the visitor to share his feelings and worries about the situation and his future. The visitor was hurt and emotional about his treatment. In his words, the experience made him feel "insignificant."

The ombuds and the visitor discussed options at the individual level and actions that could be taken at a systemic level. The ombuds presented possible options at the visitor's level, including requesting a review of the investigation, creating a plan for future interactions with this coworker, building and strengthening the network of support at work for the visitor, refocusing the visitor's effort on high performance, transferring to a new department, and finding an ally supervisor/manager with whom the visitor could have a difficult conversation about the realities of racial tensions in the work environment. In this case, the visitor decided to get more involved with plant diversity and inclusion (D&I) initiatives and to focus his efforts on doing a great job while preparing to apply for a job in another department.

At the systemic level, the ombuds and the visitor discussed local D&I activities and organizations. The visitor gave the ombuds permission to raise the issue as a systemic issue while not identifying the visitor. Since the ombuds had received information from a number of visitors about racial tensions, the ombuds concluded that these comments represented a systemic issue of both micro- and more blatant aggressions in the workplace centered on race.

The ombuds was able to include this general information in providing upward feedback to senior leadership and several key D&I leaders locally. The ombuds was also able to refer managers and D&I leaders to local racial justice initiatives and training resources for incorporation into the organization's future. The D&I leaders were extremely receptive and several enrolled in antiracist workshops that were recommended.

The Ombuds Can Help Mediate Mid-Level Staff Conflict that Would Otherwise Impede Important Work in a University Department

A female staff member in the Office of the Dean of the Graduate School at a large public research university contacted the ombuds for help with what she called a "difficult" working relationship with a male Information Technology (IT) staff professional following a conversation she described as "terrible." The IT staff member routinely provided technical support for two large departments at the university, but two months previously had also began assisting the Office of the Dean of the Graduate School.

Among her many other responsibilities, the visitor to the ombuds had been assigned the task of administering the annual survey of graduate students. Among the first assignment given to the IT staff member by the Graduate School was to help the visitor develop and analyze the graduate student survey, which this year was likely to receive intense scrutiny from administrators and the public because of disturbing and numerous highly publicized allegations of sexual harassment and bullying of graduate students by faculty members across numerous academic departments. The climate for graduate students had become a hot topic on campus.

The visitor told the ombuds that while she was initially happy to have the IT staff member's technical help with the survey, she knew he could only give 20 percent of his time to the work for the Graduate School Dean's office. She said that she and several colleagues had found the male IT staff member to be completely unresponsive to emails. She said he was rarely available. He didn't seem to recognize the constraints of the office's budget because he had mentioned wanting to use some cutting-edge software that she thought they probably could not afford. She said that the "terrible" conversation occurred when he came to her office after learning she had asked someone else to help her with the graduate student survey while he was away. When he demanded to know why she "went around his back" she answered, "Because, I have to get this survey done and I haven't even seen you for at least a week. Besides, you never answer my emails. So, I asked someone who agreed to help immediately, and, by the way, she used software we already had." According to her, his response, before walking away, was, "Oh? Now I see why I was warned about you."

The visitor was concerned about this exchange and asked the ombuds if mediation between the two of them might be a possibility. The ombuds asked if she would be willing to give the IT staff member an ombuds office brochure and invite him to call the ombuds for an appointment. She agreed, took a brochure, and left. The IT staff member called before the end of the day and arranged an appointment the next day.

When he came for his appointment, he also was clearly upset. He said he'd been doing his best to keep up with his work generally but having the Graduate School Dean's office added to his workload had made an already hectic schedule even crazier. He explained that he had never been told how much time to give the Graduate School. He met with the female staff member in the Graduate School soon after he took on the Graduate School responsibility to find out about the survey. He said he assured her he could provide the technical help she needed;

especially if the office could purchase new software that he was anxious to try because it would likely provide very robust results. He said she had seemed hesitant about purchasing the new software but said she'd investigate it. He never heard back from her about that. He acknowledged that she did send him several emails about the survey, but he said she never included any deadlines or due dates. So, with all he had to do for the other two departments, he assumed he would tackle her request after his wife had their first child, which had only occurred a week ago. He had then taken a week off from work because of the child's birth. He said he was sleep deprived when he returned to work, so he was "not at his best" when he tried to talk to her about the survey. Also, even though part of the survey work was now done, he was still going to be providing technical support for the analysis and, frankly, without the new software, he said he had less confidence about the quality of the data analysis he could provide.

After listening to his perspective, the ombuds asked if he would be interested in trying mediation with her. He readily agreed.

They both came to mediation ready to do the work required to improve their working relationship. They listened respectfully to one another, spoke honestly, asked good questions, took responsibility (and apologized) for their individual contributions to the conflict, and focused on what they could do differently in the future to improve their communication. With the assistance of the ombuds they resolved to take a variety of actions both to address the task at hand and to work more productively with each other in the future. Among the commitments they made were that the original visitor said that she would tell the Dean of the Graduate School that her IT colleague had not been told he was expected to work 20 percent for the Graduate School. They also committed to meet for coffee every two weeks to keep the lines of communication open.

RELATIONSHIP AND REPUTATION ISSUES

Ombuds Mediation Restores Respectful Communication

An employee came to the ombuds concerned about how one of her colleagues spoke to her. She said she liked him and respected him, but he didn't seem to respect her. She did not like the way he spoke to her in meetings.

The ombuds discussed various options, including conflict coaching, mediation, shuttle diplomacy, filing a grievance or Title IX complaint, or bringing it to her supervisor. The visitor did not trust the Human Resources department because they had violated her confidentiality in the past. She said that on a prior occasion her supervisor had been called by HR and told of her meeting with HR before she even returned to the office from the meeting. The visitor did not feel sufficiently confident to initiate a conversation with the person who she felt was disrespecting her, and she didn't want to get him in trouble since she was new to the department. She didn't think the matter rose to the importance of formal processes or telling their supervisor. She felt most comfortable with the mediation option.

The visitor invited her colleague to a mediation, and he readily accepted. The ombuds, however, first met with the second visitor in order to learn his perspective on the situation. In the mediation, the colleagues readily participated in the discussion with openness and authenticity. When the initiator said she did not appreciate it when he "mansplained" to her, he immediately and genuinely apologized. By the end of the discussion, both parties were smiling and complimenting each other. As it turned out, they learned from each other that their supervisor was causing divisiveness in their workgroup.

When the ombuds asked if there were any more issues to discuss when their time allotment was over, both parties said they enjoyed mediation and were looking forward to working with each other. The ombuds followed up with both of them over the next three months and they reported they were getting along fine. They also reported that they had initiated a team retreat to address the divisiveness.

Both the department and the individuals benefited from their visit to the ombuds.

Communication Chaos

The faculty in a university department hired a new professor following an extensive search. At first, everything seemed to be working well with the professor's teaching and research. However, a few months later, problems started to arise.

The department's administrative assistant felt that this professor was too closed off and unfriendly. The assistant had invited the professor to group lunches and other gatherings, and each time the professor politely declined. The assistant began taking this personally and spoke with the department chair and other faculty about the behavior.

While most faculty didn't see a problem, some of them were also concerned. Instead of approaching the new professor directly about their concerns, colleagues communicated with him in a passive-aggressive and indirect manner. The new professor began to feel as though he had made a mistake in taking the position and didn't know what to do. He decided he should start looking for another position and spoke to a colleague about his situation. The colleague advised him to talk to the ombuds.

In the first meeting, the professor described behaviors that he thought were hostile and directed at him by the administrative assistant and some of the faculty members. He could not imagine why they appeared to be acting this way, as even though he tended to keep to himself he always made it a point to say "hello" and to be polite to everyone in the office, including student workers. The ombuds asked permission to speak to others in the department and the professor agreed.

In the subsequent meetings, the ombuds discovered that the others who were upset with the professor had made many assumptions about his manner, behavior, and choices to not join group activities. They took his absence as a personal affront, assuming he did not want to get to know them or befriend them. At least one of them expressed the wish that the professor would leave the university.

After sharing their concerns (with permission) with the professor, the professor acknowledged that their basic description of his actions was accurate, but he believed that they had misunderstood his intentions. He told the ombuds about his education, which took place in another country and culture, and also about his work experience where professional distance was strictly adhered to. In his training, faculty did not mix business with pleasure except in rare circumstances. Furthermore, he had young children at home and preferred to spend his meals with them and his wife as they were still struggling to feel comfortable in this new community.

The ombuds asked him if he would be willing to meet with the ombuds and some of the other people to help clear the air about his behavior and intentions, as well as theirs. He agreed, as did the others. At that meeting, each person was able to talk about what they experienced, what the department's norms were, and began to understand better each other's behavior and assumptions. They apologized, shook hands, and learned some important lessons in cultural communication. With the greater understanding the new professor ceased looking for a new job and intradepartmental communication improved.

Facilitated Conversation Between a Faculty Member and his Department Chair Clarifies Expectations and Builds a Better Relationship

A faculty member responsible for directing an academic center was very disappointed with his salary increase. The increase was below the average percentage that year. His performance review was good, not great. He reached out to the ombuds to express his disappointment and ask for guidance on how to proceed. He felt he was getting a message from his department chair but was not sure how to approach the chair. He enjoyed his job very much and did not want to resign but was considering it. He was feeling insecure and did not feel confident enough to speak to the chair on his own. He left after speaking with the ombuds about various options, wanting to think about what he wanted to do next.

The faculty member called the ombuds the next day to ask if the ombuds would reach out to the chair to set up a meeting with the department chair, him, and the ombuds. The ombuds agreed to do so, and when the ombuds spoke with the chair, the chair was very receptive.

The chair confidentially told the ombuds that the faculty member was a valuable member of the department and indicated that it would be a challenge replacing him in a timely manner to teach his courses. The chair also expressed concern that he had found it very difficult to give constructive feedback to the faculty member

During the meeting arranged by the ombuds, the chair assured the faculty member of his value to the department and highlighted some of his contributions. It also became apparent during the meeting that there was an honest misunderstanding. The faculty member was always trying to "please" the chair by asking many questions and following directions. The chair, however, wanted to see the faculty member take more initiative and demonstrate more leadership.

As a result of this meeting, the chair agreed to make a minor adjustment to the faculty member's salary, and the faculty member decided not to seek other employment and became more confident in taking initiative. The faculty member called the ombuds about four months later sounding much more confident and expressing gratitude for a better and more open relationship with the chair.

Mediated Discussion about Racist Comments Leads to a "Mountaintop Experience"

The ombuds received a call from two Black women employees who were offended by comments made by a White male employee who had called their office for assistance. At the end of the call, the White male employee had made some racist comments. The two women were quite disturbed by the man's comments and decided that they wanted to address the issue with him. They called the ombuds for guidance on what they might do.

After listening to the women and discussing various options, including a possible mediation, the two women indicated that they would like the ombuds to explore whether a mediation was possible. When the ombuds contacted the male employee about a possible mediation, he agreed to participate.

Both women and the man came to the ombuds office on the day of the mediation willing to engage in a mediation process. The result was heartfelt reconciliation. The women were most forgiving. The man sincerely apologized. The process was such a powerful and poignant "mountain top" experience that it has remained one of the most significant experiences in the long career of the ombuds involved and inspired the ombuds to develop resources on the power of apologies and use an anonymous version of this matter as an example in discussing mediation as an option with subsequent visitors.

Healing Old Grievances

Two employees had been avoiding each other for ten years. One of them approached the ombuds to discuss how this rift might be healed. When the ombuds discussed various options with the employee, the option chosen by the employee was to see if the other employee would consider a facilitated conversation to discuss their differences and grievances with each other.

When the ombuds approached the other employee, that employee agreed to participate in a facilitated conversation led by the ombuds. When they all met, the ombuds described the process and then let each person, in turn, speak. In the course of leading this discussion, a number of misperceptions that had turn into grievances against each other came to light.

At the end of the mediation, the parties had mended their relationship and reconciled. The discussion itself was transformative. In other words, the structure of the mediation session, which was designed to be fair and balanced, gave the parties a framework for addressing, hearing, and resolving not only their past grievances but also any problems that might arise in the future.

A Department Chair Wants Information Confidentially to Figure Out How to Correct a Mistake

The chair of an academic department came to the ombuds and disclosed that he had had a challenging relationship with another senior faculty member in the same department for a number of years. Over the years, the two of them had had very public heated disagreements, and he admitted that their disdain for each other was well known.

The issue that brought the department chair to the ombuds involved a dispute over the leadership of a national project, during which the chair made some decisions in haste and anger that adversely affected the other senior faculty member. The department chair conceded to the ombuds that he had made a mistake in judgment and needed additional information to decide how best to manage "damage control," but he was not willing to seek the information himself or disclose his mistake without considering this additional information. He asked the ombuds to approach HR, the general counsel's office, and the provost's office to request both general and specific information but to do so in a way that would not disclose who was asking for the information, identify the department involved, or reveal why the information was being sought.

The ombuds was able to obtain the information sought and then to discuss options with the department chair about what to do. In gathering the data, the ombuds also gained insight on the best way for the department chair to speak with someone in each of those areas, which he eventually did.

Relationship Reset: Restoring Accurate and Direct Communication

A faculty member contacted the ombuds to report a simmering dispute causing concern in a moderately sized academic department. The caller, tenured in the same department, shared widely known facts that the chair had tried unsuccessfully to broker a resolution of the dispute and after many attempts was now part of the problematic dynamic. The caller explained that the two peers, one male and one female, were deeply entangled in a disruptive conflict and (1) both were tenured faculty members, (2) they had not spoken directly to each other for several months despite occupying nearby offices, and (3) their disdain for each other had become so uncomfortable for all that the chair had canceled faculty department meetings for the semester.

After discussing different strategies and options with the ombuds, the caller decided to refer one peer to the ombuds. That peer met with the ombuds and confided that she was contemplating taking formal steps to seek redress for reputational damage caused by the other faculty member, who she said was "falsely accusing" her of sexual harassment violations. During meetings with the ombuds she contemplated potential options and outcomes and ultimately decided that she wanted to pursue a direct dialogue with her peer.

The ombuds also received a call from the male peer who had been to the chair, who had suggested the ombuds as a helpful resource. In confidential dialogue with the male peer, it became clear that several significant misunderstandings had occurred and were exacerbated by indirect and highly inaccurate communication. Before contacting the ombuds he had been considering filing a claim against the other faculty member. When asked about his ideal outcome he stated a preference to resolve the communication disconnect and move past this time-consuming distraction hampering his research and teaching.

Recognizing that each peer wanted to find a pathway to restore direct communications, the ombuds asked each individual, in confidence, how they wanted to proceed. Eventually a mutually agreeable process was facilitated by the ombuds to informally discuss the communications disconnect. The ground rules were determined by the peers and agreed to in advance of the meeting.

The ombuds then facilitated a 90-minute informal, off-the-record meeting, allowing the two tenured peer faculty members to communicate directly. During the meeting, one party told the other that they could never forgive how they had ignored a prior heartfelt apology. In reply, the other party explained that the apology was, in fact, never heard because of a hearing impairment. This breakthrough enabled the parties to realize that both perceived the other as having broken the relationship. Sincere apologies followed and open communications were restored. Department meetings resumed and the chair enjoyed the renewed engagement of his colleagues in the department.

RETAINING TALENT

Ombuds Helps Clinical Fellow Stop Unwanted Attention from a Senior Colleague

A new female clinical fellow contacted the ombuds to discuss her discomfort with attention she was receiving from a senior male clinician. The senior clinician, an internationally recognized physician and author of a popular medical textbook, had been repeatedly contacting the fellow by phone and text, complimenting her appearance, and offering her a valuable collaborative clinical research opportunity during her fellowship. The fellow did not wish to make a formal complaint because of the impact on her career, the embarrassment it would cause the senior clinician, and because the senior clinician had not asked her out, touched her, or said anything exceedingly inappropriate. However, she had a clear sense he was interested in her romantically and may cross those boundaries in the future. She said she only wanted a professional relationship and to be able to complete the fellowship. She indicated that she had not talked to anyone else affiliated with the hospital about the situation and presently had no intention to do so.

The fellow and the ombuds discussed keeping a record of the texts and a journal of the inordinate contact as a backup measure and then began exploring ways the fellow could more clearly communicate her discomfort to the senior clinician either directly or through an intermediary. She decided that as a first step, it would be most appropriate for her to respond to a text message she received that she's noticing he's contacting her quite a bit and that it makes her somewhat uncomfortable and that she'd prefer to communicate with people with whom she had professional relationships by email only. As a secondary measure if the excessive contact persisted, she indicated that she may ask the ombuds to speak to the clinician confidentially on her behalf. Several weeks later the fellow returned to ask the ombuds to speak to the senior clinician so he would stop.

The ombuds subsequently asked the senior clinician to meet and explained the "off-the-record" nature of the ombuds office. When they met, the ombuds simply said that the ombuds was asked by a fellow if he, the senior clinician, would honor a request made of him about communicating by email. The senior clinician, understanding the confidentiality and informality of the ombuds office, expressed gratitude for the message.

The fellow reported back to the ombuds a few months later that the excessive contact from the senior clinician had stopped and she was now more comfortable dealing with her colleague.

Procedural Irregularities in Tenure Process

An associate professor sought promotion to full professor. Upon review of the associate professor's exemplary dossier that checked all the boxes, the associate professor's department and primary unit's evaluation committee unanimously recommended promotion. The dean, who had the responsibility of making recommendations to the vice chancellor's advisory committee (responsible for the campus's tenure and promotion review and making recommendation to the chancellor), met with the candidate and indicated that they would likely affirm the department and committee's recommendation but had not made a final decision.

Upon receipt of the department's recommendation, however, the associate dean in charge of faculty affairs and responsible for managing the tenure and promotion process for the university, wrote a lengthy report opposing the department's recommendation and discounting most of the faculty member's many publications. This report, however, was not in accordance with established tenure review procedures, and the associate dean had based it on his own desired publication requirements rather than adhering to what university policy required. The report also accused the department of a sloppy evaluation process. In light of this report, it was unclear what decision the dean would reach on the tenure question.

The associate professor up for tenure was angry and confused. She did not feel safe going to the dean's office and was prepared to seek legal counsel if she did not receive the promotion. Before moving forward, she decided to visit with the ombuds because she wanted an impartial, independent, and confidential place to make sense of the situation and explore her options.

After taking the time necessary to hear the faculty member's story and ask questions, the ombuds thought that while this could be a bad-faith effort to defeat the tenure recommendation and undermine the department's process, the associate dean also could have been basing his response on information not in the professor's dossier. The essential questions were whether the associate dean's actions were a personal vendetta or a legitimate concern and whether the department's tenure recommendations had gone awry.

The associate professor initially wanted to resolve the matter before the dean made a decision. The ombuds, however:

1. Provided and explained the current university policy regarding the tenure and promotion process.
2. Explained the role of academic affairs, which included overseeing faculty tenure and promotion.
3. Explained the current internal appeal process available to the faculty member if the dean rendered an adverse decision.

The visitor and ombuds also explored various options, including:

1. The associate professor or the ombuds (with the associate professor's permission) could meet with the associate dean in an effort to understand more fully their perspective and concerns.
2. The associate professor or ombuds (with the associate professor's permission) could speak with the associate vice chancellor for academic affairs to discuss the procedural irregularity involving the associate dean's report.

The associate professor, not previously aware that a review by the associate vice chancellor of academic affairs was an option, decided to contact academic affairs (rather than have the ombuds initiate the contact) and ask them to review the situation, render an opinion, and, if appropriate, address the associate dean's behavior and ensure a fair process.

The associate professor chose this option, to give the associate vice chancellor and the dean the opportunity to "do the right thing." She indicated that if the dean then rendered an adverse decision, she would use the information the ombuds provided and avail herself of the university's internal appeal processes rather than file a lawsuit.

Rebuilding Trust and Realigning Productive Focus

A renowned and distinguished researcher had pursued several claims and disputes with the university involving significant sponsored research issues. Some years had passed since lawyers on both sides staked out positions and a "cold war" commenced. With major underlying issues unresolved, intense emotions on both sides continued to smolder, fueling further misunderstandings. Communications between this well-funded researcher and faculty member and key stakeholders in the administration had strained to the breaking point. Inevitably, university leadership allowed distance to develop between them and the researcher.

The faculty member felt increasingly *persona non grata.* Consequently, his honed research skills were diverted to detecting and dwelling upon the university's mistakes and perceived flaws in the research area. The brilliant intellect that had previously garnered mutual accolades for a rising star and growing university became laser-focused on the bitter mission of exposé.

The proverbial last straw came when administrators denied the faculty member travel and related requests for professional development opportunities that were personally important to him. This led the faculty member to reach out to the ombuds, resulting in a series of meetings between them.

The ombuds made it clear that they were not authorized to receive notice of any claims against the university, but the faculty member told his side of the dispute and expressed his feeling that this was the first time that someone with the capacity to fully understand his concerns had listened to the *whole* story. The first meeting took almost seven hours, and the initial narrative was filled with emotional nuance intertwined with technical issues and lots of data. The terms of service having been agreed to up front meant that the informal operation of the ombuds removed pressure on the faculty member to "prove their case" as a matter of regulatory sufficiency. Thus, key points and perspectives voiced were heard and understood. The faculty member was thankful no time limits had started to run regarding potential peer misconduct. The faculty member was also looking into other potentially substantial compliance concerns involving federal grants.

After several follow-up sessions, the faculty member began to realize that the years of unresolved conflict with the university had shifted focus to "looking backward," which was counterproductive. Upon clear and mutual agreement, the ombuds and faculty member agreed that the ombuds would reach out to leadership in the research office to gauge receptivity to a meeting. The "good offices" reputation of the ombuds enabled a productive one-to-one meeting between the faculty member and a senior leader in the research office. Prior to this meeting the ombuds held a session with the senior leader, under the normal terms of service. The confidential dialogue enabled this leader to express regrets and concerns without fear of negative consequence or embarrassment. The leader determined that restoration of a productive collegial relationship with the researcher would be welcome. The meeting took less than one hour and resulted in an agreement to release reasonable travel funds in support of professional development opportunities of benefit to both the individual and institution.

With direct dialogue restored between leadership and the researcher the two parties continued to communicate openly about future plans. This enabled them to reach a formal settlement agreement, working directly with the university's general counsel, resolving all past outstanding issues. Some years later, no additional lawsuits, claims or adverse personnel actions have occurred between this researcher and the university's research administration.

The Ombuds as a Sounding Board

An employee from the campus computing center office came to the ombuds concerned about her workload. She said her team was being asked to produce much more than was reasonable. She described working long hours and feeling under immense pressure. She said she was getting headaches and felt tightness in her shoulders.

When the ombuds asked if she had ever missed a deadline, she admitted she had. When asked what the consequences were for missing a deadline, the visitor paused, obviously thinking, and said, "I guess nothing. I never thought about that. Nothing happens. We just get lectured and we continue working on the project until it is completed."

The visitor thanked the ombuds for the insight. She said she could now go back to her office and work on projects without feeling the pressure because now she realized that there were actually no consequences.

This employee had been considering starting a job search, and after this discussion was able to recommit herself to her job. Eventually this employee became the president of the campus-wide staff organization. Sometimes just having a confidential resource available to talk through an issue is all a visitor may need.

HELPING PEOPLE EXIT GRACEFULLY

Help to Exit Gracefully and Avoid Reputational Damage

A faculty member at a university was denied tenure. Prior to coming to the university, she had held an important role in the community and still had many significant connections in the area. In her discussion with the ombuds, she explained that she did not feel that the tenure process had been fair in that the policies regarding expectations in the area of professional development had not been sufficiently clear.

After discussion and exploring various options with the ombuds, the visitor decided that she did not wish to appeal the denial because she did not want to continue working with a department that apparently did not want to retain her. She did, however, want to share her concerns about the process that had been used in her tenure denial decision. After further discussion, she decided to write an email to the president and provost of the university to notify them that she did not wish to appeal the tenure decision but also to indicate that she wanted to meet with them to share her concerns over process and policy in the tenure decision.

The ombuds helped her craft the email to make it as constructive as possible and then followed up with the administrators to encourage them to accept her request to meet. The president and provost agreed to meet with her, and they subsequently had the discussion she had sought. The faculty member was grateful for this assistance, as she had a chance to be heard by senior administration. This allowed her to leave on a somewhat more positive note.

In its annual report, the ombuds office addressed the systemic issues raised by the faculty member's concerns and recommended that all academic departments develop clear guidelines regarding discipline-specific expectations for tenure.

Helping a Nontenured Faculty Member Focus on What Was Important to Her Avoids a Discrimination Lawsuit

A faculty member came to see the ombuds about what she considered to be racist or discriminatory treatment. She was a junior faculty member with multiple degrees, one of which was from the campus where she currently worked. As a contract employee of the university, she felt she was being left out of important meetings and treated differently than her male peers. They were being mentored and she was not. She had also found out she was being paid less than others to do the same work and now she had been advised that her contract had been canceled. She was considering suing the university for discrimination.

The ombuds listened and heard all the pain the visitor felt from being marginalized and left out. The visitor was ambitious and had dreams about doing research and having her own lab. She didn't know where to go for help. Human resources on that campus did not assist faculty, and she had already spoken to the department chair, the dean, and the provost. The dean had promised to help her but had done nothing to date. The department chair was new and said he was just supporting the decision of the previous chair to cancel her contract. The provost listened and said the dean has the right to make decisions in his school.

At this point, she was very angry and wanted to get even. As a minority woman, she felt fairly certain that she could win in a lawsuit because she had not been accused of any wrongdoing, yet her contract was being canceled.

The ombuds asked the visitor to think about what she most wanted, encouraging her to think about what her life would be like, on that campus if she sued and won, or elsewhere if she sued and lost. The ombuds asked her if all the negative time and energy was worth the time it would take out of her career and moving forward on her research and writing projects.

The visitor did some thinking and reflecting on the advice from the ombuds and came back a week later. She asked the ombuds if the ombuds would help her find resources to assist her with her resume and job search. The ombuds gave her a list of local and campus resources and met with her a few more times to give her chances to vent her anger.

A few months later, the visitor secured an assistant professor position with her own lab and mentor at a prominent university. She was so excited about her new opportunity that she was no longer interested in suing the university.

The ombuds, in this case, helped spare both the university and the faculty member from the cost and stress of a discrimination lawsuit and, with the counseling from the ombuds, enabled the faculty member to realize her dreams.

Helping an Employee Exit Gracefully

A longtime employee came to the ombuds office, wanting strict confidentiality. After the ombuds explained to the employee how the ombuds office worked and that confidentiality would be honored, the employee shared that they were being released from the company after many years of service and had received a "separation agreement" from HR. They said that they had a certain number of days to sign and return the agreement, or it would be invalidated, and any severance compensation would be greatly reduced. One of the stipulations of that agreement was a confidentiality clause, so the employee was not certain it should even be discussed with the ombuds. After some discussion, the employee confided that their desired outcome was a "retirement" separation, as opposed to a "termination" or "reduction of force." The employee asked if the ombuds could help him achieve that outcome and still retain the provision for monetary compensation.

In this case, it was critical that the employee understand what the ombuds could and could not do on their behalf, and what information should be shared by the ombuds. After explaining this to the employee, and with the employee giving the ombuds permission to approach HR, the ombuds inquired of HR whether the reason for the separation could be adjusted from a "termination" to a "retirement." HR agreed to do so, resulting in a successful outcome for both the employee and the organization.

Effective Counseling Avoids a Lawsuit

An employee came to the ombuds with concerns that his boss was discriminating against him because of his sexual orientation. He was adamant that he did not want to raise this issue with anyone in HR or with his boss, for fear of further retaliation. He was fully aware of his legal rights and was close to a decision just to quit the company and bring a lawsuit against the company and his boss for retaliation.

The ombuds worked with the employee for an extended period to try to identify options that the employee could feel comfortable with to deal with the issue. Finally, the employee and the ombuds were able to identify a manager in another area who was willing to work with the employee to help him look for another job both inside the company and elsewhere.

The employee was very grateful to have had help in finding a manager with whom he could discuss his concerns and from whom to seek advice. The employee ultimately located another job outside of the company, and a lawsuit was avoided.

Ombuds Facilitates Conversation between Senior Management and an Employee with a History of Threatening Behavior and Employment Litigation That Included Disparaging Statements in the Media

A professional with a respected resume was hired into an organization, even though he had been involved in litigation against his prior employer, about which he had spoken very publicly and disparagingly in the media. Once in his new position, this employee became the subject of multiple complaints to management from staff members, colleagues, and business partners regarding the employee's inappropriate and threatening behavior, demeanor, and actions.

In connection with the organization's decision to terminate this employee's employment, visitors in management positions came to the ombuds to explore the ways in which they could engage in a productive conversation about separation from the organization with the employee. The employee involved also independently visited with the ombuds to discuss the situation. The employee then followed up with demands that the ombuds invite and engage senior directors in a facilitated conversation. When the ombuds declined to do as the employee demanded, adhering to the ombuds office's ethical principles of informality and impartiality, the employee engaged legal counsel and threatened to publicly denounce the organization and its management in the press and on social media.

After several additional conversations and at the request of the employee and management, the ombuds agreed to facilitate a discussion between a senior member of management and the employee. In an opening statement, the ombuds reiterated the ombuds' role as a neutral facilitator and emphasized the voluntary nature of the conversation, taking an unusual step to request that the visitors acknowledge these principles in an agreement regarding the facilitated conversation. This document included specific statements regarding the ombuds' standards of confidentiality and informality, as well as acknowledgments that the ombuds office was not an office of notice for the organization, that the participants would not call the ombuds as a witness in any administrative or judicial proceedings, and that the conversation would not be recorded.

As a result of this facilitated conversation, the employer and employee proceeded to resolve the matter and the employee separated from the organization without litigation and without adverse publicity or a media campaign against the organization.

FORMAL CHANNELS AS PART OF THE PROBLEM

Speak-up Culture

An employee who had been with the company more than fifteen years called the ombuds. He wanted to have a confidential and off-the-record conversation with someone because he felt he had been threatened by his supervisor and sent to HR when he refused to undertake an assignment. He indicated to the ombuds that he had refused the supervisor's direction because he had not received the training required to do this work and was concerned about safety. The employee believed that the HR manager he spoke with had not listened to his side of the story to understand the safety issue or the training requirements involved. He also felt that the HR manager had not listened to other employees on the floor who had been trained.

The employee expressed his frustration and disappointment over how poorly this incident had been handled, especially in light of company policies that required an employee to obtain proper training and be certified to perform the work that he had been asked to do. The employee told the ombuds that the environmental health and safety department (EHS) previously had been involved in this issue and had agreed that it was a policy violation for management to ask an employee to do things that they were not trained and certified to do. The employee also indicated that EHS had previously instructed his supervisor to make improvements. However, almost a year later, this issue had not been resolved. This situation made the employee think the culture of the company was to punish employees who reported issues and to permit management to disregard its responsibility to address policy violations and safety concerns.

In discussing possible ways to proceed with the employee, the ombuds asked if the employee would be willing to speak directly with an

EHS representative to follow up on this issue and help identify the root cause for why this issue had not been resolved. The employee agreed that he should be more proactive and agreed to do so. The employee told the ombuds that he would schedule a meeting with EHS to follow up on the issue. Since the employee did not contact the ombuds office again, the ombuds concluded that the employee had apparently resolved his issue.

Meanwhile, the ombuds was aware that the employee's concerns were not the first case arising in his facility involving management's failure to follow company policy in ways that raised safety issues. Another employee had previously contacted the ombuds about similar management issues. Since the HR manager involved was planning to retire very soon, the ombuds decided to visit the facility after the replacement HR manager came on board and host a focus group to solicit employees' perspectives and insight on the organization's culture overall and then work with the new HR manager on the safety issues identified by employees.

After the new HR manager came on board, the ombuds hosted two on-site training sessions (one for salaried and hourly employees and another one for managers and supervisors) to speak about the company's ombuds program and to create more awareness of how and when to use ombuds services that were available to everyone. The ombuds also hosted a separate focus group where employees were given an opportunity to provide extra feedback on company's practices.

With this information the ombuds then met one-on-one with the new HR manager and provided a summary of the feedback from the employees. The ombuds and the HR manager reviewed safety and quality training records and identified individuals who had not received training that they should have received. And finally, the ombuds and the HR manager reviewed the supervisor on-boarding process and identified areas in which the company had not provided appropriate leadership training when someone was promoted to manage a group of people.

During the meeting with the new HR manager, the ombuds recommended that all shop floor employees be given refresher training on EHS and quality control cardinal rules, as well as giving some groups refresher technical training. The ombuds also recommended that mandatory leadership training be part of the on-boarding process for new supervisors and that new supervisors be assigned to a senior manager mentor to improve their management style and skills.

By proceeding this way, the ombuds enabled the employee who first brought the issue to the ombuds to resolve his issue directly but then went further to address on a broader level these systemic issues with the new HR manager.

Ombuds Arranges for an Anonymous Call to a Formal Channel at the Request of an HR Team to Address the Conduct of their HR Vice President

A few employees on a regional HR team had been talking among themselves about the arrogant, dismissive, and disorganized behavior of their HR VP, which they thought indicated a lack of accountability. The HR team had more than twenty people; some of them worked in the same office as the HR VP and others worked in offices in different states. The employees working in the same office as the VP, in particular, were able to observe these troubling behaviors by the VP, including the extreme favoritism he showed to certain individuals.

With frustration mounting and many of the employees finding it increasingly difficult to focus on their jobs, three employees from this HR team contacted the ombuds to confidentially discuss their concerns because they greatly feared retribution from the VP if he were to learn that they had spoken up about him. They also said that they did not trust any of the other resources in the organization to address their concerns. In their conversation with the ombuds, they said that they were looking to find a way to raise their concerns anonymously. After listening to the concerns expressed and understanding what the employees had already attempted to do to resolve the problem, the ombuds discussed various options.

The option selected by the employees was for the ombuds to contact an ethics and compliance representative, to avoid conflict within the HR organization, to arrange for an anonymous telephone call between the employees and a VP counsel for the company, a compliance representative, and a senior compliance investigator. The understanding was that the ombuds would make all of the arrangements for the call and that the HR employees could speak to the company representatives without identifying themselves. The ombuds coordinated the call and once all participants were connected, the ombuds dropped off the call so as not to be part of a formal, but unusual, teleconference. As a result of the conversation, an investigation was begun into the leadership behavior of the VP. The investigation confirmed deficiencies in the VP's leadership and management style that were then referred to corporate HR leadership.

The VP was provided coaching by the corporate HR leadership to address his behaviors. When the ombuds followed up with employees to see how they were doing, they thanked the ombuds for the opportunity to raise this issue confidentially with the ombuds. Also, the compliance team reached out to thank the ombuds for coordinating the call and providing them a chance to speak directly with concerned employees. They said that it had made a big difference.

Ombuds Helps HR Employees Surface Abusive Treatment by a New HR Manager

The ombuds heard from at least eight different individuals over a three-week period about the turmoil in the HR department with the arrival of a new high-level HR manager. These individuals were in different roles in HR, and each described the mean, dismissive, and noncommunicative behavior of this new HR manager toward them and others. They also expressed that this new manager had selected a few favorite employees who were treated very well. This new manager also made critical changes in the department after being there only a few weeks. More specifically, with no explanation, the new manager removed long-time managers to individual contributor positions and also moved several employees, who had never had any management experience, to managerial roles.

While the ombuds worked with each individual to come up with some options for moving forward, after several weeks, it was clear that this new manager was perceived by many to be wreaking havoc. Most of the employees who had talked with the ombuds were concerned about retaliation (based on a recent situation in the department regarding someone who had challenged the new HR manager), but after learning that a number of people had come forward, seven of the eight employees gave the ombuds permission to bring the issue to the head of HR and the head of employee and labor relations.

The two HR leaders listened to the ombuds' perspective and indicated that they were somewhat surprised by what they were hearing. They had noted the new leader had a different style and that it was this change that may have been causing some of the trouble. They also indicated that each of them had an extremely heavy workload and not enough time to tackle the issue alone. They did decide, however, to hire an outside consultant to interview the whole staff and issue a report.

This report found widespread discontent among the staff since the arrival of the new leader and included suggested practical next steps for the new HR manager and the entire department to take to improve the situation. The new manager was ultimately asked to leave the organization.

When a Supervisor and HR Are Part of the Problem

A mid-level manager came to the ombuds with concerns about how she was being treated by both her direct supervisor and her local HR representative. She felt that both were undermining her and not supporting her as she attempted to correct employee behaviors and improve the morale and production of the team she supervised. She felt very unsafe raising her concerns to anyone within the formal structure and reached out to the ombuds so she could have confidential conversations there. She had repeated conversations with the ombuds regarding options and strategies.

Conversations with this manager continued over the course of approximately three months, after which time she had built up enough confidence and trust to reach out to her VP of HR with the assistance of the ombuds. As a result, a personal visit was made to her supervisor by the VP of HR, and changes were made in the HR department that addressed the concerns of the manager, as well as similar concerns of other employees that had surfaced through discussions with the ombuds.

WORKING COOPERATIVELY WITH FORMAL CHANNELS

Ombuds Arranges for an Anonymous Call to a Formal Channel at the Request of an HR Team to Address the Conduct of their HR Vice President

A few employees on a regional HR team had been talking among themselves about the arrogant, dismissive, and disorganized behavior of their HR VP, which they thought indicated a lack of accountability. The HR team had more than twenty people; some of them worked in the same office as the HR VP, others worked in offices in different states. The employees working in the same office as the VP, in particular, were able to observe these troubling behaviors by the VP, including the extreme favoritism he showed to certain individuals.

With frustration mounting and many of the employees finding it increasingly difficult to focus on their jobs, three employees from this HR team contacted the ombuds to discuss their concerns confidentially because they greatly feared retribution from the VP if he were to learn that they had spoken up about him. They also said that they did not trust any of the other resources in the organization to address their concerns. In their conversation with the ombuds, they said that they were looking to find a way to raise their concerns anonymously. After listening to the concerns expressed and understanding what the employees had already attempted to do to resolve the problem, the ombuds discussed various options with them.

The option selected by the employees was for the ombuds to contact an ethics and compliance representative, in order to avoid conflict within the HR organization, to arrange for an anonymous telephone call between the employees and a VP counsel for the company, a compliance representative, and a senior compliance investigator. The understanding was that the ombuds would make all of the arrangements for the call and that the HR employees could speak to the company representatives without identifying themselves. The ombuds coordinated the call and once all participants were connected, the ombuds dropped off the call so as not to be part of a formal, but unusual, teleconference. As a result of the conversation, an investigation was begun into the leadership behavior of the VP. The investigation confirmed deficiencies in the VP's leadership and management style that were then referred to corporate HR leadership.

The VP was provided coaching by the corporate HR leadership to address his behaviors. When the ombuds followed up with employees to see how they were doing, they thanked the ombuds for the opportunity to raise this issue confidentially with the ombuds. Also, the compliance team reached out to thank the ombuds for coordinating the call and providing them a chance to speak directly with concerned employees. They said that it had made a big difference.

Compliance Issue Outside of the United States

An employee shared with the ombuds that he had been asked by his manager to do something wrong. Specifically, his manager had requested that employees on his team surreptitiously gather information about customers, in violation of the company's corporate policy. The company is global, and the manager explained that this was a very common practice locally and that employees should not worry about the corporate policy. The employee explained to the ombuds that he did not want to hurt his relationship with his manager by reporting the misconduct, particularly because he was up for a promotion. So, the employee had gone ahead and gathered the information, as requested.

After several months went by, the employee learned that a different employee on his team had received the promotion instead of him. The employee was furious and reached out to the ombuds office for guidance. He said he had decided that he was going to report his manager for the earlier inappropriate conduct, but he was also concerned that he would be in trouble too because he had done as his manager had requested.

The ombuds listened to the background, clarified the issues, and reviewed the information presented. She discussed the pros and cons of possible next steps with the employee. The ombuds advised the employee that, pursuant to company policy, he had a duty to report his manager's request when it was first made and that the company's global corporate policies apply irrespective of any local custom to the contrary. The ombuds encouraged the employee to report the issue to a formal channel now and provided him with several ways in which to do so. He could bring the issue to his second-level manager or HR and explain his reluctance to come forward earlier due to his manager's advice that the corporate policy did not apply and his fear of retaliation. He was also provided with other options by which he could report the issue anonymously either through the company's compliance hotline or the compliance website.

The ombuds stressed the importance of honesty in the event that the employee was interviewed as part of a formal investigation. Failure to provide truthful responses to questions asked during the investigation would be grounds for disciplinary action against him, up to and including termination. The ombuds candidly told the employee that it was likely that he would be disciplined in connection with the inappropriate gathering of information but if he reported the issue that might be considered a mitigating factor.

The employee left the meeting saying that he intended to report the concern through the compliance hotline right away.

The Ombuds Helps the HR and Equal Employment Opportunity Offices Cooperate with Each Other

A new ombuds was hired by an organization ostensibly to offer an additional, independent, informal, confidential, and expedient channel for employees to try to resolve personal workplace issues. Once in place, however, the ombuds realized that there was more context than that: the organization was plagued by a lack of transparency and trust between the equal employment opportunity (EEO) and HR offices, both of which were relatively independent, with strong charters and headstrong leaders. Understanding that their inability to cooperate with each other was neither good for people with HR or EEO issues nor for the organization, the ombuds saw this as a systemic issue that might benefit from ombuds involvement.

The ombuds first spoke with the HR director (and expended some of his initial good will there) about his proposed plan to help establish better relations between the two formal channels by serving a "bridging" role between them. He then did the same with the EEO director (expending more of his initial good will). In each of these meetings, the ombuds tried to emphasize that his goal was to help create more transparency and trust between the offices.

With tacit permission from each of these offices, the ombuds then looked for ways to help them cooperate with each other. One of the first projects he took on was to work to directly assist the EEO office's intervention in a long-standing systemic problem that was also of interest to the HR office. The ombuds' position as a "new kid on the block" with organizational conflict resolution and interpersonal skills resulted in helping to reframe and resolve certain issues that otherwise would have continued to plague the organization.

Of course, none of this would have been possible without the cooperation and active participation of both the HR director and the EEO director. Although the mandates of their responsibilities differ, when they and the ombuds understand that part of their missions is to help improve the organization, they can have a positive impact. In this example the EEO director became so trusted because of transparency with management around best practices to avoid disruption of productivity from EEO complaints that she was routinely invited to consult with senior management and also became a positive influence for change.

Policy Interpretation

A male employee contacted the ombuds because he had begun a romantic relationship with a coworker. He found his way to the ombuds after first starting to explore the issue with HR. The HR representative, however, was sensitive to how uncomfortable he was discussing the issue with HR and offered him the option of contacting the ombuds first, explaining that he could discuss the matter there in complete privacy.

To complicate matters, the employee's spouse also worked for the organization. The employee regarded his relationship with the coworker as private, but he also understood that it could have an effect on his professional life. He was unsure of what he was required to disclose to the company and what he could keep private. He was also nervous about what the organization would do once he disclosed the relationship. He was particularly concerned that the organization would reveal the relationship to his spouse.

The ombuds was able to leverage his experience in the organization and expertise with policy to provide the employee with guidance on the aspects of the relationship with the coworker that would be relevant to the organization. For example, it was important to ensure that the relationship did not present any conflict of interest. Because the coworker was not in his reporting line and did not work with him on a regular basis, the ombuds advised that it did not appear to be a conflict of interest that would require reporting.

The ombuds explained that he would be able to obtain a definitive answer confidentially from the organization if he desired to do so. This could be accomplished anonymously through the compliance hotline or a compliance interactive online tool. Finally, in view of the fact that he was married and embarking on a new romantic relationship, the ombuds provided him with the contact information for the Employee Assistance Program where he could obtain counseling and guidance on the impact of this on his personal and family life.

Surfacing an Issue Without Becoming a Whistleblower

An executive assistant (EA) to a senior executive called the ombuds to discuss their concern which they said could not be taken forward to management through *any* formal channel. In particular, the EA believed that, at a time of corporate restructuring to save costs, the senior executive with whom the EA worked was making fraudulent claims on his monthly expense claims.

When asked how the EA was aware of the alleged fraudulent claims, the EA said they prepared the monthly claims from the information provided by the senior executive but knew that some of the information was false. The EA believed that this conduct was not appropriate and that it should be reported. Yet, since only the senior executive and the EA were privy to what was on the monthly expense claims before they were submitted, the EA was also extremely afraid of what would happen personally to them if they were identified as the whistleblower in any investigation into the expense reports.

The ombuds and the EA discussed a number of options to surface the EA's concerns, including an option in which the ombuds could ask the internal audit team to carry out a review of the monthly expense claims of all the other people at the same level as the senior executive throughout the business and without identifying who had brought this issue to the ombuds, the specifics of the false claims, or the identity of any particular senior executive about whom there was concern. The EA gave permission to the ombuds to take the matter forward on this basis.

The ombuds alerted the internal audit team to this concern and made the request for the internal audit, and the internal audit team audited the expense reports of all the senior executives at that level. With all the senior executives at that level included, no one could have thought that any particular person was being targeted.

The results of the audit demonstrated that the senior executive was not alone in submitting fraudulent expense reports; others had done so as well. All of those senior executives were fired. The EA who brought the issue to the attention of the ombuds was never identified and subsequently was assigned to work for the replacement of the senior executive for whom the EA previously worked.

Downgrading of New Role

A female employee contacted the ombuds office with concerns about a new role she had applied for. She was pleased that she had been offered the role, but an aspect of the offer didn't seem right to her. In the job posting to which she had applied, it said that the role was at the level of senior manager. Since she was currently a manager, the senior manager job would be a promotion for her. However, when she was offered the role, it was at a manager level. That meant no promotion and no salary increase.

She found it odd that the organization would post the role at a senior manager level and then decide to offer it to her at a lower level. She wanted to take the role, but also wanted to be treated fairly. She challenged the decision to offer her the role at a manager level to both the hiring manager and to the HR representative who had been involved in the process. They both maintained that the actions they had taken with the job offer were appropriate. They encouraged her to take the role but were inflexible about hiring her at the senior manager level.

The ombuds helped her understand that what had happened was not consistent with the organization's practices and that roles needed to be offered in the manner set forth in the details of the job posting. The ombuds encouraged her to reach out to a senior member of the organization's HR department to have her situation reviewed. Although she was nervous about doing so, she decided to do it.

A week later, she called the ombuds with good news: her meeting with the HR leader had gone very well. The leader immediately acknowledged that what had happened to her was not fair or consistent with the organization's policies and practices. As a result, she was offered the role at the senior manager level, which she happily accepted.

An Ombuds' Careful Listening Helps Spot Possible Financial Abuse

A woman came to the ombuds for help on how to deal with what she perceived as discrimination in her work group. The visitor felt that women with children were being given more flexibility in work schedules than women without children. As a single woman, the visitor wanted to have flexibility for vacation time or flex hours either to go to school herself or take care of relatives. She claimed her supervisor always considered her requests behind those of women with children and their associated needs.

During the discussion with the ombuds, the visitor mentioned some financial behaviors she attributed to her supervisor and coworkers that, if true, could be breaches of the financial practices of the company. The ombuds tucked that information away and focused on coaching the visitor on how to advocate for her own needs.

At the end of the conversation with the visitor, the ombuds asked if she could ask a bit more about the financial behaviors the visitor had mentioned earlier. The visitor agreed to share more details with the ombuds and then described expensive meals, travel, and unapproved use of car services. The visitor later gave the ombuds permission to alert the internal audit group of these potential abuses.

The ombuds did alert internal audit to the possibility of financial abuse in this unit without disclosing the identity of the visitor, and an investigation was initiated. After several weeks, the ombuds learned that the investigation had uncovered vast fraud and abuse. Three people were terminated in the unit and disciplinary action was taken against others. The head of internal audit expressed great appreciation to the ombuds for bringing this issue to their attention. The discrimination issue first raised by the visitor became moot in light of the terminations and other disciplinary action that was taken.

Prompt Action by Ombuds Assists Leadership on Control Issues

A visitor scheduled an appointment with the ombuds to discuss a stressful work environment that focused on results over quality. At the start of the meeting, the visitor communicated that this was their last day with the organization.

The visitor presented the ombuds with a lengthy document detailing instances where the work climate had resulted in policy breaches over the past few months. As the ombuds questioned the visitor about each item, the ombuds learned that the visitor and colleagues had spoken up as each issue occurred and line management had, in fact, addressed them. However, the ombuds also learned that employees now felt pressured about continuing to speak up and, in some cases, were told specifically not to discuss anything with HR or the ombuds.

When the ombuds asked if there were any open issues that hadn't been reported, the visitor pointed to the final item and said, "That's why I'm here. I wanted to put it on the record, confidentially, before I leave today," and then proceeded to communicate a recent breach of controls that, if left unchecked, could take the organization out of regulatory compliance.

As the ombuds reiterated that speaking with this office did not constitute "putting it on the record," the visitor began to back off, stating that they'd done their job and weren't willing to do more. Then the visitor stood up to leave, and the ombuds quickly asked, "What if I were able to arrange for the head of compliance to speak with you *right now*, assuming they are available? Would you be willing to repeat what you've just told me?" The visitor was hesitant and didn't fully believe that would happen but gave permission for the ombuds to try. The ombuds then immediately got the head of compliance on the phone to speak with the visitor and stepped out of earshot, so as not to be part of the notice chain as the visitor made their report.

A few days later, the ombuds learned that the internal audit team had been engaged to investigate the visitor's allegation. They identified a control issue, as described by the visitor. The head of the business was notified, and appropriate controls were restored, just days before a regulatory audit began. New processes were put in place to shore up both the control environment and the climate in this group, freeing individuals to continue to speak up before any issue became significant.

NAVIGATING THE BUREAUCRACY

Helping an International Graduate Student Navigate the Bureaucracy

An international graduate student came to the ombuds after he was moved to a new residence hall following an incident in which he had been involved at his previous residence hall. The student's move to his new room occurred shortly after another student who had been occupying that room moved out. The student who moved out left the bathroom and kitchen in a filthy condition, as documented through video evidence shared with the ombuds. Both the graduate student visitor and his mother, who also contacted the ombuds from abroad, shared their concerns about the condition of the room and the lack of response by the university.

In essence, the graduate student visitor had been unsuccessful in getting the residence life office to provide the typical room cleaning that occurs when there is a transition in residents. Unlike most room transitions, however, this transition had occurred in the middle of a semester. The assumption by residence life seemed to have been that the outgoing student would have cleaned the room before his departure and that there would be no need for the type of cleaning that was usually done at the end of the semester. The visitor and his mother were very frustrated at the lack of response to the student's requests.

The ombuds discussed with the visitor options to address this issue, including contacting the director of facilities, who oversees custodial services, to ask if they could help resolve the issue. The ombuds was familiar with the director of facilities and thought the director would likely respond positively even though the student had not been able to get a response by contacting the residence life channels. The visitor had been unaware of the role of the facilities office. At the request of the visitor, the ombuds sent an email to both the director of residence life and the director of facilities requesting assistance for the student. Once the director of facilities heard of the issue, he directed his crew to provide the desired cleaning, for which the student expressed his appreciation to the ombuds.

The Ombuds Helps a Foreign Post-Doctoral Fellow Accused of Plagiarism

A post-doctoral fellow came to see that ombuds in a panic because he was being accused of plagiarism. He was African and had published academic papers in his home country and in another country before coming to the United States. He said his current professor had asked him to write a paper on a certain topic and then accused him of using others' work without citing them. Further, he was told that if he was found guilty, some or all of his past publications could be rescinded very publicly.

When the ombuds asked if he had spoken to anyone else about this, the fellow said he had only spoken with his wife. He said that this situation was so humiliating to him that he didn't want anyone else to know about it. When he heard the ombuds kept information confidential, it was the only option he would consider other than hiring an attorney to defend himself.

The ombuds asked him whether he had been formally accused or not and he did not know the answer to that question. Part of his panic had to do with not understanding what was happening and being new to the United States. He didn't know where to turn.

The ombuds asked him if he had spoken with his supervisor and his department chair. He said he had spoken with both, and they were awaiting the outcome of an investigation so they could not tell him anything. The ombuds also asked if he had spoken with anyone in the Academic Dishonesty Office, and he said he had not heard of that office.

The ombuds gave him the contact information and the location on the campus for that office. The ombuds also advised that the office's website outlined the investigation process. Just being able to read about the process provided some relief for the fellow.

A few weeks later, the fellow called the ombuds to say thanks for the help and to report that he had been cleared of any accusations in the investigation. He reiterated that it was such a huge help to him to have an office where he could talk confidentially about something that was so embarrassing without having to worry about the information being shared with others. Before he found the ombuds, he said that he thought his only option was to hire an attorney, but he did not have the money to do that. Had he done so, however, the university would have had to defend the lawsuit. As it was, he was exonerated, and his career was not ruined.

Ombuds Provides Resources to a Foreign Student to Resolve Problems with his Living Arrangements

During the COVID-19 pandemic, the ombuds received a voice message from a first-year international student residing with his extended family in a poor Eastern European country. His parents lived in a rural community two hours away, and he had been living for the past two years with an aunt and his father's parents. The student explained to the ombuds that he was feeling emotionally drained by family members who he perceived had some mental health issues. In the course of the conversation with the student, the ombuds learned that the student had limited space in a small apartment and that the aunt and grandparents were yelling constantly at him and his nine-year-old cousin. When the student tried to inquire about the anger, he was told that if he didn't stop the questioning, the aunt and grandparents would kill themselves.

The student had tried to schedule an appointment with the college's counselling and mental health office (CMHO). He was directed to the ombuds office, however, because the CMHO was restricted from offering any services outside of the state where the college is located.

The ombuds met with the student by online video conferencing and helped him think through and role-play a discussion with his elder relatives. The ombuds also located an on-call telehealth service that the student could use as a resource and provided the student with white papers on attentive listening and difficult conversations that the student could read and use as self-help. The ombuds stayed connected by setting up follow-up conference calls over the next few weeks.

With access to these additional resources, the student was able to negotiate removing himself from his relatives' apartment and moved back to his parents' home and continued to participate in remote virtual classes from there for the remainder of the semester.

Ombuds Helps with Bureaucratic Obstacles

The wife of a former 29-year employee who had retired due to a job injury called the ombuds because they had not received his retirement check for the months of November and December, even though they usually received his check every month "like clockwork." She said that she called the ombuds office to see if it could help after making numerous frustrating calls and leaving messages at local and national organization levels, during which she reported being given the run around.

After hearing what she had tried to do to address the issue and understanding the importance of two months' pay to a retiree (especially with Christmas approaching), the ombuds asked for and was given permission to make inquiries to the head of retiree benefits. Although he was unavailable when the ombuds called, the ombuds was able to speak with a retiree analyst who explained the process for getting the checks reinstated. With a couple of additional phone calls and emails, the ombuds was able to get assurance that the December check would be forthcoming.

The November check was different, however, because the organization claimed that the retiree had not responded in a timely manner to paperwork that had been sent, so that the only avenue was an administrative appeal in the organization to an overseeing board. The board was scheduled to meet that week but then not again until the first quarter of the next year, so a regular appeal would be considered then. The ombuds explored whether the paperwork could be submitted by fax and considered by the board at the meeting scheduled for that week and learned shortly thereafter that it would be permitted.

The paperwork was faxed and approved by the board, and the checks were issued before Christmas.

RISK MANAGEMENT

Surfacing an Issue and Resolving a Dispute that Easily Could Have Resulted in Expensive Litigation and Reputational Damage

The visitor was a long-time university employee whose daughter had just entered her freshman year at the same institution and had been going through new student orientation. During the daughter's first weekend on campus, she attended a fraternity party with a group of friends. While there, she drifted away from her friends, and after a few drinks of "punch" found herself dizzy, drunk, and surrounded by a group of boys. Two of them forced her into a bedroom and sexually assaulted her. After a few minutes, because the boys were more intoxicated than she, she was able to get out of the room and run back to her dorm. She was deeply embarrassed and didn't want to tell her friends what happened. The next day she decided to call her parents and tell them what happened. Not wanting to risk ever running into the boys again, or to have this first-week episode haunt her for four years on campus, she told her parents she wanted to transfer to her second-choice school. Her parents promptly got her medical treatment to ensure that she was physically alright and scheduled her an appointment with her therapist to discuss the incident.

Ordinarily, the office of student life services posts monitors at all on-campus parties (which must be registered in advance) to ensure that there is no underage drinking and that party participants behave appropriately and safely. The placement of these monitors has resulted in a significant reduction of incidents of injuries, bad behavior, and other problems that had historically occurred at fraternity parties. In this instance, although the party had been registered, no monitors had been assigned due to a scheduling error on the part of the student life office.

When the parent came to the ombuds office, he was aware of the university policy requiring preregistration of these events and the assignment of monitors. In the case of the party his daughter attended, he also had learned that, although the party had been registered, no monitors had been assigned as was required. He stated that he understood and respected his daughter's decision to transfer and stated that he did not want to make trouble for the university, even though he also stated that the incident very likely could have been prevented. The main concern that brought him to the ombuds was that if his daughter were to transfer to another college, she would lose the tuition benefit he was entitled to receive from the university (full tuition for four years, but not transferrable to any other institution). He wanted the university to compensate him to the extent of the tuition for four years at the new school. Otherwise, he said, the only other option would be for his daughter and him to bring suit against the university. With the father's permission, the ombuds contacted the risk management office for a consultation.

Because the girl's father met first with the ombuds, the ombuds was able to work with risk management to quickly resolve the issue, with the university agreeing to cover the tuition costs at the new school. Because of this resolution, both the family and the university avoided litigation that could have been costly to both sides, but which posed a real risk of loss to the university in light of the absence of a monitor at the event. In addition, potential reputation-damaging publicity was avoided on both sides and good relations with a long-standing employee preserved.

Safety

Over the course of several consults, a visitor shared with the ombuds their concerns over safety issues related to a remote campus building used for both research and summer camps. The visitor had tried to raise the concerns directly with their supervisor on several occasions, but the issues remained unresolved.

By the time the visitor brought these concerns to the ombuds, the summer camp season was fast approaching. After discussing various options to address these concerns, the visitor gave the ombuds permission to go to the provost and make an anonymous report, knowing the supervisor would likely connect the dots.

When the ombuds made this report to the provost, the provost and the ombuds were then quickly able to work together to identify ways to address the situation as discreetly as possible. The option selected by the provost was to have the building inspected. The subsequent inspection revealed that the building was not up to code. As a result, the university canceled the impending summer camp and made the necessary repairs. The ombuds' prompt and effective working with first the visitor and then the provost thus helped the university eliminate a risk that could have resulted in injuries and been both expensive and damaging to the university's reputation. By having an inspection of the building before taking any action, the ombuds and the provost were able to help protect the identity of the visitor who had raised the issue.

Not Wanting to Be a Whistleblower: Risk Management and Anonymous Reporting

A technician in a biology lab that was studying the way that COVID-19 is transmitted between people came to the ombuds to discuss whether to report concerns about a breach of protocol in the lab; and if so, how to do so without hurting his job or academic career.

The technician told the ombuds that a principal investigator from a different lab in the same building had on several occasions asked housekeeping staff, after regular business hours, to provide her with entry into the COVID-19 lab without the knowledge of the principal investigator in charge of the COVID-19 lab. He had learned this from one of the housekeeping staff members who confided in him when they happened to cross paths during the day. The housekeeping staff member stated that she did not feel she was in a position to question the faculty member who she knew worked in the same building, and she assumed it was on the up and up.

The visitor was quite concerned about this breach of protocol and the safety issues it raised. The visitor indicated, however, that the "intruding" investigator was also a tenured professor and that he was a student in one of her classes, which was a required course for his graduate program. Further, he was concerned about the risk of exposing housekeeping staff to negative repercussions. He said he wanted to discuss with the ombuds how to anonymously report this activity without being discovered to have been the whistleblower.

The ombuds and the visitor discussed the nature of the protocol breach in university-required lab operating procedures, and the visitor came to the conclusion that the intruding principal investigator had clearly violated stated safety practices and put community members and the university itself at great risk. He also stated that if the investigator's behavior led to adverse consequences, he would never forgive himself for not speaking up.

The ombuds explained that the student had at least two choices for reporting this behavior. One would be to reach out to the university's risk management and mitigation team to report what he knew. However, it would be difficult to do so anonymously because they were not set up to receive anonymous reports. Alternatively, he could call the university's safety compliance hotline to report anonymously. Because of his fear of exposure as the whistleblower, the visitor was inclined to go with the anonymous hotline. He had a concern, however, that this still could result in the housekeeping staff member suffering repercussions.

The ombuds inquired whether there might be a way to cast a wider net, such that it would not be evident that this particular lab was the target and so that it would appear that the report could have come from a variety of different directions. They discussed whether, for example, the visitor thought he may be able to anonymously identify the building at issue and state that he had observed serious safety violations. He could then recommend that the safety compliance team conduct a building-wide safety audit, which should include a review of video cameras that run continuously in the building during the window of time of the violations. This approach would serve to protect both the visitor and the housekeeping staff member and lead the safety team to observe the principal investigator entering the lab of concern. The visitor stated that he felt that this approach would enable an effective report to be filed and at the same time protect the individuals involved in the reporting, and he stated that he would move forward with that approach.

The visitor never returned to the ombuds office to report any outcomes or changes, but there were no further reports of incidents caused by safety violations in the labs of that building.

GAPS IN COMMUNICATIONS, POLICIES, AND EXPECTATIONS

Help to All in Times of Organizational Change

Broadly speaking, the ombuds can be particularly useful during times of significant organizational change and help everyone (leaders on down) work through how to deal with significant change and transformation. The ombuds office's goal is to help everyone address areas of confusion and frustration, bridge communication gaps, foster collaboration, increase transparency, and, with a view of early resolution, share micro and macro instances where outcomes do not match the intended goal.

When significant change occurred in one organization, it soon became clear that a number of new programs and initiatives had interrelated contingencies and overlapping responsibilities. As a result, there was a lot of confusion about how it was all supposed to work, and even those implementing it were trying to figure it all out. It was at this point that the program managers collectively approached the ombuds for assistance. They admitted that they knew that their task to "build the plane while flying" was extraordinarily difficult, but they sought out the ombuds because they also had a deep appreciation for the help the ombuds could provide.

The program managers acknowledged the challenges they were facing and wanted to work proactively with the ombuds to help them manage the process to make it work better for employees and the organization. With assistance from the ombuds, they were able to implement a constant cycle of communication to employees in the organization. They also encouraged and allowed the ombuds to serve as an intermediary between leadership and employees affected by changes in processes and the resulting decisions and actions.

A Supervisor Seeks the Ombuds' Assistance with New Production Rules

A supervisor sought assistance from the ombuds after senior management introduced new production rules that contradicted the process and guidance given by subject matter experts in his group. The new rules led to confusion about the work process and were causing concern and disruption in the supervisor's group.

The ombuds discussed various options with the supervisor and also engaged in conflict coaching to help the supervisor better address the concerns both with employees in the group and with senior management. The supervisor decided that the option that would be the most helpful was to give employees in his group an opportunity to share their concerns anonymously with the ombuds, with the understanding that the ombuds would then share those concerns, without attribution, with senior management. Many of the employees participated in this process and were reassured that their perspectives, but not their identities, would be shared.

Once the ombuds had heard from most employees in the supervisor's group, the ombuds provided senior management (and the supervisor) with a broad range of comments from the supervisor's work group, including compliments, concerns, and recommendations. In other words, this feedback included what the work group was doing well and should continue, areas of improvement, and most importantly, anonymous feedback from employees about what changes would be most valued and make the biggest impact.

This feedback led to an interactive process among senior management, the supervisor, and his work group aimed at improving the work process and clarifying the group's mission, strategic goals, and internal processes. Overall, this process helped improve trust among the work group. Whereas the employees were previously concerned about providing critical feedback, they saw improvements to how the supervisor responded. Specifically, and with some coaching from the ombuds, the supervisor and senior leaders were genuinely thankful for the feedback and responded by developing and executing an action plan. This in turn made the employees more comfortable about speaking up in the future.

How Does a New Senior Manager Deal with a Lack of Support?

A senior manager scheduled a meeting after a lengthy phone conversation about how the ombuds office conducts its business (confidentiality, neutrality, informality, and independence). When he then met with the ombuds, he disclosed that he was new to the organization and had been hired after a national search. He said that both during the search process and after accepting the position, he had had many discussions with the people above him about how his unit had not been performing well for many years. He said that he was told that his predecessor had been in the position for many years and was popular with employees but regarded as entrenched and resistant to change. The new manager believed he had been given a "mandate" to make systemic changes within his unit.

After he accepted the job and began work, the manager experienced a great deal of resistance (covertly and overtly) from employees at various levels in the organization. Not fully appreciating the culture of the unit or the broader organization, he admitted to having made some tactical missteps that compromised his legitimacy and the respect of the employees. He felt unsupported by those above him and undermined by those below. Though given a mandate to make significant systemic changes because of the unit's history of poor performance, that mandate was never articulated to the employees in the unit. Rather, senior officials in public speeches praised the "wonderful work" that previously had been done by his unit. This created a perception that the changes were unnecessary. As a result, his initiatives were perceived by the employees in his unit as being motivated by his need to "reinvent the wheel" and to put his stamp on the unit. He felt very isolated and was seriously considering resigning. He said that he felt he could not discuss these issues either with those to whom he reported or those who reported to him (directly or indirectly).

During the course of many meetings to discuss options, strategy, and implementation, he and the ombuds also addressed the organization's culture, how to develop "buy-in," rebuild his reputation, and nudge those to whom he reported. While there continue to be challenges with his position, the manager did not resign and has reported that his situation has improved immensely.

Coaching Helps Visitors Develop Bystander Training Initiative

Leaders (almost all scientists) from an established women's resource group wanted to address common issues they were facing in the workplace and were feeling very discouraged by what they felt was unconscious bias in hiring and promotion in their fields. Representatives of the group approached the ombuds looking for suggestions and guidance about how they could start a conversation in the organization to begin a dialogue on these issues.

The ombuds provided the visitors with references to articles, analytical models, and other materials on topics such as microaggressions, psychological safety, dignity in the workplace, and ways to engage witnesses and bystanders to take action. The ombuds also proved guidance and other tools on how the visitors could begin creating awareness of the importance of speaking up about issues people observed and unconscious bias in the workplace. The leader of the women's resource group was then able to use the articles and tools that the ombuds had provided to create traction around these concepts in various units in the organization.

One result of her efforts was an initiative that led to the formation of an employee resource group to raise awareness of the importance of active bystanders speaking up. This "bystander" employee resource group then took on the task of providing training to employees about how to combat microaggressions and unconscious bias by speaking up when they observed such behavior.

While neither the women's resource group nor the bystander training group operated under the direction of the ombuds, the ombuds had provided the tools and guidance that was a catalyst that empowered these groups to make a constructive and positive impact on training employees on these critical issues.

The Ombuds Helps an Employee Raise Issues About Inappropriate Workplace Activity

An employee contacted the ombuds after an inappropriate, offensive, and discriminatory video was shown in the workplace. The employee did not feel that the situation had been properly addressed and wanted to have a confidential conversation to learn what options were available to pursue the matter further.

The ombuds and the employee discussed several options and the pros and cons of each. The ombuds also provided contact information for equal employment opportunity personnel in case the employee wanted to file a formal complaint. The employee, however, expressed concern about potential backlash for raising this matter, being labeled as a "complainer," and how addressing it could potentially disrupt what had been a great team and make things incredibly uncomfortable. The employee was clearly caught in the middle between wanting to raise this issue and fearing the repercussions from possibly doing so.

It was only in the course of several such confidential conversations that the employee decided to address the matter directly with the first-line supervisor. These conversations revolved around the ombuds helping the employee think about if they wanted to raise it, with whom, and the best way to frame the matter. The employee also suspected that the supervisor knew about the situation and wasn't doing anything about it, which if true, called into question the supervisor's integrity.

When the employee ultimately decided to raise the issue with her supervisor, she learned that the supervisor was completely unaware of what had happened, and moreover was shocked and appalled once it was reviewed. The employee was very pleased to have talked to the ombuds, which helped her have the courage to raise the issue in the most productive way. She reported back the ombuds that the supervisor was immediately responsive to the matter, that the video was taken down immediately, and although the supervisor said he couldn't divulge personnel matters, he also said "appropriate measures were taken to ensure this never happens again."

The Ombuds Works with HR to Resolve the Visitor's Issue on a Systemic Basis

An employee came to the ombuds saying that they were at least a year overdue for a step increase in compensation. The visitor did not feel comfortable going to HR himself because he thought the supervisor would be upset when he found out and possibly retaliate against the visitor. The employee had already asked the supervisor about the promotion several times but was always brushed aside.

The ombuds discussed various options to address this issue with the visitor, but because the ombuds did not have permission to use the visitor's name, the available options were limited. The visitor, however, did give the ombuds permission to go to HR with this issue if she could keep his identity anonymous.

The ombuds went to HR and asked for details regarding how step increases were supposed to happen, who played what role in making the increases happen, and what could be done if a supervisor did not take care of a proper increase in a timely manner. Eventually, the ombuds asked HR to run a report of all employees who were overdue for a step increase. When the report was run, it identified the visitor along with several others. HR followed up on these delinquencies, and the visitor (and presumably the others) got their step promotion.

FACILITATION/MEDIATION

Facilitated Conversation with Ombuds Addresses Abusive Colleague's Behavior

Almost all residents in a highly respected training program complained about a second-year resident to faculty clinicians, including the program chair of residency training. The complaints centered on abrasive peer interactions, shirking of clinical duties, prioritizing moonlighting over clinic responsibilities, and speculation that the resident was more abrasive toward women and minority peers. The resident was among the least favorite among attending clinicians and was considered arrogant, though his clinical performance was considered slightly above average. The residency program chair had spoken to the resident on several occasions about these perceptions but had not issued discipline as there was no evidence of clinical or academic deficiencies. The chief resident, who had also tried to coach the resident, informed the program chair that the second-year resident's negative behavior had become more frequent and that it was time for the program chair to drop the resident from the program. The other residents felt that the program leadership was demonstrating a lack of care for their well-being and a lack of follow through about expectations of professional standards. Several residents indicated that they were considering submitting a formal complaint about discrimination to the Equal Employment Opportunity office; others were circulating a draft of a letter to the ACGME (Accreditation Council for Graduate Medical Education).

The program chair contacted the ombuds to seek assistance, understanding the informal, confidential, and neutral posture of the office. Several options were discussed, including more aggressive intervention by the chair, referral to a hospital-wide review committee, and a facilitative intervention process organized by the ombuds. The chair wished to pursue the voluntary facilitative process before attempting more formal options and a plan was agreed upon whereby the chair would ask if the chief resident and the second-year resident would be willing to talk individually with the ombuds about the situation. Both were willing to participate.

The second-year resident was adamant that he believed there was no basis for the complaints but was willing to participate in a dialogue with the other residents if they thought it would help. The ombuds met with the chief resident and asked for background and the chief resident agreed to arrange several small meetings between the ombuds and the other residents. The residents agreed to abstain from submitting any formal complaints or letters until the facilitative process had an opportunity to proceed. After hearing from the residents and the second-year resident, the ombuds began serving as a go between, shuttling preliminary requests to and from the second-year resident, the program chair, and the other residents. Ultimately, the ombuds facilitated a group meeting that included the program chair, chief resident, and all other residents to discuss "ground rules" for behavior and a three-step protocol on how to respond to violation of those ground rules by any member. The entire process took place over six to eight weeks.

The ombuds was available to the residents for the next eighteen months and was contacted a few times by various residents for updates and conversations about what was better and what remained difficult. Ultimately, no complaints were filed, and all the residents graduated on schedule.

An Opportunity to Be Heard and an Apology

An internal formal reporting program referred the visitor to the ombuds. Prior to talking to the ombuds office, the visitor had decided to file a complaint against a manager for retaliation. The visitor perceived that they had been retaliated against by their manager when the manager dismissed written recommendations submitted by the visitor for their program and because of the way the manager handled the visitor's mid-year performance review in the days following the visitor's submission of the recommendations. The visitor had submitted a letter of resignation because of the conflict with the manager and had requested the help of the formal channel to facilitate an exit interview with their manager, but the manager had declined to meet with the visitor because of the resignation. The formal reporting office advised the visitor that the alleged retaliatory behavior could be investigated but that the visitor might consider consulting with the ombuds to see if a facilitated discussion with the manager could be arranged.

The visitor contacted the ombuds and shared this story. The visitor also revealed being upset about having to pay back relocation expenses to the organization because the visitor would not have worked for the organization for twelve months (after which no reimbursement would be required), being just weeks away from the twelve-month mark. The visitor specifically wanted to request an exemption for the relocation reimbursement expenses and to have a conversation to provide feedback to the manager. The ombuds informed the visitor that informal facilitation by the ombuds of that conversation was an option if the manager agreed.

Because the end date of employment for the visitor was looming, prompt action was important. The visitor requested the manager contact the ombuds, which the manager did. During this conversation with the manager, the ombuds spoke about the visitor's request for an informal facilitated discussion and the voluntary nature of the process. The manager shared with the ombuds the manager's perspective about the visitor and agreed to the ombuds' assistance with a neutral facilitation via telephone. The visitor also agreed to a telephone conference call with the manager and the ombuds prior to the final date of employment. The manager understood that the employee wanted to be heard. A telephone-based facilitation was scheduled.

After the ombuds reminded the parties of the ombuds' neutral role as facilitator and of the ground rules for the facilitation, the visitor expressed their frustration with the way the performance review had been conducted and concerns around psychological safety and lack of accountability within the department. During the discussion, the manager responded with an apology and agreed to consider the visitor's feedback to make the performance feedback process feel safer psychologically. The visitor also inquired about having to pay back the full amount of relocation expenses. The manager indicated that he had already appealed to higher-level management for a relocation expenses reimbursement exemption; however, the manager also agreed to a new request to limit any reimbursement ultimately required to only a partial reimbursement of relocation expenses based on a pro-rated model.

The manager agreed to follow up on these matters by a specific date to provide the visitor with the answer.

The visitor undoubtedly appreciated the opportunity to be heard. The manager expressed appreciation for the work the employee had done on a project and tried, as expressed in the facilitation, to help eliminate, or at least reduce, any relocation reimbursement obligation. The organization benefited from the ombuds services because the likelihood of any subsequent litigation was substantially reduced. And finally, the organization benefited by the cooperation between informal and formal channels, since the initial referral to the ombuds office was because the formal office perceived the ombuds to be relevant and useful in potentially resolving a conflict informally and without the cost and risk inherent in a formal process.

Ombuds Mediation Restores Respectful Communication

An employee came to the ombuds concerned about how one of her colleagues spoke to her. She said she liked him and respected him, but he didn't seem to respect her. She did not like the way he spoke to her in meetings.

The ombuds discussed various options with her, including conflict coaching, mediation, shuttle diplomacy, filing a grievance or Title IX complaint, or bringing it to her supervisor. The visitor did not trust the human resources department because they had violated her confidentiality in the past. She said that on a prior occasion her supervisor had been called by HR and told of her meeting with HR before she even returned to the office from the meeting. The visitor did not feel sufficiently confident to initiate a conversation with the person who she felt was disrespecting her, and she didn't want to get him in trouble since she was new to the department. She didn't think the matter rose to the importance of formal processes or telling their supervisor. She felt most comfortable with the mediation option.

The visitor invited her colleague to mediation, and he readily accepted. The ombuds, however, first met with the second visitor in order to learn his perspective on the situation. In the mediation, the colleagues readily participated in the discussion with openness and authenticity. When the initiator said she did not appreciate it when he "mansplained" to her, he immediately and genuinely apologized. By the end of the discussion, both parties were smiling and complimenting each other. As it turned out, they learned from each other that their supervisor was causing divisiveness in their workgroup.

When their time allotment was over, the ombuds asked if there were any more issues to discuss. Both parties said they had enjoyed the mediation and were looking forward to working with each other. The ombuds followed up with both of them over the next three months and they reported they were getting along fine. They also reported that they had initiated a team retreat to address the divisiveness.

Both the department and the individuals benefited from their visit to the ombuds.

HIGH IMPACT CASES/POTENTIAL LITIGATION/THREATS TO ORGANIZATIONAL REPUTATION

Extended Communications with the Ombuds Allows an Employee to Agree to Report

The ombuds received a call from a compliance officer at an unrelated but affiliated organization about possible financial misconduct by the president of that organization. The inquirer was so concerned about her identity being compromised that she made the call from a public telephone at a mall. She was the compliance officer of her organization; but it was a relatively small organization, and she was afraid that she could not successfully accuse or investigate the president of the organization without being victimized herself.

After discussing various options to surface the issue, the inquirer remained uncomfortable with her identity being disclosed and was unwilling to select any of the options suggested by the ombuds. The conversation ended with the caller remaining anonymous and with the ombuds encouraging her to call back later so that they could continue to discuss how to raise the issue. Similar conversations took place several times over the next few months, with the inquirer calling from a mall to avoid Caller ID and remain anonymous.

The inquirer also continued to be unwilling to select an option to permit the issue to be raised. At the end of each conversation, the ombuds encouraged another call from the inquirer after they each had more time for reflection. After several such calls, however, the inquirer began to appreciate the fact that significant misconduct may be involved and that it needed to be reported. As she began to trust the ombuds more and more to preserve her confidentiality (especially since no word had leaked out about her calls), she grew more comfortable with the idea of initiating an investigation.

She finally gave the ombuds permission to reveal basic information, including the identity of her organization and the nature of her concerns, to other formal channels who could conduct an investigation. With this permission, the ombuds then made the authorized disclosure, and an investigation and audit commenced. The investigation revealed a multimillion-dollar fraud that ultimately sent the organization's president to prison. Throughout all of this, the inquirer insisted on remaining anonymous, even to the ombuds.

Patience, the Promise of Confidentiality, and an Ombuds' Proactive Engagement Helps the Ombuds Surface Issues that Led to Transformative Systemic Change

A case that resulted in significant systemic change at a university began innocuously.

From an initial contact, the ombuds learned over time and from many other conversations that a department on campus had a common practice where some managers offered temporary and permanent positions to women in exchange for sex and to both men and women in exchange for money. The practice was generations old. The habits that helped sustain this behavior over time had become a part of the organizational culture in this one unit and were accepted and enabled by both managers and employees in this unit as "that's the way it is here." Most people felt nothing could be done and resistance was pointless because previous attempts to address the matter over time had been ruthlessly suppressed. The people who paid bribes or exchanged sex for their jobs needed the jobs and had a legitimate fear of losing them or of suffering some other form of retribution if they spoke up. Also, the shame of being forced to do what they did kept many quiet and feeling powerless.

Nothing about bringing an end to these practices happened quickly. It took time before other individuals in the department would speak in confidence openly and honestly with the ombuds. It took time to collect their experiences and the effect they had on individuals and the department collectively. The ombuds determined that it was necessary to express empathy and sorrow, as well as to provide assurances that something could, in fact, be done to address this situation. It took time for the ombuds to understand the history and culture of the department and the concerns and interests of the people involved. As more and more people from the department came to speak with the ombuds and strategize ways of managing the problem, they learned to trust the ombuds because he kept his word that the communications were confidential and because he spoke a language they could understand and appreciate—not a language based on different ethnic and cultural groups but, rather, a language that fostered cross-cultural communication. It was the universal language of empathy, honesty, and humanity.

It also took time for the ombuds to understand the dynamics that allowed this to happen and learn the diverse perspectives of people outside the department who shared responsibility for what happened. Since the ombuds office was new to the campus, it also took time to develop trust across the university community so that the ombuds would be listened to. It took time to connect the dots, to see how some seemingly unrelated issues were all relevant, and to plan a strategy for how and when to involve others and explore ways to make the appropriate people at the university aware of this issue in a way that was acceptable to the ombuds' visitors.

After a significant period of time gathering information and building trust, the ombuds identified the visitors' goals and considered where they overlapped with the institution's goals and where there was space between them. It took a lot of strategic thinking and planning to move forward. With this strategic plan in mind, the ombuds then worked hard to foster collaboration between those who had been wronged, their allies, and those who had the authority to initiate and oversee change.

When these exploitive and abusive practices ultimately were exposed, the university did not hesitate to take appropriate action, including terminating the employment of those involved in perpetuating these practices. The outcome, some of which became public, was beneficial to everyone involved, with the exception of those who lost their jobs because their wrongdoing had been exposed.

This outcome was transformational in many ways. First, a significant set of employees was no longer subject to the unacceptable and extortionate actions of their supervisors. These beleaguered employees could come to work without fear of being subject to the demands and whims of their supervisors. The university made changes in structure and policy, as well as in personnel. Formal support systems were put in place. Administrators were praised for the direct way they dealt with the problem. The ombuds office was praised for bringing the problem to light and for offering thoughtful options for resolution. The perspective and guidance of the ombuds was actively promoted and sought, particularly when oversight groups struggled with the dichotomy between "fairness," which was often policy and procedurally driven, and "doing the right thing," which was human rights and justice driven.

Second, many people across the campus became aware of the ombuds office and the important role it filled on campus to find creative solutions to sensitive and complicated problems. Conversations and consultations with the ombuds office by both decision-makers and those who felt powerless demonstrated that the ombuds office could be trusted and that it could help address significant issues. The ombuds office also strengthened its already positive relationships with the human resources professionals and the attorneys representing the university by demonstrating honesty, good judgment, and common sense.

Once the most senior leadership of the institution was made aware of the scope and nature of the situation, significant systemic change occurred, and it was transformational. And what was the ombuds role? Starting with one person who came to the ombuds for help with a different matter, the ombuds was able to encourage and ultimately convince many others to come to him to speak confidentially. It was the ombuds' proactive engagement—and the reassurance over and over again that the ombuds office was a safe place and that it kept its word with regard to confidentiality—and a willingness to point out those inappropriate and unprofessional behaviors that had become a "a part of the landscape," a part of the organizational culture where many no longer viewed it as a problem, that brought about this change.

Surfacing an Issue and Resolving a Dispute that Easily Could Have Resulted in Expensive Litigation and Reputational Damage

The visitor was a long-time university employee whose daughter had just entered her freshman year at the same institution and had been going through new student orientation. During the daughter's first weekend on campus, she attended a fraternity party with a group of friends. While there, she drifted away from her friends, and after a few drinks of "punch" found herself dizzy, drunk, and surrounded by a group of boys. Two of them forced her into a bedroom and sexually assaulted her. After a few minutes, because the boys were more intoxicated than she, she was able to get out of the room and run back to her dorm. She was deeply embarrassed and didn't want to tell her friends what happened. The next day she decided to call her parents and tell them what happened. Not wanting to risk ever running into the boys again, or to have this first-week episode haunt her for four years on campus, she told her parents she wanted to transfer to her second-choice school. Her parents promptly got her medical treatment to ensure that she was physically alright and scheduled her an appointment with her therapist to discuss the incident.

Ordinarily, the office of student life services posts monitors at all on-campus parties (which must be registered in advance) to ensure that there is no underage drinking and that party participants behave appropriately and safely. The placement of these monitors has resulted in a significant reduction of incidents of injuries, bad behavior, and other problems that had historically occurred at fraternity parties. In this instance, although the party had been registered, no monitors had been assigned due to a scheduling error on the part of the student life office.

When the parent came to the ombuds office, he was aware of the university policy requiring preregistration of these events and the assignment of monitors. In the case of the party his daughter attended, he also had learned that although the party had been registered, no monitors had been assigned as was required. He stated that he understood and respected his daughter's decision to transfer and stated that he did not want to make trouble for the university, even though he also stated that the incident very likely could have been prevented. The main concern that brought him to the ombuds was that if his daughter were to transfer to another college, she would lose the tuition benefit he was entitled to receive from the university (full tuition for four years, but not transferrable to any other institution). He wanted the university to compensate him to the extent of the tuition for four years at the new school. Otherwise, he said, the only other option would be for his daughter and him to bring suit against the university. With the father's permission, the ombuds contacted the risk management office for a consultation.

Because the girl's father met first with the ombuds, the ombuds was able to work with risk management to quickly resolve the issue, with the university agreeing to cover the tuition costs at the new school. Because of this resolution, both the family and the university avoided litigation that could have been costly to both sides, but which posed a real risk of loss to the university in light of the absence of a monitor at the event. In addition, potential reputation-damaging publicity was avoided on both sides and good relations with a long-standing employee preserved.

Avoiding a Class Action Lawsuit

A female professional staff member contacted the ombuds office with concerns over actions by the predominantly male staff in her group. She had only been with the organization for a few years but was highly educated and at the cutting edge of her scientific field. She had also received high ratings as an employee. She related that she and other women in her group had experienced demeaning, disrespectful, and dishonest treatment by the male professional staff in her group. She thought one of the worst offenders was her former mentor, who was also a highly valued staff member responsible for bringing in millions of dollars of new business. She and the other female scientists and technical staff had been ignoring the demeaning behavior by him and the other male colleagues because they needed his skill and research projects.

The female staff member also mentioned an episode six months earlier in which a male staff member had created a dangerous condition in the lab with only women present. Although the incident had been investigated and the male staff member transferred to another group, a verbal threat on her life had been made to her to prevent her from speaking about the episode. That event clearly had traumatized her, and she had not reported the threat. Since that time, however, she had been keeping a record of the incidents and comments. In addition, the women in the group had been advising potential new recruits to the organization that they could not recommend working at the organization.

The ombuds discussed various options with her on several occasions. During this time, the staff member urged other women in her group also to speak with the ombuds. The ombuds thought that the facts outlined by the women created a real possibility of a class action lawsuit against the organization and was trying to find a way to help get the issue to senior management. While most of the women insisted on anonymity, two of the women with whom the ombuds spoke were willing to speak about their concerns with management.

The ombuds helped coordinate a meeting between those two women and the CEO. As a result of those conversations, an investigation was undertaken to deal with the issues in that group. In addition, senior management engaged workplace consultants to work with staff throughout the organization to raise awareness of and deal with gender-related communication and interaction.

IMMINENT THREAT OF SERIOUS HARM (BREAKING CONFIDENTIALITY)

Breaking Confidence Due to an Imminent Risk of Serious Harm

Late one afternoon, the ombuds received a phone call from a very disgruntled employee, who had been "released unfairly" from his job location. The ombuds, in asking questions and gathering information from the employee, learned that this employee had apparently made some threats to his management that afternoon and was terminated.

The employee, however, also advised the ombuds that if "someone didn't do something right now . . ." and proceeded to make another threat against the management of the location where he worked, as well as the physical site itself. The employee stated: "that he would not wait much longer."

The ombuds talked quickly about the role of the ombuds and voiced a concern about the level of the threat being made during the conversation, explaining the "imminent risk of serious harm" provision. That explanation was barely completed when the employee told the ombuds to do whatever needed to be done and hung up the phone.

The ombuds decided that this indeed fell under the imminent threat of serious harm clause of the Standards of Practice, justifying disclosure, and called the management at that location, who in turn notified the local authorities. The management knew the identity of the individual without the ombuds having to reveal that information.

An Imminent Threat of Serious Harm

A maintenance worker came to the ombuds with issues relating to conflict with supervisors and coworkers that had been going on for years. The issues were about disrespect and a feeling that he was being treated differently than others. The visitor had raised issues over the years and felt he was now being seen as a "troublemaker." The visitor wanted the supervisor and coworker to be removed or that he would not have to have any contact with either of them.

During the conversation with the ombuds the visitor repeatedly said, "I may have to take care of this on my own and deal with it outside." Each time he said this the ombuds stopped the conversation and asked the visitor what this meant. He replied that he could take the individuals outside and settle it like men. During the conversation he also mentioned he had a gun license. The ombuds told the visitor that when she heard things like this, she took them seriously. When asked about his real intent, the visitor would laugh and say, "Well, I'm not serious." Yet, the visitor also repeatedly pounded on the table while telling his story.

Due to the physical and verbal behavior of the visitor, the ombuds decided to bring the issue to the safety department because she felt that action should be taken immediately while the organization tried to find a longer-term solution. Safety gave the visitor three days of paid leave and asked him to stay at home. They later changed the assignment of this visitor, so he did not have contact with the supervisor or coworker.

Raising Systemic Safety and Recordkeeping Issues Where There Is an Imminent Threat of Serious Harm

Several employees of a federal agency came separately to the ombuds with concerns about a safety protocol not being followed and recordkeeping not reflecting the fact that safety steps were being skipped due to time pressures. Each of the visitors was unsure what to do but all expressed a fear of retaliation if they were to formally report their concerns.

After several visitors had discussed with the ombuds similar concerns and fears, the ombuds raised the issue to the head of safety. The ombuds made this decision based on their knowledge that lives were at risk if this situation was true and not resolved.

An audit was scheduled immediately under the guise of an opening in the audit schedule. The audit revealed several gaps in protocol. The operation was completely shut down until the safety gaps were resolved.

Breach of Confidentiality Because of Personal Safety Concerns

An employee learned that a supervisor was going to be attacked at work the next day by other employees. Concerned that her own safety would be at risk if she reported this to anyone, she felt that she could tell the ombuds about it confidentially and that the ombuds could take the issue from there.

With such a short time to act and no other reasonable option, the ombuds determined that the situation presented justified invoking the exception to confidentiality and notified security of the allegation and the identity of the employees who allegedly were involved.

Security responded quickly and diffused the immediate threat to personal safety. A broader investigation was also commenced that revealed extensive drug trafficking at this location. Local police were informed, and several arrests were made, resulting in a safer and more productive work environment. The person initially reporting the incident was satisfied that her identity was never revealed.

Breach of Confidentiality Because of Risk of Harm to Others

The ombuds was contacted separately by five different individuals. Each one reported concern about the unusual or troubling behavior of a high-status female employee. Each of the odd behaviors, including sharing a risqué photograph, finding an "accidental" fire in a trash can, keeping a knife in a desk drawer to slice fruit at lunch time, and making what might be interpreted as veiled threats in an email, had been investigated by the compliance office, but in each case, there was insufficient evidence for a sanction harsher than a warning. However, when the bystanders discussed their concerns with the ombuds, they were able to provide more context and explain why they felt afraid of this employee. Moreover, the ombuds was the only person in the organization who had enough information to "connect the dots" and see a pattern.

In light of the number and type of complaints about serious and inappropriate conduct that had been raised, the ombuds approached the female employee and encouraged her to seek psychiatric help. When she refused, but demonstrated anger, despair, and fascination with violence, the ombuds was concerned that this person may pose an imminent threat of serious harm to herself or to others and that confidentiality could not be maintained.

The ombuds disclosed to the HR director and the general counsel some—but not all—of the information that suggested the seemingly disparate instances might reflect a pattern and that several other employees felt concerns for their personal safety. While the ombuds does not know what the HR director and the general counsel then did to evaluate this information, they subsequently developed a plan to remove the female employee from the organization's premises until a satisfactory psychological evaluation had been completed.

Saving a Life and Saving a Career

A graduate student and her faculty advisor developed an intimate relationship. After several months, the graduate student tried to break off the relationship, but the faculty advisor threatened to prevent the student from graduating. In addition, the faculty advisor had planned an out-of-state trip and was demanding that the student share his hotel room. It was at this point that the graduate student contacted the ombuds office. She said she was on the verge of taking her own life.

In light of the student's fragile condition, the ombuds concluded that there was an imminent threat of serious harm and made limited disclosures to get the student access to mental health counseling. After her condition stabilized, the ombuds discussed options she might use to deal with her advisor. The option selected was to give the ombuds permission to contact the administration about the advisor. Since there had been other complaints about that advisor, the ombuds was able to indicate that concerns had been expressed by students generally, though no other details were provided.

The administration conducted its own investigation and determined that there was merit to the concerns raised. As a result, the faculty member was stripped of all advisor assignments. Since all of his advisees were reassigned to other advisors, neither this graduate student nor any of the other students who had complained were singled out. Once this episode was behind her, the student went on to graduate and is now a highly respected scholar in her field.

PERMISSION GIVEN TO MAKE DISCLOSURE (BREAKING CONFIDENTIALITY)

Limited Disclosure Solves the Problem and Protects the Informant

An employee came to the ombuds to report that he suspected that one of the subcontractors working on plant renovations at the facility where he worked was not doing the work to code. The employee felt that this should be brought to the attention of the company for safety reasons but because he was a union member in the same trade as the subcontractor, he was unwilling to be the one to raise the issue with a formal channel. He was certain that he would suffer retaliation by other members of the union if it became known that he had been the person who reported the issue.

After discussing various options, the employee agreed to permit the ombuds to contact the facility manager to advise him that it would be advisable to have an inspection of the construction work by the local building inspector, but no other information was revealed. The manager arranged for the inspection, which uncovered the defective work, and the company required the subcontractor to correct it. Since the inspection appeared to be a routine inspection by the building inspector, the identity of the employee who came to the ombuds was protected.

Policy Clarification Wanted But Fear of Asking

The organization had a drug-testing policy for safety-sensitive positions. An employee came to the ombuds to ask whether he would have to take the drug test if notified to do so. He said that he objected to the drug test on principle, not because he had any fear of the results. He was afraid to ask for a clarification of the policy, however, because that may mark him as a "dangerous druggie" or cause him to lose his sensitive duty status or even his job.

The ombuds reviewed the policy with the inquirer. Among other options presented by the ombuds was the possibility that the ombuds could make an inquiry of the director in charge without naming any employee to see if there were any exceptions or "wiggle room" in the policy. That was the option selected by the inquirer. When the ombuds made the inquiry, the answer was that no exceptions were permitted because the test was required by federal policies. When this information was communicated back to the inquirer, he understood and very much appreciated the chance to raise the issue without being the person identified with doing so.

A Desire to Protect Others but Uncertainty Over Whether Problem Continues

A female employee had filed a formal complaint about a male employee's sexual harassment of her, including his inappropriate touching of her. The male employee was reprimanded and moved to another location. The female employee was given coaching and additional protection, including an escort to her car at the end of the workday.

Some time later, the female employee came to the ombuds because she believed that the male employee, in his new work location, was engaged in the same conduct with another female employee, but the suspected conduct did not involve her, and she had no direct proof. She also did not want to be identified in any complaint, but she indicated that she was trying to protect other women from what she had gone through. After discussing various options with the ombuds about how this issue could be addressed, the female employee permitted the ombuds to contact HR to advise them that a person who wished to remain anonymous had concerns—but no direct proof—about sexual harassment by the male employee.

HR conducted its own investigation and concluded that the male employee was, in fact, sexually harassing another female employee. His employment was subsequently terminated.

Safety

Over the course of several consults, a visitor shared with the ombuds their concerns over safety issues related to a remote campus building used for both research and summer camps. The visitor had tried to raise the concerns directly with their supervisor on several occasions but the issues remained unresolved.

By the time the visitor brought these concerns to the ombuds, the summer camp season was fast approaching. After discussing various options to address these concerns, the visitor gave the ombuds permission to go to the provost and make an anonymous report, knowing the supervisor would likely connect the dots.

When the ombuds made this report to the provost, the provost and the ombuds were then able to work together quickly to identify ways to address the situation as discreetly as possible. The option selected by the provost was to have the building inspected. The subsequent inspection revealed that the building was not up to code. As a result, the university canceled the impending summer camp and made the necessary repairs. The ombuds' prompt and effective working with first the visitor and then the provost thus helped the university eliminate a risk that could have resulted in injuries and been both expensive and damaging to the university's reputation. By having an inspection of the building before taking any action, the ombuds and the provost were able to help protect the identity of the visitor who had raised the issue.

Identifying, Surfacing, and Correcting a Potentially Serious Hazard

The visitor was a staff member who was concerned after observing that a studio made available over the years to students to use power tools to build art installations and theatre scenery had become very loosely supervised. Historically, full-time staff had been responsible for supervising the studio, and the studio had regular hours and had been carefully locked when the supervisor was not present. The visitor stated that in the last year the full-time supervisor had retired and was replaced with student supervisors. The visitor thought that the student supervisors had been trained but that the studio doors were often left open, apparently as favors to accommodate students' schedules, and that students were often alone in the studio without supervision.

The visitor decided to visit the ombuds office after becoming aware of an accident at another university where a student had been hurt by a power tool in a similar studio. The visitor had not been able to determine who was currently in charge of the studio and did not want to get anyone in trouble. The visitor was not directly involved in the studio but was concerned about using the ethical tip line because they didn't know how it worked and didn't trust that it was really confidential. Those were the stated reasons for going to the ombuds rather than somewhere else to raise this concern.

During their conversation, the ombuds and visitor come up with several options:

- The visitor could go online and use the confidential ethics and compliance reporting system (or print it out and put it in campus mail).
- The visitor could inform the environmental health and safety (EHS) department.
- They could figure out which department had oversight of the studio and let them know.
- With permission from the visitor, the ombuds could do any of the above and relay the information while not disclosing the identity of the person who brought the issue to the attention of the ombuds.

The visitor requested that the ombuds go to EHS and let them know of the concern without saying where the information came from, and the ombuds agreed to do so.

EHS and the ombuds had a good working relationship from previous interactions, and EHS was very welcoming of the information. The situation was remedied quickly without repercussions for any individual.

REPORTS TO SENIOR MANAGEMENT/ IDENTIFYING TRENDS AND SYSTEMIC ISSUES

Patience, the Promise of Confidentiality, and an Ombuds' Proactive Engagement Helps the Ombuds Surface Issues that Led to Transformative Systemic Change

A case that resulted in significant systemic change at a university began innocuously.

From an initial contact, the ombuds learned over time and from many conversations that a department on campus had a common practice where some managers offered temporary and permanent positions to women in exchange for sex and to both men and women in exchange for money. The practice was generations old. The habits that helped sustain this behavior over time had become a part of the organizational culture in this one unit and were accepted and enabled by both managers and employees in this unit as "that's the way it is here." Most people felt nothing could be done and resistance was pointless because previous attempts to address the matter over time had been ruthlessly suppressed. The people who paid bribes or exchanged sex for their jobs needed the jobs and had a legitimate fear of losing them or of suffering some other form of retribution if they spoke up. Also, the shame of being forced to do what they did kept many quiet and feeling powerless.

Nothing about bringing an end to these practices happened quickly. It took time before other individuals in the department would speak in confidence openly and honestly with the ombuds. It took time to collect their experiences and the effect they had on individuals and the department collectively. The ombuds determined that it was necessary to express empathy and sorrow, as well as to provide assurances that something could, in fact, be done to address this situation. It took time for the ombuds to understand the history and culture of the department and the concerns and interests of the people involved. As more and more people from the department came to speak with the ombuds and strategize ways of managing the problem, they learned to trust the ombuds because he kept his word that the communications were confidential and because he spoke a language they could understand and appreciate—not a language based on different ethnic and cultural groups but, rather, a language that fostered cross-cultural communication. It was the universal language of empathy, honesty, and humanity.

It also took time for the ombuds to understand the dynamics that allowed this to happen and learn the diverse perspectives of people outside the department who shared responsibility for what happened. Since the ombuds office was new to the campus, it also took time to develop trust across the university community so that the ombuds would be listened to. It took time to connect the dots, to see how some seemingly unrelated issues were all relevant, and to plan a strategy for how and when to involve others and explore ways to make the appropriate people at the university aware of this issue in a way that was acceptable to the ombuds' visitors.

After a significant period of time gathering information and building trust, the ombuds identified the visitors' goals and considered where they overlapped with the institution's goals and where there was space between them. It took a lot of strategic thinking and planning to move forward. With this strategic plan in mind, the ombuds then worked hard to foster collaboration between those who had been wronged, their allies, and those who had the authority to initiate and oversee change.

When these exploitive and abusive practices ultimately were exposed, the university did not hesitate to take appropriate action, including terminating the employment of those involved in perpetuating these practices. The outcome, some of which became public, was beneficial to everyone involved, with the exception of those who lost their jobs because their wrongdoing had been exposed.

This outcome was transformational in many ways. First, a significant set of employees was no longer subject to the unacceptable and extortionate actions of their supervisors. These beleaguered employees could come to work without fear of being subject to the demands and whims of their supervisors. The university made changes in structure and policy, as well as in personnel. Formal support systems were put in place. Administrators were praised for the direct way they dealt with the problem. The ombuds office was praised for bringing the problem to light and for offering thoughtful options for resolution. The perspective and guidance of the ombuds was actively promoted and sought, particularly when oversight groups struggled with the dichotomy between "fairness," which was often policy and procedurally driven, and "doing the right thing," which was human rights and justice driven.

Second, many people across the campus became aware of the ombuds office and the important role it filled on campus to find creative solutions to sensitive and complicated problems. Conversations and consultations with the ombuds office by both decision-makers and those who felt powerless demonstrated that the ombuds office could be trusted and that it could help address significant issues. The ombuds office also strengthened its already positive relationships with the human resources professionals and the attorneys representing the university by demonstrating honesty, good judgment, and common sense.

Once the most senior leadership of the institution was made aware of the scope and nature of the situation, significant systemic change occurred, and it was transformational. And what was the ombuds role? Starting with one person who came to the ombuds for help with a different matter, the ombuds was able to encourage and ultimately convince many others to come to him to speak confidentially. It was the ombuds' proactive engagement—and the reassurance over and over again that the ombuds office was a safe place and that it kept its word with regard to confidentiality—and willingness to point out those inappropriate and unprofessional behaviors that had become a "a part of the landscape," part of the organizational culture where many no longer viewed it as a problem, that brought about this change.

Fraud, Amorous Relationship, Conflict of Interest, and Fear of Reporting

The ombuds worked with a visitor for two years. At first the issue presented was a benign interpersonal conflict. After the ombuds established trust with the visitor, the visitor began sharing documentation and information that revealed a fraud scheme apparently orchestrated by the visitor's leader, a well-regarded tenured professor who brought in millions of dollars for the university each year. The visitor did not want to be a whistleblower because of fear for their position, career, reputation, and physical safety.

The ombuds presented the visitor with various ways the issue might be surfaced or investigated. Eventually the visitor gave the ombuds permission to raise the issue anonymously to the university's financial compliance department, which had the ability to discretely review records to determine whether the concerns had merit. If they concluded that the concerns might have merit, they could intervene or refer the matter to internal audit for a formal investigation. In this case, given the positive working relationship between the financial compliance analyst and the ombuds, the analyst took all of the information provided by the ombuds and immediately initiated an informal and extremely discreet review of the leader's unit's records. Literally, no one else knew it was happening.

Ultimately, this review surfaced a myriad of concerns, including conflicts of interest (using university position and resources for personal gain), financial fraud (funneling money to a private business), and sexual misconduct (an amorous relationship between the leader and a direct report). The financial compliance analyst then referred the matter to the university's internal audit department and a formal investigation ensured. The compliance department told the leader under investigation that it had discovered information during a routine check. Once internal audit released its report to the vice chancellor of research, the university terminated the leader, restructured the unit, and imposed new restrictions and policies to address the types of transactions at issue.

Inappropriate Conduct by Senior Leader

During a site visit in Latin America, several employees visited the ombuds with concerns involving a senior leader who was providing inappropriate directives to their team and violating company policy by making inappropriate "agreements" with government officials.

The employees who came to the ombuds were extremely fearful of retaliation. They did not trust their leadership chain, because they were unsure whether more senior leadership was aware of and supported the senior leader's conduct. Most of the employees who came to the ombuds for guidance had tried to advise the senior leader directly of their concerns. He responded, however, in a threatening manner and told them that he was their supervisor and they needed to abide by what he was telling them to do.

The ombuds discussed with each visitor the options they had for notifying the company of their concerns and how they could go about doing so. However, each felt that, because they had already expressed concerns to the supervisor in the past, he would know who it was that was complaining. The ombuds also had explained to the employees at the outset of each of their meetings with the ombuds that part of the ombuds office charter required that where three or more visitors approached the office with the same issue, the ombuds must raise that systemic issue to leadership for action.

In this situation, because the ombuds had had multiple employees come to the office with the same concerns, the ombuds was able to raise this "trend" to the most senior leader of the business unit for action. The ombuds also advised the visitors that it was important to document and gather any communications that they had with their supervisor on this topic so that they would be prepared to answer questions once the investigation was underway. They discussed how best to manage through the current environment, such as seeking clarity from the supervisor if he made additional similar requests so that conduct and guidance would also be documented.

After raising this "trend" to the most senior business leader, the matter was investigated. The investigation determined that the supervisor was indeed violating company policy, placing the company at risk. The supervisor's employment was terminated, and the employees moved forward with performing their jobs in a manner consistent with company policy without fear of retaliation. Having the ombuds office bring forward this trend allowed the company to take corrective action and avoid a potentially major impact to the organization.

NOT WANTING TO BE A WHISTLEBLOWER

Where Does a Vice President Go with Concerns About the President?

The ombuds of a multinational organization received a call from a regional vice president with concerns about an international region president. The inquirer expressed concerns that the regional president was acting strangely and making improper comments about people at an offsite meeting where over a dozen other vice president–level organization officials were present, together with several outside counsel, professionals, and other consultants to the organization. The inquirer was concerned that the regional president could have a drug problem, as the strange behavior had been evident for at least the preceding few months. The vice president making the call, however, was also obviously concerned that he may be wrong and was worried about the possible impact on his own career.

The ombuds discussed various ways this issue could be surfaced and investigated. The inquirer gave the ombuds permission to convey information about the regional president's conduct at the off-site meeting (but not the inquirer's identity) to the top levels of the organization at its international headquarters. When this information was relayed to the president of the entire organization and the head of HR, they instigated an investigation almost immediately by having many of the attendees of the offsite meeting interviewed. The regional president was also interviewed.

As a result of this investigation, they made the decision to remove the regional president from his position and announced that he was relocating back to the organization headquarters. He retired from the organization not long thereafter.

Surfacing an Issue Without Becoming a Whistleblower

An executive assistant (EA) to a senior executive called the ombuds to discuss their concern, which they said could not be taken forward to management through *any* formal channel. In particular, the EA believed that, at a time of corporate restructuring to save costs, the senior executive with whom the EA worked was making fraudulent claims on his monthly expense claims.

When asked how the EA was aware of the alleged fraudulent claims, the EA said they prepared the monthly claims from the information provided by the senior executive but knew that some of the information was false. The EA believed that this conduct was not appropriate and that it should be reported. Yet, since only the senior executive and the EA were privy to what was on the monthly expense claims before they were submitted, the EA was also extremely afraid of what would happen personally to them if they were identified as the whistleblower in any investigation into the expense reports.

The ombuds and the EA discussed a number of options to surface the EA's concerns, including an option in which the ombuds could ask the internal audit team to carry out a review of the monthly expense claims of all the other people at the same level as the senior executive throughout the business and without identifying who had brought this issue to the ombuds, the specifics of the false claims, or the identity of any particular senior executive about whom there was concern. The EA gave permission to the ombuds to take the matter forward on this basis.

When the ombuds alerted the internal audit team to this concern and made the request for the internal audit, the internal audit team audited the expense reports of all the senior executives at that level. With all the senior executives at that level included, no one could have thought that any particular person was being targeted.

The results of the audit demonstrated that the senior executive was not alone in submitting fraudulent expense reports; others had done so as well. All of those senior executives were fired. The EA who brought the issue to the attention of the ombuds was never identified and subsequently was assigned to work for the replacement of the senior executive for whom the EA had previously worked.

Bullying and Hostile Work Environment

The ombuds received a number of visitors from one office who expressed concerns about a specific leader's treatment of people and whether the leader made ethical business decisions. None of them wanted a formal investigation, which would likely require their on-the-record testimony. They were comfortable raising the issue with the ombuds but did not want to become enmeshed in a formal investigation. Several also said that they "did not want anything bad to happen" to the leader. Rather, they just wanted to see the behaviors change and the environment improve.

The ombuds met with more than ten current and former employees from that office who described the conditions in that office using expressions such as a "reign of terror," "a remarkably toxic atmosphere," and an "abusive" and "hostile" environment. Among other comments expressed by employees was that they felt the leader "created fear," "beats people into submission," was "extremely condescending," "intentionally makes you feel like you're stupid" by "constantly pointing out mistakes, making you feel terrible about it," where "nothing you do is ever right . . . ever." These vivid and graphic descriptions clearly reflected an extreme and difficult work environment.

With permission from the employees, the ombuds compiled the comments without attribution and shared them with a more senior executive in that office for information and action as appropriate. The ombuds reiterated that it was up to the senior leader to initiate any investigation but that these comments suggested that there was an opportunity to address perceptions and reinforce expected leadership behaviors. The senior executive confirmed with the ombuds that a number of other issues had been raised before, but nothing this serious and widespread. The ombuds confirmed that a large number of employees were doing everything they could to stay in the good graces of this leader, which meant not speaking up for fear of retaliation, which colleagues stated took the form of low performance evaluations.

The senior executive: 1) used the ombuds' nonattributable feedback to put the leader "on notice" about expected behaviors surrounding respectful treatment; 2) created an open door for all employees to make direct contact freely; and 3) gave the leader a one-year ultimatum to improve or find another opportunity. While things improved slightly for a short amount of time, ultimately the bad habits did not change, and the leader left the organization.

Fear of Retaliation Is so Great that Employee Will Trust Only the Ombuds

An employee was concerned that a supervisor was misappropriating funds by submitting false entertainment vouchers. The employee was extremely concerned about possible retaliation and the consequences of raising these issues about her supervisor. She said that she was not prepared to submit any documents or to speak to anyone other than the ombuds because the ombuds' communications were confidential.

After several rounds of conversation with the ombuds during which they discussed options for raising the issue, she finally agreed to speak with an internal auditor but only anonymously. The ombuds arranged for an anonymous call between her and internal audit. The employee, communicating through the ombuds as an intermediary, was also able to provide internal audit with other information they needed to commence the investigation, but the employee's identity was never disclosed.

The audit revealed misconduct and the supervisor was terminated.

Local Management Misconduct and Fear of Retaliation

Employees at one unit of the company had been using company products and equipment to create their own personal business, resulting in a loss of customers and revenues for the company. Some of the people involved in the scheme were members of the local management. As a result, employees who knew about this misconduct felt that they could not report it to local management and were afraid to raise it through formal channels. They were not sure how to contact or approach higher levels of management or if higher management might also be involved.

Some of the employees who knew about the scheme came to the ombuds office because they understood that it was independent and confidential. After discussing the issue with the ombuds, the ombuds, at their request, facilitated contact with the compliance office, which investigated and eventually terminated the employment of those involved in the scheme. The employees who came to the ombuds office stated that the experience made them more comfortable raising issues with the company's compliance office.

FEDERAL AGENCIES

Author's Note: Included in this category are examples that uniquely involve federal agencies. Several of the examples in other categories are drawn from federal agencies, but the fact that those examples occurred in a federal agency was irrelevant to the issue addressed in that category because there was no difference between the ombuds' practice in the federal agency and those of corporate or university ombuds programs.

An Ombuds Helps Resolve a Problem that Could Have Led to Congressional Action Against a Federal Agency and Its Political Leadership

A visitor came to the ombuds at a federal agency concerned about what to do about their supervisor, who was creating a hostile work environment. In addition to discussing the conduct of the supervisor, the visitor also disclosed during this first meeting that the visitor was like family with an influential Member of Congress who had already been notified about the visitor's issues with the supervisor.

After discussing various options on how the visitor might proceed with this concern, the visitor asked the ombuds to see if the supervisor would be amenable to having a facilitated conversation with the assistance of the ombuds. The ombuds approached the supervisor, who indicated their willingness to participate.

All of the visitor's concerns were successfully addressed through facilitated conversations and shuttle diplomacy. In addition, larger systemic issues were elevated to the highest level of the organization. As the visitor felt heard and was satisfied with the outcome, the Member of Congress backed off on potentially taking action adverse to the supervisor, who was a presidential appointee.

An Ombuds Helps Get a Presidential Initiative Back on Track and Improve Communication in a Federal Agency

Relying on the confidentiality of communications with the ombuds, a visitor came to the ombuds in a federal agency with information that a presidential initiative at the agency was way off track and not meeting the expectations stated to Congress and the citizens of the United States.

The visitor and the ombuds discussed options for taking further action, and the visitor authorized the ombuds to elevate the issue (while protecting the identity of the visitor) to the head of the agency. The ombuds did so and then worked with senior leadership in the agency to identify why the head of the agency was not receiving accurate information about the progress of the presidential initiative. With the assistance of the ombuds, the agency was able to identify systemic breakdowns in communications, and the ombuds helped in recommending solutions.

By surfacing this issue, which had been brought confidentially to the ombuds, the ombuds helped the agency avoid public embarrassment and helped ensure that the goals and expectations of the initiative, as outlined by the president of the United States, were achieved on time and within budget projections.

Ombuds Helps Contractor Address Attempts by Government Employee to Have an Inappropriate Relationship

A government contractor came to the ombuds with concerns about a government employee who allegedly had expressed an interest in engaging in a personal relationship with the contractor. The contractor explained that the government employee also had been designated as the contractor's point of contact with the government agency involved and oversaw the contractor's work. The contractor reported that when the government employee tried to shift the working relationship to something personal, the contractor immediately expressed disinterest to the government employee and asked for him to stop.

The government employee continued to show interest, however, both directly and indirectly. As a result, the contractor looked to the ombuds for guidance on what else the contractor might be able to do to make the unwanted attention stop. Sadly, the contractor also divulged this situation to the company's HR office, which did not want their employee to "cause a problem" and risk the government looking unfavorably on their company.

Among the options discussed was having the ombuds make the management of the government agency aware of the contractor's concerns. Luckily, the ombuds had prior experience with managers in this area who were consistently supportive and responsive to broad organizational concerns, and especially to concerns related to ethics and harassment. The contractor was reassured by this insight and selected this option. With permission from the contractor, the ombuds made management aware of the contractor's concerns and requested that the situation be investigated, or other appropriate action taken. The government supervisor took immediate action to ensure that the contractor was in a safe environment, and also talked to the company about being more forthcoming when situations like this arise.

Ombuds Helps Government Contractors Avoid Retribution for Raising Issues with Government Supervisor

Three contractors of a federal agency came together to the ombuds with claims of retribution. The contractors had raised concerns inside their company regarding the behavior of their civil servant supervisor at the federal agency. The company had then raised the issue with the agency's HR personnel. A month later, the contracts of these three contractors were terminated, and the explanation given to them by the federal agency was that there wasn't enough work for their contracts to continue.

With the permission of the three contractors, the ombuds looked into the situation on both the agency and the contractor side and found different explanations were being given for the decision. From the questions posed to the agency's management, the ombuds concluded that the firing decision had been made by the contractors' civil servant supervisor with little oversight from either higher management or HR. However, based on the questions that had been posed by the agency ombuds, higher management reviewed the decision to terminate the contractors. Although this review concluded that the project that they had been working on did not need them, there was other work in the area for which they were well suited, and they were rehired.

CROSS-CULTURAL ISSUES

Information and Guidance from the Ombuds Makes a Difference

A post-doctoral fellow came into the ombuds office worried that her boss was going to fire her. She was from another country, and she did not want to go home in disgrace. She said her boss yelled at her and always criticized her written work. She also reported having no friends and feeling lonely. She said she didn't know how to make friends and missed her family.

The ombuds talked with her about ways to get suggestions before she wrote a paper and discussed resources on campus such as clubs that she could join to meet others. The ombuds also mentioned the Employee Assistance Program in order to deal with her depression and perhaps to talk about assertiveness (in response to her statement about it being difficult being a woman in science.)

The visitor was very excited about the idea of getting help with assertiveness and thanked the ombuds effusively for her various suggestions.

The university avoided losing a post-doctoral fellow, and the student was able to build her confidence. On follow-up, the fellow reported that she was now getting along with her professor and publishing a paper.

Facilitation Leads to an Awareness of Different Cultural Perspectives

Two employees came to the ombuds because they were concerned about what they perceived to be a threat made by another person who worked for the company. The two visitors, a man and a woman, were both from an Asian country and were at the company's US headquarters on a one-year temporary permit.

They reported that they returned to their building late one night after enjoying a break for dinner. The security guard had left, so they used their electronic employee badges to enter the building. As they entered, they noticed that an African American man slipped into the building behind them. Concerned about security, especially post 9-11, they decided to follow the man to see where he went. They said that they tried to be discrete as they followed him up the internal staircase in the building. When the man entered an office, they became very alarmed and stood in the hallway, discussing what to do next. They noticed an office directory on the wall by the staircase and checked the name associated with the office the man had entered. At that point, the man suddenly burst forth from the office and shouted at the visitors. Startled and tremendously frightened, they ran down the stairs, retreating to the office they shared. They considered reporting the incident to their superiors but did not because they were unsure of themselves and because they did not know if the man who had been in the office was the person listed on the directory. They decided to come to the ombuds to ask for confidential guidance on what they should do.

After discussing various options, the visitors gave the ombuds permission to contact the person listed in the directory. The ombuds did so and learned that he was the African American man who they had seen enter the office. The man told the ombuds that he had been very disturbed and offended by the two visitors' behavior and that he had questioned their motives.

The ombuds presented all three people with an option to have a mediation in which to discuss their concerns, and they agreed. The African American man explained that he found the behavior by the other two to be both threatening and racist. He described experiences in being followed and harassed by police and explained how insulting he found it to be that the others assumed that he did not belong in the building. He also explained that he had felt threatened by their actions in following him and that he actually feared for his own safety. It had occurred to him that *they* might be terrorists, since they looked vaguely Middle Eastern or South Asian.

The visitors explained to him that they were not familiar with issues of race in the United States and had no idea that their actions would be interpreted as they had been. They assured the man they had not intended to cause him alarm, and that they would have done the same no matter who had slipped in behind them. They stated that they appreciated the cultural lesson and had learned much from it. They also were glad that the ombuds was available for them to talk about their concerns.

Ombuds' Sensitivity to Cultural Issues Gives Inquirer More Options

A female doctoral student from a Muslim country came to the ombuds only after carefully checking out the documentation available about the program's confidentiality. After the initial conversation about the office and how it operates, the visitor engaged in a somewhat extended conversation about her home country during which the ombuds demonstrated a sensitivity to her culture and customs.

Only after this extended conversation, during which the ombuds perceived that the visitor was trying to determine whether or not to trust the ombuds, did the visitor reveal her principal concern: she had become sexually active while at the university, but she was going to be completing her program soon and her family expected her to return home to an arranged marriage. She was terrified of the potential ramifications for her, her family, and the planned marriage. While there were other places that the visitor could have gone to discuss the personal and cultural issues involved, her desire for confidentiality and the ability to explore options were paramount and led her to the ombuds.

The ombuds reaffirmed the principle of neutrality and, without making value judgments, indicated a willingness to discuss a full range of potential options with the visitor, from going home to the arranged marriage as planned to rejecting the arranged marriage and not going home.

The option selected by the visitor, and one she had not previously considered, was to pursue a position in a post-doctoral program, which would give her more time to assess the situation and decide how she wanted to proceed ultimately.

Help Me Understand

The ombuds received a call from a US-based expatriate executive asking for help in understanding the culture in China. The caller told the ombuds that he was not having much success or cooperation in his new organization and felt like it was due to his lack of understanding of the norms and culture of the country. Because the caller was new to the organization, he was unwilling to raise these concerns through any of the formal channels and was afraid that his failure to understand the culture would adversely affect his evaluation.

The ombuds was able to provide the caller with helpful information about local practices, background, and cultural norms in China. The ombuds was also able to suggest a website and other resources that had extensive information about doing business in China and the cultural norms and practices in the area. The executive was pleased to be able to obtain this guidance without going through formal channels. Without it, the caller said, he would have continued to struggle with living and working in his new environment or disclose his difficulties to higher management.

Help for Pregnant Employee and in Enforcement of Global Policies

An employee from a location outside of the United States contacted the ombuds to say that her boss had called her into his office to tell her that he noticed that she was pregnant and that he knew she was unmarried. She said that the boss had told her that if she was not married by the time the baby was delivered, she would be fired. Such conduct was not illegal in the country where she worked but violated the company's policies. She was uncertain what to do, afraid of losing her job, and feared retaliation by management of the company in her country, who she felt would support her manager.

The ombuds assured her that such action would violate company policy and discussed various options for how to proceed. With her permission, the ombuds forwarded her issue to a formal channel at the company headquarters, which intervened with local management to reinforce the company's policies and reiterated to local management that retaliation against her for bringing this issue to the attention of the company would not be tolerated.

The ombuds also worked with those responsible for the company's newsletter, which was sent to tens of thousands of employees around the world, to address the issue prospectively and generically (no reference to any names or locations) in a question-and-answer format to advise everyone in the company that it would violate the company's policies for a supervisor to discipline a female subordinate for being pregnant and unmarried and that attempting to do so would subject the supervisor to discipline, including possible dismissal. Such clear and direct guidance not only helped reinforce the company's global policies but may have spared other women throughout the world and in these circumstances from having to deal with the threat of termination or retaliation.

UNDERGRADUATE ISSUES

Author's Note: Included in this category are examples that uniquely involve undergraduate students. Examples in other categories may involve undergraduate students but were placed there because they were also relevant to that topic and due to space limitations. Please review other categories and the PDF downloads for additional examples involving undergraduate students.

Guidance for a Foreign Student on Dealing with Professorial and Peer Pressure

An undergraduate student in a political science class addressing politics and academic freedom came to the ombuds to discuss how to deal with pressures from his professor and classmates that he participate in a demonstration that he feared, as an international student, could adversely affect his visa status.

The student said that the class had been encouraged by their professor to take part in a peaceful demonstration at the state capitol to raise awareness about climate change. Because he was an international student, he was reluctant to attend the demonstration for fear of jeopardizing his visa status. Nevertheless, he felt a great deal of peer pressure and consternation and was even called out in class by another student as being a "climate denier." He said that he was concerned that his refusal to participate may affect his grade, particularly because the professor did not intervene when he was shamed in class. The student wondered whether he should take the risk and attend the demonstration to avoid both social and academic consequences.

The ombuds and the student explored various options. He could attend the demonstration, but he quickly ruled that out because the risk was too great. He could soldier on and hope that once the demonstration had come and gone the class would move on, although there was no assurance that the issue would blow over. He could also request a mediated conversation with the professor to share what he was experiencing in the hope that she would back down. The option selected by the student was to have the ombuds reach out to the professor, hear what she had to say, and if both were in agreement, facilitate a conversation between the two of them.

When the ombuds met with the professor, it became apparent that she was not aware of the student's full story and, in particular, the visa concern. Regarding the in-class shaming, she stated that she did hear an exchange among students and the use of the phrase "climate denier" but did not know the context so let it go. She also stated that it was her intention to let the students decide for themselves if they wanted to attend the demonstration. However, because it required canceling class the day of the demonstration, those who were not going would be required to write a short paper on climate change.

The professor acknowledged that her manner of delivery regarding those factors may not have been sufficiently clear. In sum, she felt sorry about how events unfolded for the student and wanted very much to meet with him to say so directly. Additionally, she stated that she planned to emphasize to the class that every individual could choose whether to attend and reinforce that not participating in the demonstration could be for a whole host of reasons and did not equate to climate denying.

The ombuds hosted the facilitated conversation soon thereafter. The professor listened intently to the student's account; and when he was done, she apologized for her lack of awareness, particularly with respect to the reaction of some of the class members regarding the student's decision not to attend the demonstration. She asked the student whether he would be comfortable with her making a statement to the class about these points, and after some discussion, he agreed provided she did not single him out or refer to him personally. She agreed to the caveat, and they both left the meeting having a much better understanding of each other. It also resulted in a teachable moment for the class regarding mutual respect and recognition of diversity of thought.

Successful Student Team Dismantles

A student team created intellectual property and won a large monetary award as a result. The team then decided to create a limited liability company to commercialize what they had created and used the monetary award to start their business. After starting the business, however, they fired one of the team members. This action caused a significant disruption in the business, along with resentment and hurt feelings.

A faculty member attempted to intervene to help resolve the issues but succeeded only in violating university policies and losing the students' trust in the process. The individuals involved reached out to the ombuds for help with the unresolved questions regarding the team's class "agreement," issues related to the intellectual property, allocation of winnings, etc.

Over the course of the next few months, the ombuds met with the team members and conducted several mediations. Ultimately, the parties were able to address the emotional issues, restore their relationships, and agree upon terms to part ways amicably. Each side retained legal counsel to review the terms of a settlement agreement and settled the matter. This resolution saved the university significant negative publicity (and possible expense) and resulted in revising the structure of that particular class so that similar issues would not occur again in the future.

Undergraduate Student Grade Dispute

An undergraduate student who was planning to hire an attorney and sue the university came to the ombuds with a complaint about the grade the student had received from a professor with a highly irregular approach to a class that the student had been enrolled in.

The professor had an unconventional grading scheme, with no syllabus, no grading rubric, and no requirements for the class. The professor did not take attendance and assigned grades to students based on undefined parameters, although the professor had expressly told the students that participation in class would earn an A. He also said that if students were not meeting his expectations, he would email them to let them know.

The visitor to the ombuds had received a B in this professor's class but thought they deserved an A. When the student raised the issue with the professor, he provided reasons that did not align with his prior statements and practices.

The ombuds explained internal processes available to the student for raising this issue with the university, including the fact that the student had three levels of appeal. After learning of the internal appeal options, the student decided to engage in internal processes to pursue the matter further.

Ombuds Helps Student and Helps Preserve Evidence of Wrongdoing

A student employee came to the ombuds to describe a situation she did not know how to handle. She wanted to discuss the matter confidentially with the ombuds before taking any action.

The problem arose in connection with her job in the campus housing office. Her manager told her when she started work that his mother was sick and could not afford food or medicine, so he wanted to add six hours each week to her timesheet and assured her that she would still be paid for the eight hours a week that she in fact worked but that she would give him back the extra money so he could give it to his mother. The student agreed, and they operated under this arrangement for several months. When she received her W-2 form, however, she realized that not only would she owe taxes on the extra money because her earnings were so high, but she would also no longer be eligible for her scholarship.

The ombuds advised the student to turn herself in to the dean's office, but also offered options on how to deal with the misconduct of the manager. The ombuds was aware of the need to preserve evidence, an issue that had not occurred to the student. They agreed that, before the student went to the dean, the ombuds and the student would go to the senior vice president in charge of student life. Because of the ombuds' knowledge of the university, the ombuds felt that going to the most senior level first was the best way to proceed and was able to arrange for such a meeting. The senior vice president immediately arranged for HR and security to gather the necessary information in a professional and discreet manner before alerting the manager involved. The ombuds had been concerned that a less thorough or easily noticed investigation might have been done if the matter had been reported at a lower level.

Only after this was accomplished did the student report the incident to the dean and deal with her own situation. Since the university had already obtained the incriminating documentation on the manager, there was no risk that he could destroy the evidence or flee.

He was subsequently confronted, arrested, and later terminated from employment. The student's assistance led to some leniency in terms of disciplinary action by the university and the financial aid office helped her explore other sources of financial aid, but her W-2 form was not changed, and she was ineligible for her scholarship for the following year.

GRADUATE STUDENT, POST-DOC, FELLOW, AND RESIDENT ISSUES

Author's Note: **Included in this category are examples that uniquely involve these students. Examples in other categories may involve graduate students, post-docs, fellows, and residents but were placed there because they were also relevant to that topic and due to space limitations. Please review other categories and the PDF downloads for additional examples involving students in this category.**

Unpaid Labor

Through a series of visitor consultations, the ombuds identified a pattern of unpaid labor for graduate students. Because this issue appeared to be a systemic issue involving multiple locations in the university, the ombuds brought this issue to the university's legal counsel without providing any identifying information relating to any of the visitors who had raised the issue with the ombuds. As a result, the university's counsel was able to investigate the issue and then develop a resolution of the matter campus-wide.

Ombuds Helps Clinical Fellow Stop Unwanted Attention from a Senior Colleague

A new female clinical fellow contacted the ombuds to discuss her discomfort with attention she was receiving from a senior male clinician. The senior clinician, an internationally recognized physician and author of a popular medical textbook, had been repeatedly contacting the fellow by phone and text, complimenting her appearance, and offering her a valuable collaborative clinical research opportunity during her fellowship. The fellow did not wish to make a formal complaint because of the impact on her career, the embarrassment it would cause the senior clinician, and because the senior clinician had not asked her out, touched her, or said anything exceedingly inappropriate. However, she had a clear sense he was interested in her romantically and may cross those boundaries in the future. She said she only wanted a professional relationship and to be able to complete the fellowship. She indicated that she had not talked to anyone else affiliated with the hospital about the situation and presently had no intention to do so.

The fellow and the ombuds discussed keeping a record of the texts and a journal of the inordinate contact as a backup measure and then began exploring ways the fellow could more clearly communicate her discomfort to the senior clinician either directly or through an intermediary. She decided that as a first step, it would be most appropriate for her to respond to a text message she received that she's noticing he's contacting her quite a bit and that it makes her somewhat uncomfortable and that she'd prefer with her professional relationships to communicate by email only. As a secondary measure if the excessive contact persisted, she indicated that she may ask the ombuds to speak to the clinician confidentially on her behalf. Several weeks later the fellow returned to ask the ombuds to speak to the senior clinician so he would stop.

The ombuds subsequently asked the senior clinician to meet and explained the "off the record" nature of the ombuds office. When they met, the ombuds simply said that the ombuds had been asked by a fellow if he, the senior clinician, would honor a request made of him about communicating by email. The senior clinician, understanding the confidentiality and informality of the ombuds office, expressed gratitude for the message.

The fellow reported back to the ombuds a few months later that the excessive contact from the senior clinician had stopped and she was now more comfortable dealing with her colleague.

An Advisor's Failure to Advise

A female graduate student came to the ombuds to talk about concerns she had about completing her PhD. Her advisor had left employment at the university to join industry but was still advising students by distance. The student had heard about the ombuds through a presentation at the graduate college and decided to bring her concerns to the ombuds because of the confidentiality afforded by the office. As a graduate student, she feared retaliation by her advisor and, possibly, her committee members should she use formal channels to complain.

The graduate student described a pattern of neglect by the advisor, who often made comments about the student's financial status as well as comments about her immigration status. The student believed that the advisor assumed the student was international, when in fact, she was a US citizen. Since the student was self-funded, the advisor refused to treat her the same as those students on grant projects and left her without adequate assistance. As the student prepared for the defense of her dissertation, the advisor canceled meetings and ignored email and voice mail. Although her dissertation was accepted and she was a 4.0 student, she failed her oral defense and was given only two weeks for a second defense, with no advice from her advisor. The external member on her committee noted the irregularity in the lack of support by her advisor, and the "gotcha" type of questioning in the defense, and suggested she reach out to the department chair.

At that point, the student decided to speak to the ombuds. After hearing the student's concerns, the ombuds asked to speak to the external committee member and received permission. The external committee member confirmed what the student had reported and added that the advisor also said that if the student was going to return to her country of origin, then the advisor would pass her, but not if she stayed in the United States. The external committee member was from the same country as the student but knew she was a US citizen and was appalled by the statement. None of the other committee members said anything. He convinced the student to file a discrimination complaint with the Title IX office, which she did but held off on the investigation, fearing retaliation.

After being coached by the ombuds during meetings over the course of four weeks, the student spoke with the department chair and the graduate advisor, both of whom refused to listen to the student and tried to convince her to accept a master's degree instead. Finally, the student allowed the ombuds to speak to the vice provost and the dean of the graduate college about the situation, her fear of retaliation, and need for an advocate in her department. The graduate dean was able to convince the department to provide a new advisor, cancel the second defense due to the comments made and lack of advisement, and provide a stipend to the student to stay and defend again and pass her defense. The student, after being awarded her PhD, chose to drop the discrimination complaint against the university.

Checking Out the Process Can Be Very Involved

The ombuds was contacted by a woman who said that she was employed by the organization but who disclosed neither her name nor the area in which she worked. She said that she was gathering information about what the ombuds office did and did not do, but she was quite thorough: the initial call lasted forty-five minutes. This is a fairly typical action by some people who, before doing anything, want to "check out the process."

A few weeks later, the same woman called again, although the ombuds knew this only by recognizing her voice (and later confirmed it); she made no reference to having spoken to the ombuds before. She scheduled an appointment with the ombuds office but used an assumed name. When she met with the ombuds, she did not disclose either her position or where she worked in the organization. Her concerns focused on a number of issues she said she had been having with colleagues and her supervisor, including a general lack of civility (basic rudeness) and the need for clarification of responsibilities. She said that her issue with the supervisor was that he was not engaged as a manager and not managing staffing problems. The ombuds provided coaching for her and gave her options on how she could address the issues.

Approximately a month later, she returned for another discussion with the ombuds. They discussed how things had been going and strategized other options for her. More coaching was provided, and she left again to address her issues on her own.

When she returned again approximately a month later, the ombuds assumed it was for another debriefing and further guidance, but at this point the woman revealed that all of the prior discussions had not been on the "real issue" and that she had resolved all of the other matters. During this discussion she disclosed that she was a post-doctoral graduate student working in a lab under the direction of a principal investigator, who was well known both in their particular specialized field and at the organization as a major researcher and senior faculty member. In addition, only at this point did she disclose that from the beginning, her true issue was sexual harassment by this principal investigator. She admitted that she had raised all the other issues to see if the ombuds really knew what the ombuds was talking about, appreciated the political realities of her position, and was "truly confidential."

She said that she had gone through the extended "checking out the process" period because she was extremely concerned at how vulnerable her position was. The principal investigator was eminent in his field and had the power to make or break her career. She was clear that she did not want to engage any formal process, but she wanted the harassment to stop.

After long discussions on a few occasions about various options, she finally decided that she would attempt to leave his lab and find another one. In the research world, this approach can be very problematic on many levels, especially if the principal investigator of the lab being left attempts to prevent someone from transitioning to another lab or poisons the person's reputation. To address this issue, she asked the ombuds to speak with the principal investigator to see if he would consent to her departure.

The ombuds then had a confidential, informal, neutral, and frank conversation with the principal investigator and helped him realize that it was in everyone's best interest for him to support her leaving his lab as a great opportunity for her "intellectual and professional development." He agreed and she found a new lab, where she has flourished.

Helping a Graduate Student Disengage from a Sexual Relationship with a Faculty Member

A graduate student pursuing a PhD in an engineering department came to the ombuds seeking guidance on how to terminate a sexual relationship she had had with a faculty member without ruining her career. She reported that during the past year (her third in the program) she had engaged in an affair with a faculty member who was married and who also served on her dissertation committee. The affair began when they both attended and presented at a conference in another city.

After three months, she decided to end the relationship, believing that it was not healthy and that it was interfering too much with her academic progress. She said that, unfortunately, the faculty member continued to pursue her, calling frequently and even cornering her in a hallway when no one else was around. When these overtures did not succeed, the faculty member conveyed that he was quite angry that she was sticking with her decision to end the affair and told her "you will pay for this."

She did not report the harassing behavior at the time, because of fear of retaliation, including his power to ruin her academic career, and because she didn't want to get him in trouble or do anything more to interfere with his marriage. The student had recently come to the conclusion that the faculty member was now retaliating against her by disparaging her to other faculty members and creating roadblocks in the progress of her dissertation. She was not sure how to handle the situation and asked the ombuds for guidance on what were her options.

The ombuds informed the student of university policies regarding graduate students. First, romantic relationships between a student and a faculty member where there is a direct academic connection (e.g., advisor, dissertation committee member) is prohibited. Accordingly, the faculty member could be subject to disciplinary action from his department or the university. The student quickly interjected that she did not want to hurt the faculty member professionally, and that was a factor that had to be taken into consideration. Second, the ombuds said that it was university policy that the student has the right to exclude faculty from her committee if she so desires. The student expressed concern that removing the faculty member from her committee could provoke him further. She simply wanted him to back off and leave her alone.

The ombuds inquired whether the student had any close relationships with senior tenured faculty members in whom she could confide. She stated that there was—a department chair in a different field of study, as well as one or two others. The ombuds asked whether the student could share her story with the department chair and ask whether the department chair might approach the other faculty member on the student's behalf. The idea would be to let the faculty member know that other faculty members were aware of the affair, that the university could be facing serious legal exposure because of his affair with the student, and that his continuing behavior could be construed as retaliation. The student was comfortable with the idea and said she would reach out to the department chair.

Several weeks later, the student returned to the ombuds office to provide an update. The department chair had spoken to the faculty member about the affair and then let the student know that she should move forward with removing him from her committee and identifying someone else, which she did. The student was appreciative because she thought she would be making good progress on her dissertation in the coming weeks and months. Because the faculty member had ratcheted down the behavior that had been fueled by his anger at being rejected, the likelihood that the student would have to resort to legal action to protect her academic career was significantly reduced.

FACULTY ISSUES

Author's Note: **Included in this category are examples that uniquely involve faculty issues. Examples in other categories may involve faculty issues but were placed there because they were also relevant to that topic and due to space limitations. Please review other categories and the PDF downloads for additional examples involving faculty issues.**

Difficult Boss and Policy Guidance Regarding Annual Reviews

A faculty member came to the ombuds with a myriad of issues regarding her department chair. One of the issues involved the chair's practices around the annual review process. The faculty member explained that at annual review time, her department chair would expect her to read, digest, and sign her review in front of him. He essentially would give her no time to respond or clarify the review before expecting her to sign it.

In the discussion with the faculty member, the ombuds explained that the faculty handbook policy allowed a faculty member to compose and submit a written response to a review if they so desired. The ombuds also explained that the policy provided that signing a review did not necessarily mean that a faculty member agreed with it; it simply meant that one had read it.

The ombuds helped the visitor consider various options for how to proceed and, ultimately, the visitor decided that she would like the ombuds to contact the dean (the department chair's supervisor) to inquire as to her expectations regarding how chairs should conduct annual reviews with their own supervisees. The understanding was that the ombuds would not identify the faculty member or department in question.

When the ombuds spoke with the dean, the dean explained that she expected the annual review to be a conversation and that that conversation should be seen as an opportunity to make any reasonable edits to the review. As a result of the conversation with the ombuds, the dean agreed to remind all chairs of her view of how the process should work, as well as of the policies regarding faculty's right to submit a response.

The faculty member's improved understanding of her rights in the process, along with the dean's reminder to all chairs, allowed the faculty member to have a more productive conversation regarding her performance and made the process fairer for all, without compromising confidentiality.

Ombuds Helps Provost and Senior Leaders Resolve Issue with Senior Faculty Member

An internationally recognized faculty member was referred to the ombuds by his department chairperson. The faculty member had been granted lab space and a stipend to run the lab in a new research center. The new research center director, however, determined that this was not a good use of resources. She needed to use the lab space to court new hires and for more cutting-edge projects. It appeared to her that the faculty member was not even using the space and not doing any work to justify the stipend. Plus, she felt that the new work that would be done there was not in his area of expertise.

The faculty member felt slighted by this. He felt that this was age discrimination and a sign that the university's leadership was trying to push him out before his time. He complained to the director and the dean above her. They said it was really out of their hands and that they had to do what they could with limited funding.

On the advice of his department chairperson, he went to the ombuds to discuss what he could do, although he said he had little hope of the ombuds doing anything. In his conversation with the ombuds, he threatened to have his attorney sue the university and he also threatened a social media campaign against the university. It became clear to the ombuds in the course of this discussion that prestige, respect, and recognition were of utmost importance to the faculty member.

One of the options the ombuds presented to the faculty member was to take the matter to the provost, which he did. He also gave the ombuds permission to speak with the provost. In speaking with the provost, the ombuds indicated that giving the faculty member an audience, listening, and acknowledging his importance and contributions might go a long way towards resolution. The provost subsequently invited the faculty member in to state his concerns. After listening empathetically to his concerns, the provost offered some nominal compensation.

The faculty member felt respected and declared to the ombuds that he had "won" the argument. He also stated that he had dropped his claim against the lab and the lawsuit. The director, dean, and provost were pleased to have the matter resolved.

Facilitated Conversation Between a Faculty Member and His Department Chair Clarifies Expectations and Builds a Better Relationship

A faculty member responsible for directing an academic center was very disappointed with his salary increase. The increase was below the average percentage that year. His performance review was good, not great. He reached out to the ombuds to express his disappointment and ask for guidance on how to proceed. He felt he was getting a message from his department chair but was not sure how to approach the chair. He enjoyed his job very much and did not want to resign but was considering it. He was feeling insecure and did not feel confident enough to speak to the chair on his own. After speaking with the ombuds about various options he left, wanting to think about what he wanted to do next.

The faculty member called the ombuds the next day to ask if the ombuds would reach out to the chair to set up a meeting with the department chair, him, and the ombuds. The ombuds agreed to do so, and when the ombuds spoke with the chair, the chair was very receptive. The chair confidentially told the ombuds that the faculty member was a valuable member of the department and indicated that it would be a challenge replacing him in a timely manner to teach his courses. The chair also expressed concern that he had found it very difficult to give constructive feedback to the faculty member.

During the meeting arranged by the ombuds, the chair assured the faculty member of his value to the department and highlighted some of his contributions. It also became apparent during the meeting that there was an honest misunderstanding. The faculty member was always trying to "please" the chair by asking many questions and following directions. The chair, however, wanted to see the faculty member take more initiative and demonstrate more leadership.

As a result of this meeting, the chair agreed to make a minor adjustment to the faculty member's salary, and the faculty member decided not to seek other employment and became more confident in taking initiative. The faculty member called the ombuds about four months later sounding much more confident and expressing gratitude for a better and more open relationship with the chair.

LINK TO FULL COMPILATION OF EXAMPLES

Due to space limitations, the printed version of this book contains only a sampling of all the actual ombuds examples that were collected. The full compilation of examples is available at: http://ambar.org/Howard-ombuds-examples.

Index